To DARREN;

Remember all our fun times.
Chamblee, Blairsville, Gulfshores,
Mardi Gras — All those years.

ONE STEP TOO FAR

Love always,

Vern ≥ Brackett

ONE STEP TOO FAR

A NOVEL

—BASED ON A TRUE STORY—

VERN E. BRACKETT

ISBN: 1-58500-553-3

An Overview

American book-readers and tv-viewers are seeing more and more documentaries and books covering only the violent activities of the illegal drug cartels or, separately, the bottom-level street crimes created by dealers and users. But, little, if any, has been shown or written about the people within the four inner-levels between the top and the bottom: The people that export the products from Columbia; or the people transporting narcotics between countries; or the folks handling the contraband on the coasts; or the men and women making up the intra-country pipelines just above the street-peddlers. Yet, thousands are involved in the middle where the odds of being caught are 100 to 1!

One Step Too Far is a mainstream action/thriller novel, based on a true story, about a family of cabinet-makers living on Alabama's Gulf Coast in the 1980s who, unwittingly, got pulled step-by-step into a level of drug distribution, called "Off-loading and Raking", that submerged them in smuggling, murder, intrigue, and betrayal. Why they were, after making millions, forced by the cartel's drug czar to retire (or be shot) and then set completely free makes an exciting story that warrants and gets a very explosive ending!

ONE

When Celia and Colt decided to move to the Alabama-Florida gulf coast from Virginia in 1973, they were glad their only son, Rick, then 23, had chosen to go with them. All went well for Rick until 1983 when he was told: "Talk to no one about this or you will find yourself on a one-way walk in that Mobile River Delta Swamp of yours! You should have taken our secret oath, Omerta, when it was offered to you. You cannot leave us, Rick; not alive! You know too much. But now, so do we!"

Mickie, 27, had been reared in Pensacola and completed three years at Pensacola Junior College. She had been a little wild during her teenage years, also. She loved sex and had the great body and pretty face that attracted quite a few lovers. Two abortions had proved it. Then along came Rick to end her promiscuity.

She and Rick first met in 1978 at the Flora-Bama Lounge on Hwy. 182 at the Ala./Fla. state line. And it was love at first sight. They married six months later. Each had admitted that their past was tainted and should be left undiscussed, and it was. They vowed fidelity to each other and that their marriage would begin a new life and an unbreakable bond between them of true friends and devoted, faithful lovers, forever. And that's the way it was; that is, until Rick was forced unwittingly into breaking his vows to Mickie. And he would never forgive himself for it!

It started one day in 1983 when his boss in the drug smuggling business, Carlo, phoned him and told him to meet him and two more 'made' men for a drink at Nolan's Restaurant and Lounge on Hwy. 182 in Gulf Shores. About once every three months or so Rick would get a call like this. It was known among Raker-crew Team Leaders, of which Rick was one, that when called you went whether you wanted to or not.

These innocent-looking meetings were serious in as much as it was how the organization did cross-checks on its employees by having other bosses evaluate their counterpart's activities and further to see how his underlings were developing, i.e., growing towards becoming qualified for promotions to higher

1

responsibilities. Rick had been through a number of these screenings over the last four or five years and knew just how to cover for Carlo and himself. Carlo had trained him well but evidently, not well enough this time.

After the third Chivas Regal Scotch and water the usual frivolous questions about the weather, golfing, and fishing had been covered when the older of the two 'outsiders', Emilio Sanchez, opened the serious part with, "Rick, until now, we've not met. And after tonight we'll probably never see each other again. You don't know who I am or who Chico, here, is either. So, let me put you at ease. I asked Carlo for this meeting; it isn't a regular cross-check as I suppose you thought it to be. Instead, it is my way of honoring and saying thanks to you for all you have done for me and my division. I heard that you turned down the Omerta and the opportunity of becoming made. I respect you for that, for it isn't for everyone. But you are an exception to the rule.

"Usually, once a man refuses taking our Oath of Secrecy he, and his own volition, simply fades into the wood-work. We don't make them do that or encourage them that way, either. It seems that those who leave us under these circumstances feel that we want them to go. But that it is not the truth at all for they have become very valuable to the organization or we would not have spent so much time and money getting them ready for the ultimate promotion to our inner ranks."

Rick interrupted, "Emilio, let's hang onto this spot and take a bathroom break." They all rose and made a pit stop with the table talk being put on hold.

Upon returning Emilio continued, "For whatever reasons, Rick, you chose to continue serving us. You have done an exceptional job running our raking activities, showing the highest percentages of total tonnage transferred to my area among our imports and the highest percentage of damage product retrieval and with the lowest costs, and no arrests. What this means is that you, yourself, have chosen good men to help you at fair and acceptable prices; you have trained them well and have hired rakers of integrity, ones that don't rat-out to the narcs. So, we want to honor you."

Rick answered, "May I ask just who you guys are in our organization, Emilio?"

"Oh, I apologize! I skipped over that. Your division handles only the shipping and transferring of our products, as you know. My division does the receiving from yours and sells the product through a well organized sales and marketing group completely separate from yours. We place orders to our home office; they make and turn the products over to you guys and you get it to us.

"I'm leaving my Area Manager's position for a Regional Vice President's spot our west next week. Chico Constantina, here, will move up to my responsibility. I got permission from your higher-ups to see you.

"How many regular guys do you have, Rick?"

Rick answered, "Let me think. There's 18 guys and 4 gals, plus me."

"Good. Nineteen, counting you," Emilio continued. "I'll do something separately for the girls. For you guys I want to send you all on a five day fishing trip. Can you get in touch with them and have them meet us, say, right here at Nolan's, next Friday afternoon at six?"

Getting a nod from Rick, he continued. "Good. Tell them to bring their passport or birth certificate and some picture identification; they'll be needing it. Have their wives or whomever drop them off with their luggage, ready to leave for the airport from here after you guys have a couple of drinks. Chico will be going with you, and will take care of the details on my behalf. I won't be going and neither will Carlo. I'll have some limos waiting when you guys arrive and Chico will fill y'all in on the trip once aboard the plane."

Nobody in Rick's life had ever honored him like this and he really appreciated it and told them so.

Chico paid the bar tab and as they walked out, Emilio put his arm around Rick and said warmly, "Rick, if you ever decide to leave this beautiful coastal paradise and would like to come to southern California, I'll have a job waiting for you at a quarter of a million annual salary, plus perks. I could sure use a new Omerta like you, my friend."

As they began their parting, the new Vice-President said to

3

Rick, "I almost forgot. Congratulations on that great piece of work you did last month on that Delta thing!" Rick was shocked and upset that Emilio even knew about that, much less his just mentioning it in passing like that!

Now Rick was mad. As Carlo walked slowly towards his car Rick scurried to catch up with him and queried, "Carlo, what do you know about all this crap and how did he find out about that Delta thing? It was supposed to stay quiet and among just us? And why aren't you going? You run this show, not me."

Carlo answered Rick in such a way that Rick knew he was not being completely open straight, for he would not look Rick in the eyes when he spoke. "This 'crap', as you call it, is not my doing, nor does it have my blessing. Sal told me to see that it was done after Emilio called him. And he called Sal first, not me. I was forced, just like you, to go on one of Emilio's fishing trips several years back. I had no choice. Neither do you. Darn it, Rick, just do it! Go! Try to relax and enjoy yourself. I can assure you that your men will. You and I can discuss it when you return. I'm not commenting anymore on it right now.

"As far as my spreading the word about that Delta thing, the only person I said a word about it to was Sal. I had no choice but to inform him. That's part of my responsibility; to keep him informed so that you and I can have his backing should something unexpectedly happen. Sal must have repeated it. But I swear to you that I did not tell anyone other than my superior, as I am sworn to do. But I apologize to you for your embarrassment. I was shocked, too. And you can bet I'm going to discuss it with Sal. However, when I told Sal, I did not tell him that it was under Omerta, thus sealing his lips. So, I feel partly responsible for it. Please accept my apology, Rick. I feel as badly as you do."

"I wish," Rick continued, "that I could be mad at you, but I can't. You're my best friend, Boss. I'll see you when we get back from fishing. But you owe me a steak dinner on this one, Partner!"

On the way home Rick thought about all that had just transpired, but he, particularly, dwelled on that Delta thing; and with it the only major guilt, up to now that is, that he had of his entire years of dealings with Carlo, the Colombian organization, and their drug smuggling.

'That Delta thing' had begun with Rick's pager going off relaying a number from a pay phone for him to call. Rick stopped at a nearby Circle K convenience store and used the drive-up phone to call Carlo back. The voice on the other end said, "36-green-29-21." Rick repeated it and hung up. Decoding it went: Subtract today's date, the 18th, from the numbers giving: 18-green-11-3. Using the color that followed green in the spectrum (Red; orange; yellow; green; blue; and violet) he knew his instructions to be: The Winn-Dixie Shopping Center in Gulf Shores on Hwy. 182 was number 18; blue would be the color of the van parked next to a light pole there; the air-drop was scheduled for 11:00 p.m.; and three raking crews would be needed this time. Carlo would phone the other two Team Leaders, but Rick was their supervisor. Coded directions to the drop-site would be in a discarded bag of fast-food trash in the vehicle. Rick would pick up the van and have his men meet him elsewhere before leaving for that night's work.

At precisely 10:55 that night, three vans of six men each followed by an eighteen wheeler entered the pasture gate from the road about ten miles west of Foley near Fish River. No more than their just getting to the center of the grassy field a huge Cessna King-Air made a pass overhead and began a descending circle while slowing down. Rick, immediately, threw a small, lit flare on the ground signalling to the pilot that anywhere in that area would be fine. Pass after low pass was made as dozens of tightly-wrapped, heat-shrunk-plastic bales of marijuana thudded the ground as bundles of similarly wrapped cocaine hit all around the scurrying rakers as they loaded the waiting tractor-trailer.

However, unlike the bulk marijuana, the cocaine bundles contained dozens of individually packaged kilos. One raker hollered, "Rick, I have a buster over here. I got it." What that meant was that he had a bundle of cocaine that had burst and at least one of the individually-wrapped kilos had ruptured, but he could handle the raking, himself; no need to stop the others. (Had a bundle burst with no individual kilos broken, he would have called it a breaker). This guy, Jack, was from one of the other vans, not Rick's, and Rick did not know him. He was a first timer.

After the van was loaded and while Rick was checking the inventory, he remembered that the new guy was, indeed, the one that had handled and re-packed the buster. The usual practice in a situation like this one was to check the individual packages to insure that Rick wasn't zipped.

Being 'zipped' meant: A raker was expected to have some empty, zipper-type, plastic food-bags in his trousers along with a small brush and a big-bladed knife for brushing and scraping the remaining product from the ground. Once finding a buster far enough away from the others, he could easily rake a kilo into these bags and hide them in his pants or under his shirt, if he was stupid. Or sometimes, he might just hide them in the area and come back later for his treasure. He would then re-pack the broken bundle with the unbroken kilos and hide inside a few mouth-blown, air-filled zipper-bags to replace the stolen one. It worked, unless the crew's supervising Team Leader physically counted the individual kilos from the broken bundle and found the air-filled, empty bags, thus being zipped.

Rick found the air-bag inside the bundle using his flashlight. Stupid Jack did not see Rick inspecting the broken bundle. Rick walked slowly over to the #2 Team Leader named Buzzy and told him that Jack was a 'zipper' and to have his men jump him, restrain his hands behind him with cable-ties, put Jack in Rick's van, then tie his ankles, tape his mouth, find the missing kilo, bring it to him, and after leaving, follow him until they came to the first pay phone. Jack had the goods under his shirt -- a very, very serious offense.

After signing-off the inventory with the eighteen wheeler's driver, they left. Rick stopped and paged Carlo. Ten minutes later Carlo returned the call. Rick told him, "#2's team had a 'zipper'. #2 and he are with me now. All else went well. What are your wishes?"

Carlo instructed, "After dropping off the others, you and #2, drive north with that idiot. Page me in about 90 minutes from another pay phone."

An hour and a half later, they were at a convenience store's pay phone at Hwy. 59 and Hwy. 31 north of Bay Minette. Carlo phoned back saying, "Drive north on 59 just past I-65, turn left and go to Live Oak Landing. There you will be met by two men waiting in a boat who will ask you if you were the one that called to hire them to take a ride in the Mobile River Delta; drink a few Buds; and night fish a little. Answer, <u>No, but my two friends did.</u> You send them and wait until #2 gets back. Then you and #2 return to Gulf Shores. I'll advise your wife and #2's that you'll be home about daylight. Phone me tomorrow. Any questions?"

Three hours passed before Rick heard the 250 horse-power motor returning. Buzzy got out and the boat wasted no time in disappearing northwards up the Tensaw River. About all that was said going back to Gulf Shores was by #2, "Orders were that since I hired him, I had to whack him, myself, and he fell backwards into a quick-sand pit, deep in the swamp, somewhere. Where, I have no idea."

Enough had been said that night about that Delta thing.

TWO

When Rick and Mickie arrived at Nolan's at 5:45 that Friday afternoon in preparation for the upcoming fishing trip, four long, white limousines with uniformed drivers were eagerly awaiting the 19 guys with Chico overseeing their luggage transfers. After a warm and sincere good-bye kiss with his wife, Rick departed for the lounge to join the others.

After the last one arrived, Chico joined Rick saying, "A big jet is waiting for us at Jack Edwards Airport. But we don't have to hurry. Let's let the fellows have a couple of drinks to get them relaxed."

Rick asked, "Where are we going?"

"In the past we have learned it's best to inform the entire group once airborne. But, confidentially, we really aren't going fishing, at all, but to somewhere much more exciting and entertaining."

When Rick saw the huge, customized jet sitting on the ramp he was awestruck, thinking that it was as large as a Boeing 727 and additionally, about how they had landed it on only 5399 feet of runway. Too, he did not know that this chartered jet actually was built for the Drug Czar himself, Randy Martinez, Rick's dad's 'secret' best friend. Neither did Chico, for that matter. Further, he thought, Man, this has got to be costing hundreds of thousands. But why are they spending this kind of money on honoring me? I wonder if there is more to it than meets the eye?

Once inside Rick saw that this plane was made for partying. It had three fully equipped bars, four heads, expensive sofas and lounge chairs throughout its open cabin, televisions with VCRs over each and headsets, and plenty of room for fifty or more he estimated. Six uniformed Colombians were there to serve the anxious group of partiers. Once airborne, Chico took the intercom mike and told them to have some drinks and sandwiches, that it was party time. Their next stop would be in Ft. Lauderdale for fuel and 'some other things'. Then it would be on to Rio de Janeiro, Brazil where Carnival Season had just begun and he doubted if once there that anyone would want to go fishing.

9

Then he had the Colombian servers pass out an envelope to each guy that had $2,000 in it for their fun and expenses. However, all transportation would be provided as well as their hotel rooms and unlimited room service when desired. He told them that his boss was sending $5,000 envelopes to the four lady rakers that were not with them. Rick questioned their motives even more, now.

Drinks had been flowing like Niagara Falls all the way to Ft. Lauderdale. But Rick kept his scotches coming slowly; he felt that something important was about to take place and he wanted to be sober enough to handle himself properly, should he have to. But little did he know that he was already caught, once he had stepped aboard this plane, hook, line, and sinker!

At the Ft. Lauderdale International Airport, Rick was looking out the opened door at the ramp below where the refueling trucks were topping off the jet's tanks when four limousines rushed up and unloaded 20 beautiful ladies. Rick counted them as they came aboard and then the cabin door was quickly closed and locked. He was petrified when he realized that one of them was intended for him! Immediately, the engines were started for take-off. There could be no escape on his part, they were rolling! And he was furious; for now he was being trapped and he knew it. He feared what may be next!

Once at cruising altitude, Chico passed out 18 playing cards to the guys and 18 playing cards to the ladies telling the guys to find each's matching card among the ladies and to introduce yourself to your full-time playmate for the next five days.

But Rick did not receive a card; neither did Chico keep one for himself. Two gorgeous, high-class, expensively dressed young ladies sat off the themselves near the cabin front awaiting further instructions from Chico, their trip-boss. As the drunken multitude mingled finding their lovers, Chico took Rick by the arm and led him over to the two saying, "Rick Erhlichman meet Connie McMurray and Erika Von Epstein. Connie and Erika, this is my friend, Rick."

Then Chico continued, "Rick, Erika, here, is from Germany and will receive her Phd. in Computer Science next spring from the University of Florida. She will then report to Bogota where she will eventually head up our laser-based inventory control program, one that will be announced in the near future. Erika wants to be with you for the weekend; Connie will be with me. The four of us will, together, go our separate ways from the others while in Rio. However, here's the kicker: You and I will let these two beautiful ladies give us a blow job in front of this crowd. That will set up the atmosphere for all to have a good time allowing your guys and the ladies to feel free in doing whatever they want while onboard and afterwards. After our part is over, it is up to you and Erika what you two do."

Taking the mike once again, Chico asked for the noisy crowd to listen up and then said, "Alfredo, bring out all the partying stuff." Continuing, he said, "Gentlemen, there's the best Santa Marta Gold marijuana that we grow. Help yourself, but be especially aware that the cocaine on the trays is uncut. Go slow on it. And to show you that we mean what we say, that we want you to party, Rick and Erika, and Connie and I will show you what it's all about."

Erika was about 30, Rick guessed, nearly six feet tall with a gorgeous face and beautiful head of blonde hair, full but natural breasts to go along with her narrow waist, wide hips and well-exercised, tanned, muscular legs. And first, ashamed to admit it to himself, he was strongly lusting for her. Then even the tiniest feelings of restraint disappeared when she, along with Connie, slowly began taking off the blouses, their brassieres and their skirts, and the rest until both were wearing only high heals with stockings and panties; nothing else. Erika knelt and pulled Rick to her. Then the plane-wide orgy began.

Without giving it a second thought Rick slipped off his wedding band put it into his pocket and totally forgot about his beloved Mickie back home as his emotion-controlled mind slid into that private, secret, velvet-soft, oblivion that great oral sex causes a male to drift into. As Rick closed his eyes, the approving and staring crowd totally faded from his awareness. All he could think of, now, was his immediate pleasure and what he was going to do with Erika once he got her into bed, later. And just think, he had four more days with her heavenly-body!

Moments later, Rick had to handle all of this in his own

mind. This he did by convincing himself that it was his getting into this business that got him into this predicament and he could blame it on no one but himself. He had no choice but to go on this trip and he'd just have to find a way to forget all this once back home. He concluded that he had to submit to Chico's demands. And further, since that was the case, he'd put all of his scruples and reservations away and literally make the best of a bad situation. And he did just that.

By the next day Rick had grown to like Erika. She was fun. She was intelligent. She was well-up on American ways. She could converse about anything, had impeccable manners and social graces, made Rick feel like a real man, and was very, very knowledgeable about sex and how to please her partner. She and Rick talked, relaxingly, about various sexual acts and she blew his mind by showing him dozens of positions and ways that he had never seen or experienced. She even gave him a two hour professional body massage. Erika was, indeed, the very epitome of all the fantasies he had had over the years of a perfect sexual encounter and now here she was. And he truly embellished it all, never having another thought about his Mickie or his being married for his entire stay in Rio. And he could not remember ever having so much fun.

But all good things must come to an end. And so did their five days. After they had cleared Customs and dropped the girls off in Ft. Lauderdale, reality began to return to Rick and he felt worse than he had ever felt in his life, bar none. Not only was he absolutely furious with himself for violating his fidelity to his wife but he hated himself even more for having given up and for having enjoyed it so much. And he despised Chico for having trapped him!

As these feelings mounted, Rick felt he had to know the true reasoning behind all this expenditure of money and effort by the organization. So, he confronted Chico with, "Chico, this wasn't just to honor me and the guys for our good work. What's behind this?"

Chico answered, "It'll take a few minutes for me to explain it all. So, sit down and let's have a drink and I'll enlighten you. Rick, you are a very intelligent young man. You have an inquiring mind that has let you learn far more at your age than 90% of these guys. You question everything and you analyze situations that most of these guys in this plane don't even recognize as existing. All of our Omertas that have met you have stated that they want you to be made. Your future would be unlimited. But for your own reasons you have chosen not to. Yet you give us the same loyalty and faithful support as others that have taken the Oath of Silence. And you do this because you have consciously made a decision to. Yet, you have not wanted to be totally obligated to our organization. And you probably never will.

"But look at this trip like we do. We need to recruit new blood for possible future management development and they, all, do not need to be as smart as you. They just need to be willing to learn, to follow orders without questioning them, to work faithfully, and to be loyal to us. One way to move a candidate along the journey towards these goals is to seek a commitment from him either consciously, as we have done with you, or to get him mentally obligated to us like we have done this group. For they have shared something very private and secret with us that is extremely sensitive to their back-home family lives; something that they will, forever, hide from their wives. They have participated in a sex orgy of grand proportions. Because of this they will have strong feelings of indebtedness, and even inner-fear, towards us. They are mentally obligated and don't realize it. This will make it easier for us to control them should the need occur. And it will, for a few, I can assure you.

"For, my dear fellow orgy-partner, I have it all on tape should we ever need to resort to that drastic of a measure. And yes, your having oral sex with Erika in front of the crowd was filmed, as well as all those crazy positions of you and Erika in your hotel bed, too. And with sound I might add. So, just leave all this behind on this plane and stowed away, Rick. Talk about this to no one, not even Carlo. For he, already, knows what has gone on; he's been there himself. Or you may find yourself on a one-way walk in that Mobile River Delta swamp of yours! You wanted to play in the big leagues. Well, you've made it! You're there and you're obligated to us! You should have taken the

13

Omerta when it was offered to you. You cannot leave us, Rick; not alive. You know too much. And so do we, now! So, you cannot quit!"

THREE

Cecilia (Celia) King Erhlichman was born and reared in California. She was about 5' 2" bare-footed, and looked like one of the stereotypical, middle-aged Italian wives in Mafia movies (but in looks, only.): Coal-black, shiny hair, usually kept short and combed back into a duck-tail style or slightly collar-length in the winter time, small shoulders more narrow than her widening matriarchal hips that were heavier from the waist down, dark brown piercing eyes, a beautiful smile showing pearl-white movie star-type teeth, and very darkly-tanned skin.

She looked you straight in the eyes when she spoke to you and listened to you in the same way, both with such intensity that it made you feel uncomfortable, like she was looking into your mind. She walked with immense confidence and had such an aura about her that you could sense her coming into a room. She did not over dress or under dress, but dressed for the occasion and usually was very neat and unwrinkled, looking like she had just come from under a shower. You wondered if she ever sweat.

There was no lying or buffaloing Celia; you knew from first meeting her that she could detect your best try. She was very intelligent and very well read. She could converse on any subject and knew when to ask questions and how to listen intensely to every word you said in order to draw the best out of you that you were willing to give at the time. Celia seemed to be more introverted, personality-wise, than extroverted. She got along as well with men as she did with women. And she controlled the men in her life through indirect methods. She had a broad range of adaptability that allowed her to appear comfortable with the lowest level of human beings to the highest of the country club set, and everyone in between. Yep! Celia had her act together and was able to keep it that way for a long, long time. But things would change!

Coulter (Colt) J. Erhlichman was born somewhere in Virginia and was in his fifties. He was tall, 6'1" and wirey, yet very strong looking and a well-built man for his age, carrying about 175 pounds. His silver head-full of short-cropped, wavy hair matched by a similar-colored, well-trimmed, Clark Gable-type mustache on a very tanned, bronze body made him a very distinguished looking gentleman. And Colt was an extrovert from the word go.

When he spoke he had no geographical accent and used good English with a vocabulary that radiated his high intelligence level. Yet, he talked down to no one and everybody was his friend. Like Celia, he adapted very well to any environment and seemed always aware of his surroundings and sensitive to other peoples' feelings, particularly the ladies, who found him quite charming and he, them. You'd think he and Celia had gone to the same charm school of people-skill arts.

Colt was a principled man; his word was his bond. He believed in right and wrong. He hated the liberal press and believed in his country; at least the one he grew up in and joined the Navy for. He was a strong supporter of strict law enforcement and thought capital punishment was the answer to solving many of our crime-related problems, and particularly, for the drug lords. At least, that was the way he was then.

After Navy boot camp young Colt was assigned to Pensacola before being tested and assigned to cryptography school--a school for guys and gals with very high intellects who can learn how to decode secret messages. Then he was sent to San Diego, California where he, at 19, met Celia, 18, working in a jewelry store. They got married and had two girls before being transferred back to his home state of Virginia where their son was born just before he mustered out of the service. But Colt could not forget his love for Pensacola and the Gulf Coast area and vowed someday to return to live there.

Colt had learned carpentry while in the Navy by moonlighting in their craft shops and had come to love working with his hands, and was quite good at it. With that trade and talent he helped support his family of four with carpentry part-time on the outside.

After a dozen years or so in civilian life passed he became aware that in order to give his family what he wanted them to have that he must go into business for himself. So, he did; that is until several years later when one big project caused him to nearly go bankrupt. He closed down the business and took a job with a huge home builder. Several more years passed. He had worked up to become the head superintendent over all their jobs and hundreds of workers.

In 1973 Colt, now 40, was troubled, heavily stressed, and unhappy. He became a heavy drinker. He wasn't happy with having to spend so much time in the business away from Celia, for they worshipped the ground each other walked on, even after 21 years of marriage. And there would be no good-life without each other closely around. His favorite child was his first born and she had married a guy from Los Angeles and followed him there. That hurt Colt badly, loosing the apple of his eye.

Colt had developed the, then, manly habit of smoking while in the Navy. Cigarettes at the base stores were cheap and he bought his share, supporting a three-pack-a-day habit. Now, after twenty-something years of inhaling that much nicotine was taking its toll. After repeated colds, a consistent cough, and bouts with pneumonia, Colt's doctor told him that he was fast developing a serious case of emphysema. Plus being outside daily as a construction superintendent, Colt complained of being cold all the time.

Finally, while in the hospital with double-pneumonia, the doctor told him that if he did not die, then best he get out of Virginia to a warmer climate somewhere where he wouldn't be cold all the time, where his lungs could begin healing, where he could get well enough to come to his God-given senses and quit smoking and cut down and maybe even quit drinking. "If you don't do it, Colt," the doctor told him "we'll bury you this time next year."

Colt got worse and nearly died from the pneumonia. But he did recover. Two weeks after his leaving the hospital they were in the Pensacola, Florida area looking for a condo and found one on the beach over looking the Gulf of Mexico in Orange Beach, Alabama, a small resort town just west of Pensacola near the Florida-Alabama state line.

Colt followed the advice of the doctor; well, somewhat. He did leave Virginia for a warmer climate. But that's all the advice he took. He felt that playing tennis and golf regularly allowed him enough exercise to offset his smoking and drinking, and after all, he did give up one pack a day, down from three. And he did stop drinking so much; he dropped beer for scotch.

Their second daughter got married and moved to Orange Beach, too. And their son had come down, gotten married, and was out on his own.

Colt's mental and physical health was improving--no more cold spells, no more job-related stress, plenty of rest, plenty of time together with his true love, Celia, plenty of her good home cooking, and plenty of exercise with his tennis and golf in the warm Gulf of Mexico sunshine. Colt was happy once more! And his emphysema seemed to be clearing up or at least wasn't getting any worse.

What money they had saved over the years was gone, what with all the medical bills that medicines their insurance did not cover from all those trips to the doctors and to the hospitals while in Virginia. Additionally, there was the cost of moving to Alabama and the $30,000 that it cost for the down payment on the condo and furnishing it with stuff it needed that they did not have in Virginia. It was obvious they had to find a source of income pretty soon. And now being in his fifties, it would be hard for Colt to start over in carpentry in such poor health, too.

On a visit to their daughter, in California, Celia had seen a beautiful coffee table that her son-in-law had made using a cross section of a redwood tree. It was resting on a pedestal made from the above-ground redwood tree roots and its top was finished with several layers of clear polyurethane, making a crystal-clear magnification of its hundreds and hundreds of circular growth rings. Celia was in awe over the table. Here, Celia discovered an opportunity for Colt and her to go into business. All she had to do was make enough local contacts while in California to get the redwood shipped to Orange Beach and she and Colt could do the rest: make redwood coffee tables for the rapidly growing condo and tourist market in their own area. Additionally, she knew where an available, vacant building was that would just do the trick. She called Colt and the rest became history.

Soon their son joined them, and then their son-in-law, then

their daughter. And, now, three families were doing well from making coffee tables. The demand from the condo furnishing companies and retail outlets exceeded their ability to make them. And Colt kept it that way, on purpose, keeping their profits and their prices high and more people wanting them.

Several years of their working from can to can't went by with Celia and Colt's tennis and Colt's golf taking a back seat. The initial fun and challenge had gone and now, with business slowing down because of their own local market saturation and with new condo construction declining, Colt began looking for a way to make their little family business come alive again. So, they turned to specialty cabinet-making and became good at it and very profitable. And the family was having fun again.

Pretty soon, though, the cabinet business began slowing down for them due to K-Mart, Wal-Mart and a number of the other do-it-yourself retailers opening up and under-cutting Colt's prices with their pre-cut, assemble, and install-it-yourself cabinets.

Now, Colt was facing trouble again. But this time he didn't handle it as well as when they started their coffee table business. His reaction was: more scotch and back to three packs of cigarettes a day! His emphysema got worse.

FOUR

In the spring of 1983 a man and his wife came in. They were driving a new Rolls-Royce. It was about mid-morning with Colt, Celia, and the guys busy. They did not see them drive up or enter the shop. Their names were Randy and Caterina (Kat) Martinez. Dressed in the usual south Alabama beach attire consisting of deck shoes, walking shorts, and t-shirts, and lots of rings and gold jewelry, the middle-aged couple did not look any different than any of the other Latin couples in the area.

After introduction that included both their wives, Randy asked Colt, "How busy are you guys?"

Colt asked in reply, respectfully, "Why?"

Randy stated, "Because we've got a very big opportunity for an expert cabinet-maker and it will take a lot of time for the right person. Plus he will need a place to build my cabinets, about like this place. And he'll need about ten more cabinet makers to help make them in order to complete the job by the time that I want them finished. How many do you employ?"

Colt told him, "Five, all family members. And I really don't want to hire anybody else. I've been there, done that and don't want to do it again!"

Randy continued, "Well, I don't know if the five of you can get it done soon enough. But maybe if you worked hard and smart for about seven days a week for two months. But Kat wants it done in a month."

Turning to Kat, Randy asked, "Kat, can you give us two months? Hiring a family to do the job sounds pretty good to me, compared to the drug-heads and drunks that we've already talked to."

Kat replied, "I just don't know, Randy."

Looking at Celia and then at Colt and then back at Celia, Kat continued, "Celia, will you and your husband have dinner with us tonight? I'd like to get to know you better before giving you such a big job."

Colt interrupted, "Just how big a job are you talking about?"

Randy hesitated, looking puzzled at Kat, then stated, "Kat, we really don't know, do we?" Then answering Colt, Randy said "We've got about 20,000 square feet of living space with 12 bedrooms with cabinets and closets, some are walk-ins, 18 baths and half baths, four playrooms with wet bars, and three kitchens, plus several pantries with storage cabinets. Only The Holy Father knows how many cabinets are in the six-car garage, the servants' quarters, and the guest house. And oh, I forgot the pool house and bar. But there's zillions of them."

Randy continued. "Kat tried to stop me from buying the place nine years ago. She hated that cabinets. And I admit, they are cheap looking. But I promised her that if she'd go along with it, and if my business was successful enough, for our thirtieth wedding anniversary next month, she could remodel the whole place ever how she chose. And my word is my bond. And all she asked for was for new cabinets, through-out, and a little paint-work. I'm really getting off lucky."

Addressing Colt, Randy stated, "So, how much, you ask, Colt? You will have to determine that! But I suggest that we consider an arrangement with your working on my money with advance payments for material. Labor changes can be paid weekly. We'll need to agree on your labor costs per hour. I suggest for profit and overhead that you double the actual total cost of material and labor as shown by your material purchase receipts and your time sheets. Supply me with copies of the material receipts and time sheets. Plus, if Kat is extremely pleased with your and Celia's finished work, I'll give you, two, a very nice bonus in addition. Just be honest and fair to us on your charges. And do make a good profit on travel-time costs, too. That's all we ask. Right, Kat?"

Kat responded, looking at Celia, "I'm not sure about all that. Business details are a little above my head and Randy talks too fast for me to keep up. Celia, will you spend some time with me, starting with dinner tonight? We need to get to know each other, first."

"How could we say no?" Celia spoke, looking at Colt for a response.

Colt said, looking at Randy, "Name the time and place."

Randy nodded at Celia saying, "Celia, you choose."

"How about Sam's Marina and Oyster Bar on the intracoastal at seven?" was Celia's choice.

"See you guys at seven," Randy said.

As the Latin couple turned away and proceeded toward the front door, as an after-thought Colt hollered, "What kind of business are you in, Randy?"

"Import and export," Randy hollered back.

FIVE

Celia and Colt did not discuss this opportunity during the rest of the day. No reason not to talk about it, though, other than they spent time talking about the orders currently being worked on. It was as if they were, silently, waiting for the meeting at Sam's and all that it would offer and, too, to see if the couple did, indeed, show up at all. For this seemed too good to be true; and it probably was. And talking about it might make it go away.

If one drives east on Highway 182 from Orange Beach towards Pensacola about ten miles or so past the Florida line, you reach the bridge over the intracoastal waterway. Looking to your right you see on the canal several water front restaurants with dock-side drinking and dining facilities. The one with the swimming pool was Sam's. Exiting right, immediately before the bridge would get you into the parking lots of the side-by-side canal accessed establishments. The food was excellent and the service and atmosphere superb. It was not unusual to see boats and yachts of all descriptions traveling the waterway and/or docking at your feet for cold booze and bites.

It was 6:50 p.m., Celia and Colt were being seated next to the water at a four-topper table with a giant umbrella. But their shaded-canopy would not be of much help as the sun was below its edges. Celia sitting with her back to the water said, "Honey, I'll sit here so I can see them when they come in."

Colt answered, "Okay, I'll get some drinks ordered," motioning to a server. He ordered a Johnnny Walker Red Label Scotch and water for himself and a Coke for Celia and a pack of Camels.

Celia hesitated in drinking alcohol around anyone that she wasn't very close to and then wouldn't do it until after she ate, and then only wine. She resisted getting tipsy, much less drunk. She was too reserved for that. But Colt was a different case. He'd let-go whenever and wherever he felt like it regardless of who was around. Once he drank, in a couple of hours, nine Johnny-Reds at a golf club bar in Pensacola and still acted sober enough that the valet manager let him drive home.

At exactly 7:00, as if they had been waiting for the exact minute, up strolled four people; two men dressed in expensive suits, each with the size and build of an Arnold Schwarzenegger, one in front and one behind Kat and Randy. As they passed the thatch-roofed deck-bar and just before stepping onto the open, tabled-deck area, the giants separated and took stools at the bar. Celia saw them enter and motioned the Latin couple over.

Randy had picked out Celia just as Celia had seen them arrive. Randy, once the newcomers were seated and greetings exchanged, looked at Celia and said, "The two gentlemen that came in with us are employees of ours and wanted to come down for a drink and one of Sam's gourmet hamburgers. They'll stay over there, though."

Celia and Colt frequented Sam's every chance they got. It was a popular place between Pensacola and Orange Beach/Gulf Shores. Besides getting great seafood and good service, the atmosphere was outstanding with yachts of all descriptions plying the waterway. The wharf was crowded with tables. But the noise level allowed enough privacy for everyone to be able to carry on a conversation without shouting. And the female servers wore tight shorts. And the male customers didn't complain about anything!

Randy asked Celia, "What are you guys having?"

Celia replied, "Colt ordered a Johnny Walker Red and water and a Coke for me."

Randy continued, "Do you ever drink wine or champagne, Celia?"

"Yes, sometimes," was her reply.

"Good." Randy turned to their arriving server saying, "Please, bring a bottle of Dom Perignon and I'll have the same as my friend. And if you will see that we get your very best attention and you tell the bartender and the folks in the kitchen the same, I will see that everyone that helps us enjoy the evening gets a very good tip. And see those two gentlemen in the dark suits sitting at the end of the bar near the entrance? See that they get the same type of treatment and put their tab on mine. Will you handle that for me, Niki?" (Seeing her name tag.)

26

The server smiled, nodded a happy and willing "Yes, Sir!" and left stepping spryly towards the bartender to begin getting Randy's message to the others.

Randy looked at Celia with a stern facial expression but with a slightly devilish grin and said, "Let's let sometimes be now, Celia."

Changing to a big confident smile, Randy continued, "Kat and I want to know about each of your backgrounds and we want you to know about ours. Celia, where did you and Colt grow up?"

Celia ignored his question, for a feeling of being controlled flashed over her while Randy had been talking to the server. Quickly, though, she analyzed the stand that Randy was taking and still not giving up her feeling of resistance, came to a rapid decision. She would let him have his way, this time, and drink a little champagne. Her reasoning was that she did not want to put the possible order on the cabinets in jeopardy by making a scene and that they could still turn down the work, though, but not until it had been offered to them. So, she'd play along with his game, for now. But if he keeps this crap up . . .! she thought.

A similar feeling was going over in Colt's mind at the same time. Here the customer was wooing the seller, by taking control of the evening's expenses. This was starting off upside down in Colt's mind. Unlike Celia, though, Colt could not condescend; his manly-pride jumped in. "Come on, Randy! This isn't right. You are our customer. The bills are going to be mine!" Colt said firmly.

Randy was quiet for about five seconds. Then in a very low, embarrassed voice he said, "I apologize to you, both. You are right. I've been too presumptuous. And I should not have ordered that bottle without your permission, Celia. Please forgive me, folks. However, let me have my way this time and you guys can pay next time. Okay, Celia? How about it, Colt?"

Colt, looking at Celia and receiving her now-expected nod, giving Randy a light-hearted smirk that meant <u>You didn't get away with it after all, Mr. Smarty!</u> said, "Alright, Randy. This time!"

The drinks came. The bucket with the $145 bottle of

champagne was placed between the ladies and their glasses were filled when Kat, finally, came alive for the first time since arriving and said, "Our first drinks together should be something to remember, something special. I propose a toast to our new friendships! May they be long lasting and fun! Cheers!" All seconded that.

After Niki brought the second drinks to the guys, and while the ladies were enjoying their third glass of champagne, Kat asked, "Celia please tell us about yourselves and what brought you to this area, or are you from here?"

Celia answered, "Okay, but let's get some food coming before I get so tipsy that I can't remember who I am, much less all the rest."

Colt raised his hand towards the bar and another server came over. Her name tag showed "Christy." Colt asked, "Christy, would you send Niki over?"

"No problem," Christy said. "However, we intend to see that you get preferred service. So, Holly, our shift manager and hostess, assigned me to help Niki with you. What may I get for you?"

Colt asked, "Could we have some menus?" After perusing the long list of finger foods, Sam's world-famous hamburgers and fries and fried crab claws were ordered.

After ordering, Celia told about herself, where she was born, meeting Colt, having kids, their life in the military, moving to Virginia, Colt's getting out of the Navy and going into the construction business, his health problems, their daughter in California, their moving to Orange Beach, the redwood table business and now the cabinet business, their hobbies of tennis, Colt's playing golf and lastly, the rest of their family.

Randy asked to be excused for the men's room and for Colt to wait until he came back before telling about himself. On the way Randy passed Niki and whispered, "Another round of drinks and another bottle of Dom."

When Randy returned, the food and drinks had arrived. Celia saw Niki put the fresh silver bucket of iced champagne in the place of the empty one. But after having already consumed half a bottle herself, she really didn't care; well, not enough to say anything, anyway. She was having a good time. And they never did get to talking about Colt.

SIX

Celia asked Kat about her background.

Kat's maiden name was Bonita Caterina Julianne and she had no brothers or sisters. She was born in a small town near Bogota, Colombia called Funza and was educated by private tutors until she was sent to a Catholic high school convent in Durango, Mexico. Her family had been very wealthy for many years, having made fortunes in South American banana plantations and cattle ranches from as far back as her great-grandparents. She went to college at the Universidad Juarez Del Estado De Durango earning a Master's Degree in Nursing. She was fluent in Spanish, English, and a Peruvian tribal language called Kin Chabba.

She had met Randy while both were in English classes their freshman year. They were married in Bogota during their senior year. Kat worked for several years at a Bogota hospital prior to the birth of their first child. They have a son, 21, who is a junior in Agriculture and Cattle Breeding at their alma mater in Mexico at its Gomez Palacio Campus, and a daughter, 19, at Auburn University in Business Administration.

Randolph Antonio Martinez was born in Havana, Cuba to two doctors; he was their only child. His parents fled Cuba with the first wave as Castro's forces reached the city's limits. All they were allowed to take was one suitcase each, leaving a mansion home, a very successful medical practice, and nearly two million dollars behind for Castro to claim as his own once he federalized the banks. Their deal was: <u>Leave everything for the new regime and they'll let you keep your lives. Stay and you and your entire family will be shot!</u>

Once in Miami, young Randy's parents had no trouble getting a new start. They had both graduated from American medical schools and spoke very good English. So, before long, wealth returned and soon, as his parents' medical practice grew large and very time consuming, Randy was put in a military-style boarding school in Georgia where he continued through high school.

Randy did not like the military lifestyle and asked his parents to let him apply to a college in Mexico. The University of Durango accepted him and he stayed through dual Master's Degrees in Languages and Psychology. Randy studied Spanish, English, and Portuguese and also speaks two Peruvian tribal languages: Quechua and Kin Chabba.

Randy and Kat moved back to Bogota after graduation where he worked to learn her family's businesses. He travelled Central and South America for his father-in-law. He began by marketing their products and beef before being transferred into a totally new field of importing and exporting that included the marketing of electric motors, bearings, seals, lubricants, rubber and plastic hoses, hose couplings, conveyor belting, and industrial supplies, all together called Power Transmission Products.

Alfredo and Emelda (Elizondo) Julianne, Kat's parents, owned 28 stores called industrial distributors in Central and South America. They had gotten into this activity to supply their family's banana plantations, beef ranches, and slaughter plants, then began selling to others.

They had made nearly thirty million dollars selling 49% of the stock in this chain to wealthy South Americans for cash before they transferred Randy to this family holding. Randy was told to learn to fly airplanes so that he could fly himself between stores in the company's two A-36 Beechcraft Bonanzas.

Five years later, Randy was made Vice-President over the distribution stores plus their agricultural and beef operations. A year later, he was promoted to the conglomerate's President and COO and asked to move to the U. S. where he was to set-up an import and export company to sell their bananas and beef in the states and Europe. Kat's father became Chairman and CEO.

Randy convinced The Board of Directors to let him establish a central warehouse and distribution center for their U. S. beef and banana imports in Miami but to let him put their international headquarters and flight department in Gulf Shores, Alabama where he would live and work in order to bring less attention to their U. S. operations. Then he made a deal with the Gulf Shores Airport Authority and built offices and a huge corporate hanger at their Jack Edwards Airport.

Further, Randy developed a purchasing department in Miami for their 28 South American industrial distribution stores buying both U.S. and foreign products, and then formed a U. S. sales department in 1971.

Kat's father and mother died in a commercial plane crash in Lima, Peru. But sometimes before the fatal plane trip, Alfredo Julianne had set up a holding company for theirs and all the Elizondo family's business including their sugar cane farms, banana plantations, produce packing plants, cattle ranches, slaughter plants, feed and fertilizer mills, plants, and retail stores, the distribution chain of 28 stores and its import operations, all their vehicles, boats, and airplanes with a net worth of nearly half a billion dollars. Then they sold stock in it with Senor Alfredo and Kat's mother, along with her two brothers and two sisters, keeping 51% of the stock.

After the probating of her parents' wills, Kat inherited 20 percent of the holding company's stock, making her the conglomerate's largest stockholder and her personal wealth close to a hundred million dollars.

One of the first things Randy, as "El Presidente", did was to set up a leasing company to purchase from their conglomerate all the cars, boats, and airplanes they owned and lease them back to each of their separate companies on an as needed basis. This would cause each profit center manager to analyze each expenditure to determine if it was necessary or not, give upper management a better control tool, allow for more tax benefits, and, hopefully make more money for the stockholders.

Once this was completed, he began a program to buy through the leasing company all new capital expenditure machinery and the new major equipment needed by their agricultural and ranching operations and then lease it to them. At the same time he departmentalized the conglomerate into divisions and promoted and hired the necessary executives with a Division President over each to oversee the day-to-day activities. Then he computerized everything.

The Board, then, had the leasing company buy for their use a $50 million jet. It would be offered on a charter basis to other companies when not in use by Randy, his in-laws, or some of his Division Presidents. They based it in their hanger at Jack Edwards Airport along with a full-time Travel Division, another profit center.

Randy incorporated a travel agency within their Travel Division to handle all reservations (commercial airlines, motels, car rentals, etc.) for their top executives, thus making another profit for themselves that would ordinarily have gone to outside companies. Further, when on their non-company trips, the travel department would give their booking commission to the employee as a discount; thus another company benefit to the employees.

Also, their Travel Division was given the responsibility of keeping the flight department planes busy with a full lease schedule. And their qualified pilots would be available to fly the million-dollar Beechcraft King-Air that Kat and Randy bought for themselves for their 25th wedding anniversary. They put it on the lease program, too. Randy intended to charge everybody for everything, even Kat and himself!

They flew a lot: to Auburn football games, to the New Orleans Saints games, to visit their son at college in Mexico, and to bring him and their daughter home and return them to college. Kat loved flying and flew with Randy a lot.

Randy kept up his flying currency, got a U.S. license, and furthered his status with an instruments rating, commercial ticket, Certified Flight Instructor/Instruments ratings in single and multi-engine, began working on his jet-rating, and hoped to qualify for his ATP (Airline Transport Pilot) allowing him to become the Flight Department's Chief Pilot.

For his and Kat's personal use, Randy bought from the company, and flew back from Colombia, the A-36 Bonanza that he had flown all over Central and South America. Kat had flown many times with him in this plane and had shown a lot of interest in reading the charts. So Randy taught her navigation. And she became very good at it.

After Kat's father, Alfredo, was gone, his two brothers and

two sisters, (the other major stockholders in the holding company) decided that they wanted a private place in the gulf beach area with a yacht, so that they could come over, rest, play golf and conduct some of their business meetings there. And, too, the company could pay for their travelling to and from the states using the jet. Further, they could pre-tax and expense their state-side and European vacations and their frequent gambling trips to Las Vegas.

And since their U. S. operation had grown so swiftly under Randy's guidance, they wanted Randy and Kat to search out and find a compound big enough to house the whole Colombian bunch under one roof and a satisfactory yacht.

The leasing company was to pay for them and lease them back to the holding company on an annual basis. Then the holding company would in turn bill each user for the amount of time each spent there. Also, Randy and Kat would be paid a healthy managers fee for over seeing the place and the yacht.

As each major stockholder and family, including their Division Presidents and their families used the compound or the yacht, the holding company would bill their costs. However, the usages would have to total more than 50% of the time for business and business entertainment. So, quite a few top company employees were there staying in the servants' quarters, a small motel in itself, like the two Arnold Schwarzeneger types who accompanied Kat and Randy to Sam's and about six more like them ---Captain Lou and his crew when the yacht was not leased for a trip, Pablo and 'Nita and their group of ten cooks and kitchen helpers; house-keepers; grounds-keepers; and the compound's Security Guard Team, all totalling about 40.

They found 'the' place and spent 15 million dollars of the leasing company's money buying and remodeling it and got what the family wanted, except for the cabinets. Kat named it: Cinco Robles (Pronounced: 'Sin-ko Row-blace') for the five magnificent 300 year-old live oaks inside the beautifully landscaped, stone-walled 50 acres on Wolf Bay near Foley, a city north of Gulf Shores on Highway 59.

And after many family gatherings, Kat's aunts told Randy,

"Get rid of these stupid cabinets and get Kat what she wants or get yourself a job at Wal-mart and see if they'll let you play with their airplanes!"

Randy heared about the yacht from a broker in Ft. Lauderdale. It was located in St. Thomas, when Kat and Randy first looked it over. They were asking $4.5 million for it, but took 4.2 cash. The 105-foot motor-yacht was a sedan-cruiser --- the stern is enclosed and it was not a fishing boat. It was 4 years old and was built by LeFevre Yacht, Ltd. in Taiwan for a sand country oil baron who paid $6 million for it and whose wife, later, caught him using it in St. Thomas for a harem and made him sell it.

Celia, Colt, Kat, and Randy had visited on Sam's dock for four hours. It was 11:00 p. m. and the ladies were beginning to lose their well-earned giddiness when Colt said, "Celia, if we are going to get up at six in the morning and finish that cafeteria job, we best be leaving."

Kat interrupted, "Celia, there's a few more things that I want to talk to you about. And Colt's right, it is getting late for us, too. We're usually in bed by this time every night. I set out clock for 5:00. Randy likes to have coffee and read the paper in bed with me before he goes to the office at 6:30. So," as she looked at Colt, "I'm not ready to give you the order, just yet. I want to have some one-on-one time with my new-found friend without you men around so that we can talk some girl talk. Would you two take off work tomorrow and go with us on a boat ride? It's important to me and it will be worth while to you, too, Celia. I promise. We need some more time; me with you, and Randy with Colt. We definitely need tomorrow to get acquainted. Can you arrange things? How about it, Colt?"

"That's up to her, Kat," Colt responded. "She knows what we have to do as well as I do."

Celia answered, "Let's do it. We need a day away from the shop, anyway."

"Good," declared Randy. "We'll pick you guys up right here at 8:00 in the morning. We'll be on the yacht."

Randy left the table telling them that he'd clear the bill and to meet him at the gate to the parking lot.

36

About the time they started their separate ways toward their cars, Kat stopped and turned to Celia and gave her a big hug, holding onto her and whispering in her ear. "I feel like you are the sister that I never had. I've never had a real friend, not a close, true friend!" Celia was shocked! The two separated and joined their husbands.

Colt asked, "What was that all about?"

"Just girl-talk," was the answer that he got.

Celia and Colt hesitated while walking to their car, each knowing that the other was thinking about wanting to be the last to leave. The two men from the bar, walking fast, got in a big black Cadillac and sped out of the parking lot in order to fall in behind the Latin couple in their Rolls-Royce.

Colt said, "See that, Honey?"

"Yeah," was her answer.

Both were quiet as if contemplating the evening's happenings and re-thinking what needed to be committed to memory. Once several miles up the road, Colt spoke, "I think they're dopers."

Celia replied, "I thought the same thing when those two giants followed them in. There's so much money talked about. It's beyond my world! But I'll tell you what, Sweetheart; what we're going to do is make cabinets for them at a real good profit. And that is very, very legal. What they do is their business and we don't want to get involved in it. We're too old to lose everything you and I've worked for and to spend the few years that we've got left in jail."

Colt's answer was, "You got that right, kiddo!"

SEVEN

The next morning's sky was clear except for puffy, cotton ball clouds dotting the blue here and there. Thunder showers were predicted for the late afternoon hours, which was very normal, and the winds would be to 5 knots from the southeast, temperature near 90, perfect spring weather. The marine forecast that Colt retrieved over his weather band radio additionally called for seas 2 to 3 feet offshore with calm inland and on protected waters.

It was 7:45 a.m. when Celia and Colt left their Ford F250 pick-up truck in Sam's parking lot. A half dozen cars were there already even though the bar and restaurant did not open until 11:00 for lunch. These cars belonged to the day-manager, the bar-backs, the clean-up crew, the book-keeper, the morning chef, and his food-prep crew. A beer delivery truck, a bread truck, and an eighteen-wheeler from a large food broker from Jacksonville were busy unloading.

Colt appraised Celia, "I don't see the Rolls or the Cadillac. Apparently, they rode over on the yacht. I wonder where they keep it? It must not be too far from here, huh?"

Celia replied, "Probably not, if they got any sleep at all."

Colt responded, "Maybe they slept on the yacht."

Colt and Celia entered the handicapped ramp, crossed the deck, and walked over close to the dock. Only one yacht was moored there, when usually there's many all the way down past all three restaurants and continuing toward the bridge. As they approached the dock's edge they saw the yacht's name on the stern: Bonita Caterina. No doubt, they had found the right one.

The bright white sedan-cruiser was humming busy noises— Bilge pumps blowing out water, air-conditioner singing its song, a television sounding the news of last night's misery, and a deck-hand whistling a Beatles tune as he ran a vacuum on the rear deck carpet at the gang plank. The young man saw Celia and Colt approach the dock-side ramp and hollered towards the adjacent salon, "Captain, company's arrived!"

A tall, middle-aged Latin appeared wearing a captain's uniform consisting of a white, open-collar shirt with epaulets that designated his rank, white trousers, and freshly-polished white shoes. As he approached them he donned his gold-braided cap and said, "Mr. and Mrs. Erhlichman, please come up. And welcome aboard the the Bonita Caterina. I'm Captain Louiz Alvarado. Please call me Lou." He cordially shook their hands and continued, "The Senor and Senora are waiting for you in the dining room and wish for you to join them for breakfast. Please follow me and watch your step particularly through the hatches. And if I can be of service to you, in any way, please ask."

Colt replied, "Some time today, if you're not too busy, I'd like a tour of the yacht."

"Oh, absolutely. I'll appraise the Senor for a time," was the Captain's reply.

The dining room was on dock-level and after entering and crossing the elegant drawing room, Randy and Kat were viewed in the adjacent room having coffee at the dining table. The couple stood to great their guests and after 'helloes' Randy asked them to be seated and if they would join them for breakfast.

"Sure," was Celia's answer. No sooner had they sat when a door opened, apparently from the galley, and a neatly dressed, uniformed, middle-aged Latin lady appeared with a coffee decanter on a silver serving-tray offering a fresh Colombian gourmet brew to the newcomers.

Kat spoke next. "Mr. and Mrs. Erhlichman, I'd like for you to meet Senora Juanita Gomez. 'Nita was a child-hood playmate of mine. She married a local muchacho named Pablo, who became an internationally trained, gourmet chef. When we moved stateside she and Pablo would not let us leave without them. He is our head chef at home and she is our head house keeper. They love this yacht and insist that we allow them to help us here, too. Plus, they are our dearest friends. And Randy and Pablo play golf together, almost, every Sunday. And when we go to Europe on the big jet 'Nita and Pablo travel with us." Cordial expressions were exchanged.

Kat continued, "Randy and I enjoy many different kinds of food, and we adore Pablo's cooking. So, Pablo decides what he wants us to eat and therefore, it is a complete surprise each time. So be careful, he loves to cook for strangers and he'll over-stuff you if you let him! Before I send word to the galley that we are ready, are there any types of food that you cannot eat?" Both guests shook their heads. Kat nodded to 'Nita and 'Nita departed to tell Pablo to begin preparing breakfast.

About a minute later, a tall and handsome middle-aged Colombian dressed in perfect attire, even sporting a white chef's hat, came through the door. "Mr. and Mrs. Erhlichman, I am Pablo Gomez. Welcome to 'My Little Heaven'. That is what I've named this dining room, for I love it so much and the delightful and interesting people that Kat and Randy have brought to me on The Caterina. Last night, we slept aboard and I stayed up eager to hear from Kat about her visit with you at Sam's. I'm positive from what she told me last night or actually early this morning it was, and now meeting you, that 'Nita and I would like to become friends, also."

This frankness, openness, and forwardness made Celia and Colt feel a bit uncomfortable. They were not use to this much initial honesty and aggressiveness. But sincere smiles were exchanged. And Pablo continued, "Has Kat informed you two that I like to surprise our guests with the meals?"

Again, nods were given. "Good," Pablo smiled looking at Colt then back at Celia, "Would you four like something stronger than coffee, say a Bloody Mary?"

"No, thank you," was their reply.

"As you wish. 'Nita will keep your cups filled and I should be ready with your surprise breakfast in about ten minutes. Please prepare yourself with a hearty appetite and enjoy your coffee."

The four returned to light chatter about the furnishings on display throughout the dining room and where each came from representing the different cultures of South America and how she and Randy came to find these antiques among the mountains, the coasts, the pampass-grass plains, and the jungles. Each artifact was displayed separately on a special mounting or on a pedestal or enclosed in a glass case. And there was placed on each an engraved enamel plate telling the names of each piece, its make-year, its area of origin, and a description of what it was used for. One could tell by this vast array of previous life that this yacht's owners truly loved their heritage and wanted their visitors to share in their pride.

Randy asked Colt, "Do you guys have a certain time that you need to be back? I need to tell Lou."

Colt, looking at Celia for approval, stated, "We need to stop by the shop before the crew goes home to check on what was done today and to plan tomorrow's work. Would 4:30 be okay?" All nodded approval.

Randy reached for the wall phone and punched up the bridge saying to Lou, "Lou, let's cast off at your pleasure, stay inside, and plan to return-dock at 4:30. We'll want you to join us in the salon at 11:30 for cocktails and lunch. We'd like for you to get to know our new friends. Have they had time to clean the rooms, yet? Fine." Pausing to listen, he then added, "Colt did? Great! I was just about to invite them on a tour, myself. I'll buzz you after we finish breakfast."

Kat spoke next. "Pablo published a cook book a couple of years ago. We pride ourselves over his cuisine, as I mentioned earlier. So, before you leave, I'll see that you and Colt get an autographed copy from Pablo as a memento of your honoring us with your first visit aboard The Caterina. He named his book <u>La Caterina Fiesta Especial</u>. He tries out his new recipes on us first. Then if we and our guests like them, he'll have them printed and mailed to everyone who has a copy of his book. So, we're constantly trying out new meals, both here and at Cinco Robles. It's fun! Oh, don't let me forget to get you both to sign our visitors' log before docking. We use it to send special invitations for parties and Christmas cards."

From the galley, in walked 'Nita with her serving tray carrying four fruit-filled bowls and Pablo following. Kat immediately asked, "Is this a new one, Pablo?"

"Yes," was the Latin's response. "If our guests enjoy their breakfast, and so inform me, recipes for each dish will be mailed to over 50,000 of my cook book owners. The presentation will be called <u>The Bayou La Batre Delight</u>! With each addition I add a little background note about the area that the meal comes from, if appropriate. And this one will say, <u>As served and approved by Celia and Colt Erhlichman of Orange Beach, Alabama aboard</u>

42

The Bonita Caterina, with today's date on it."

Pablo continued, "May I inform you about your up-coming pleasure?" With positive responses received he explained, "Bayou La Batre is a small coastal town near Mobile in southwest Alabama close to the Mississippi state line and just inland from the Gulf of Mexico where most of their income is derived from seafood harvesting and seafood packing operations. Those tangerine-looking fruits in the bowls are called Satsumas. They are grown just north of Bayou La Batre in the towns of Grand Bay, Theodore, and Tillman's Corner and ripen in late fall. I have several crates shipped to me each year. 'Nita and I preserve them for later enjoyment. Marashino cherries and shredded fresh Florida coconut have been sprinkled in."

Pablo added, "One of the two main dishes that I want you to try is the fresh mullet flown in yesterday from Bayou La Batre. Mullet is a saltwater and brackish water vegetarian and requires expert cleaning in order to offer its unusually sweet taste. Once cleaned properly, dipped in a milk and egg marinade, and then in a mixture of half cornmeal and self-rising flour, I deep-fry it until golden brown in vegetable oil. After draining on a bed of towels, lightly sprinkle it with a creole all-purpose spice. My favorite brand that I get shipped in with the fish is Tony Chachere's Creole Seasoning made in Opelousas, Louisiana. I prefer it because it has no MSG. Serve the fish hot."

Pablo explained, "The second dish I named Cajun Country Hominy Grits. Just follow the directions on the grits package but about the time that the grits are done, add enough sharp or cheddar cheese to give it a rich cheese color. Add to the pot crushed bacon bits and about one to two tablespoons of the bacon grease. Figure three crisp strips of crushed bacon per serving. Add salt as necessary.

"Then side-dish some buttered toast using French bread cut in thin slices," advised Pablo, "and follow up with a bowl of chilled, sweet watermelon preserves.

"That's it, folks," Pablo summarized. "Enjoy yourselves. 'Nita and I will join you before you finish, for a cup of coffee and your honest opinion of the new dishes."

Not knowing that Kat had informed her, Pablo added, "And,

43

Celia, I give all my guests a personalized copy of my cook book to take home. Please leave your mailing address in our visitors' log and I'll see that you and Colt get on our mailing lists."

For the next 45 minutes they enjoyed their meals.

Then Pablo asked questions. "What was your first impression of the visual presentation? Tell me about its aroma? Was it cooked too much or too little? How did it taste? How was the temperature? Did you detect any after-taste? What other dishes could be served with it? Did you like it and why or why not? If so, would you order it in a fine restaurant? Could you prepare it easily at home yourself? Would you recommend it to others?"

Needless to say, raves were given to Pablo and two more recipes would be faxed to his publishers and in a week or two mailed out to 50,000 eager gourmet chefs and gourmet cooks all around the world, both professional and private, who in turn would send a dollar per recipe back to the publishers. Colt pondered, 'half of it, $25,000, would be sent to Pablo in a couple of months. That ain't bad for one day's work cooking breakfast, is it?'

As the last bite of the watermelon left Randy's plate he looked at Pablo and said, "My dear friend, it's about 9:45 now. I've asked Lou to drive us inside and west and he'll be joining us for cocktails at 11:30. Chuck will be at the helm."

Randy turned to Colt and Celia and continued, "Oh, did Lou introduce you guys to the young man that was on the stern when you came aboard?" Celia and Colt shook their heads no. "That was Chuck Parsons. He dated our daughter, Little 'Nita, for several years before she went off to college. You know who she's named after. And she won't let us call her "Little 'Nita", anymore; not to her face, anyway. Then as so often happens, with Little 'Nita leaving, she and Chuck drifted apart."

Randy continued, "Kat and I, Pablo and 'Nita, and Lou and Connie grew to love Chuck like a second son. In fact, there for a while we all did, indeed, think that they would eventually be married. So, after they broke up, we took him under our wings and tried to get him to let us send him to college with Tony in Durango but we didn't win. Chuck just wasn't convinced that he was college material. So, we asked him to come to work for us on The Caterina. Lou trained him and helped him get through his captain's license. He's done a good job for Lou and for us and we think of him as part of our extended family. I'll introduce you to him later. You'll like him."

Colt questioned Randy, "You've just mentioned for the first time the names of your children, 'Nita and Tony. What are their full names?"

Randy embarrassingly replied, "Oh, please forgive us, for we have talked so much about ourselves that you must think of us as egotistical boors! Please excuse our rudeness! Kat and I, after each other, consider our son and daughter before all else, as good parents should."

"Not at all!" was Celia's immediate response and Colt nodded similarly.

"Randolph Antonio Martinez, Jr. is our first born's name and Juanita Caterina is our daughter's name," Randy answered.

Celia asked, "Are you guys U. S. citizens?"

Kat entered with, "Absolutely. We all were Naturalized including Randy and me, Little 'Nita and Tony, Pablo and 'Nita, and Lou and his wife, Conchita. But Connie, as we called her, died two years ago with cancer. God rest her soul!"

Colt asked 'Nita, "Where did you and Pablo learn to speak fluent English?"

'Nita informed, "Before I answer you, Colt, may I add to what Kat just said? While we chose to be citizens of this country, all of us have chosen to keep dual citizenships. Our kin back home would be devastated if we gave that up! But God only knows what's happened to Randy's since Castro took over Cuba! Maybe one day we'll know."

'Nita answered, "In South America, we were taught to speak a local language which, depending on where you live, probably would be Spanish or Portuguese or tribal. However, English is a second language that the upper classes and the educated city workers are expected to know. But the average citizens have a great dislike for gringos. English is offered as a foreign language in some high schools. That is where Pablo and I first learned it. And to keep fresh, we, when aboard The Caterina,

45

speak only English.

"Then," 'Nita added, "if one travels the entire continent, like Randy did for ten years, speaking German or French will help you in conducting business. However, about 50% of the Peruvians speak Quechua. Plus there are over 30 other tribal languages there."

Randy picked up where he left off in advising Pablo by looking at his watch and saying, "Goodness, it's nearly 10:00! I don't know about how you people feel, but I won't be anywhere near ready for lunch in an hour and a half. How about you guys?"

Having affirmation from the two ladies, Randy turned to Pablo advising, "And since our guests need to be back at 4:30, Pablo, why don't we just skip lunch and have hors d'oeuvres and cocktails about three?" Looking at and receiving confirmation on his thinking from the others, he added, "If you would buzz Lou, Pablo, I'll invite our guests into the salon."

Pablo spoke, "Splendid! That will give 'Nita and me time to come up with another little surprise for our guests!"

Randy joked, with an air of seriousness, "Yeah, and make another $50,000!"

All rose to depart the dining room with Kat, Celia and Colt following Randy aft to the drawing room where they sat on the plush lounges and sofas, except for Randy. He went over to a small cabinet that had a hand-carved, ornate humidor as its center piece. As he put his hand on its lid, he remembered his manners and asked as he turned towards the ladies, "Do you mind if I smoke?"

"Not at all," Celia answered.

"Good," Randy continued. "Colt, would you care to join me for a Cuban cigar? These are the very best smuggled out of Cuba into the U. S. Very few people stateside have been able to enjoy them since Castro took over and the U.S. made it illegal to ship them in."

Colt thought that since he, too, loved a good cigar now and then, any fool in his right mind would not turn down a one-in-a-million chance like this. As he verbalized this thought, Randy opened the lid of the box and Colt helped himself to one of those rare jewels. After Randy gently positioned the humidor back on its altar as if that was a precious ritual that only a few are allowed to see, Colt glimpsed Randy trying to disguise his actions of sneaking the cabinet door open and retrieving something. Turning to Colt, Randy said, "Celia gets her autographed cook book as a memento of her first trip on The Caterina and you, Colt, get a container of pure gold: a box of Havanas! Enjoy them and remember that we were honored more than you!"

With both cigars having been lit, Randy took a book from another table and handed it to Celia along with a pen asking her to please sign the visitors' log and to be sure to give their mailing address. As Celia wrote, Randy politely asked, "Do you ladies wish to join us on a tour of the yacht?"

Kat spoke immediately, as if to interject her feelings before Celia could respond, "If Celia agrees, I would prefer us not to. I will show her later. I'd like to begin our one-on-one time that I spoke of yesterday, if no one objects. Celia?"

Celia felt a little surprised but hid it, for she wanted to see the yacht and had expected a group tour but willingly answered, "I'd very much like the same, Kat. I'm looking forward to our chat. See you guys, later," as the men left aft.

EIGHT

After the guys had disappeared up the stairs on the stern, Kat leaned across the sofa that they shared and whispered as if someone might hear her, "Let's go to my stateroom. I've got some secrets to tell you!"

Secrets! Celia thought, as she followed Kat to and then up the spiral staircases located in one corner of the salon then through a hatchway and down a hall and left into their master stateroom. Celia continued her private mental examination, Why are they showering us with so delicate a beginning? Or are they this polite and generous to everybody and this if just their way? Anyway, I need to be cautious with this 'secret' business and watch what I say! Secrets, huh?! What'll be next?. Celia was nobody's fool.

The master stateroom was as Celia had expected, having seen how these people spend money. It was a huge room about the same size as the salon and dining room put together; a king size bed with a hand-carved, mahogany head-board containing gobs of built-in electronic control devices within reach of the bed's occupants.

But what caught her eye next was a Grecian-style Jacuzzi next to the starboard side of the yacht with its heavily tinted window separating this oasis from the world outside. Four giant red-marble pillars surrounded the marble tub-side apron holding above it white lattice work covered with live tropical plants in ornate baskets. A beveled glass bar on the apron at tub-side and eye-level contained about every type of alcoholic beverage that the bather could desire. Next to the bar was a ceramic refrigerator that Celia imagined contained snacks and cold sodas.

After visualizing a million dollars spent in furnishing this bedroomm, her awe-struck flash waned as she asked Kat, "Why would you have a door in the side wall that appears to go nowhere?"

"When you open that hatch, a platformed, hand-railed ladder descends to the water level below. Sometimes, when we're cruising the Caribbean on a moon lit night, when anchored in one of those beautiful, crystal-clear, multi-colored green and blue island lagoons, we may go for a midnight swim. It sure does keep our frequency of love-making high. And the crew knows not to check on us if they hear us laughing or splashing later at night we have been known to go skinny-dipping. It's a real blast!"

Kat said, "Let's sit over here in the reading area. It's my favorite place to hideout when Randy is conducting business in the salon. I decorated this stateroom, myself, and I allow no one to use it, not even when the yacht is chartered."

Celia wondered silently, <u>With a queen's palace like this, why would anyone need to hide?</u>

Sitting in a $2,000, one-of-a kind lounging chair, Celia asked, "Where do we begin?"

Kat asked, getting an okay nod from Celia, "Do you mind if I control the conversation this time, Celia? I promise never to talk about myself this much, ever again. But there is so much in my background that could negatively influence how you feel about me in the future, if we are to become the best of friends. And I want you to know all of it from the outset so that you won't be hurt or ever feel that I wasn't completely open with you. And God knows how much I want and need a close friend! I said ten rosaries last night and ten Hail Marys and begged Jesus and The Holy Ghost and my Guardian Angel to help me make it happen."

Celia asked pointedly, "Why do I feel like I'm being smothered by you?"

There was a ten second pause, then Celia saw tears in Kat's eyes before she heard Kat whisper, "Oh, I'm so sorry. I know you must feel that I am a desperate, mental case and emotionally unstable. And I have been once or twice in the past, but I'm not now. Thinking about my actions, I guess that I have come on rather strangely and strongly, considering my whispering in your ear and saying things that indicated assumptions on my part. Will you forgive me and let me start over again? I promise to lighten up?"

"Sure," was Celia's answer.

Kat wiped the moisture from her eyes and continued, "Celia, do you understand I.Q. and how it represents a person's ability to learn and understand?" Kat received a nod from Celia.

Continuing, Kat asked, "Have you ever had yours tested and measured?" Again, a 'yes' answer, "Do you recall what it was?"

"Yes. I took some college-level courses on the naval base when we lived in San Diego and a couple of them were in psychology. We studied tests' make up and did a series of I.Qs. on ourselves and mine averaged 135 over five tests. But why do you ask?"

Kat said "Great! Having a high I.Q. can help and hinder. In my case I think it has not served me well. And it'll take some amount of my talking to explain what happened in my past. And because of certain events and how I let them affect me, some folks see me as being weird."

Continuing, Kat allowed, "And by the way, I've stood, sat, and laid many hours in psychiatrists' offices since I was ten years old in order for them to help me keep my sanity and to please my mother and her stupid ideas. And none of the many doctors ever deemed me anything but simply super-intelligent and a bit off the normal path, even for geniuses. I'm <u>not a danger to society but needed to be watched</u> was the way one stupid shrink in Rio wrote it in his file. I read this line when he left to go to his restroom. The jerk!

"And by the way, my I.Q. tested at 182," Kat added. "But don't let that scare you, because at 135 you've got to seem a little different to some folks yourself. With your I.Q number you are what is called a borderline genius. Haven't you felt strange sometimes because of how you can think compared to others? Don't you sometimes come over to people as a steamroller when your patience with their mental slowness is about gone? Don't you sometimes feel out-of-place and even bored in wordly group talks? And though you hate to admit it, don't you feel more comfortable talking in groups of intelligent men or women than with their mundane spouses detailing what happened to their kids yesterday in school or who beat the stew out of whom on the football field last night?"

Being surprised that someone else could feel this way and hearing her own secret feelings stated so precisely for the first time, Celia poured out in a high voice, "Oh my God, Kat! Yes!

51

Many times."

This was a very private, very personal, big admission on Celia's part; one that she had never been able to share with anyone before, not even Colt. Now, not only had she exploded her secret feelings in the open for the first time, but she was sharing them with this lonely, beautiful, middle-aged, Latin female that she had only met yesterday and whom she knew little about. Her uncontrolled and spontaneous revelation shook her innards to her bones. Trying to summarize her thoughts, Celia realized the enormity of what she was getting herself into. But she was consciously willing to let it happen as if a life-long needed release of a pent up and frustrated psychological part of her make-up was about to escape a little at a time. And it felt good. Then she turned to feeling excited.

A flash of a loss of time and place and circumstance captured Celia's mind for a few seconds. She reflected on a thought about destiny, as a fleeting feeling of strangeness came over her and disappeared. Then she realized how easily and quickly she had given away one of her inner-most secrets. She next felt a little self-loss in that she had lessened herself with this give away. But a deep seated, warm feeling of soul-closeness to Kat began easing its way in and was consciously building a recognizable foundation for a strong friendship. Celia instructed her mind: <u>Relax and go for it, Kid!</u> Celia became aware of feeling like she had known Kat and had trusted her in a previous life and that this relationship was to be. <u>Yes, we will be trading secrets!</u> Was Celia's conclusion as her thoughts returned to reality and her attention to Kat.

All this inner-thinking by this now-branded, borderline genius could not have taken over a second or two because no interruption in the flow of conversation occurred. Now back and sober from her mind-trip, Celia asked "Why me, Kat? Why have you chosen me for your friend? You don't know anything about me?"

"I'll have to explain it to you in lengthy detail. Celia, this has to be a secret between you and me. Sometimes I'll limit what I tell you, like this upcoming true story. And it can't be told to anyone. That would impart major damage to our relationship. Other times I may say, Okay to tell Colt, but nobody else. Do you have a problem with this condition and you doing the same with me?"

"Not at all," was Celia's oath of secrecy. "Would you get us a Coke from the bar?"

"Please forgive me for being nervous. I want so much for this meeting to go right. Do you smoke, Celia? I did not see you last night or this morning," Kat asked.

"I never have and never will; I hate it!" was Celia's reply. "Emphysema is killing Colt!"

"Me, either," Kat added, returning with two chilled and opened bottles. "Well, what I just said is not completely true. Sometimes, late at night out there on the ladder, I will smoke a cigar with Randy after we come out of the water. I won't allow him to smoke in here. I kind of like the taste of his cigars. But, as you know, some folks don't think cigar smoking is lady-like in public."

"Of course," she continued, "truth be known, I cannot stand to kiss or make love to a cigar-mouth; it's awful! So, if I smoke one before we come back inside, it ain't so bad." Both dying laughing, Kat added, "This is one of those secrets. If Randy knew that is what I've been doing all those 30 years of marriage and two before that, he'd kill me!"

Kat had relaxed with their laughter, but now, Celia was getting tense. Realizing this, she knew she just had to get it over with once and for all. She began, "Kat, you've set an atmosphere of trust and openness with what you have asked me and said. If it is to be that way, and I do want it to be, then there should be nothing that you and I cannot discuss except the intimacies that we enjoy with our husbands in the privacy of our marriages. Do you agree?"

"Absolutely. What are you leading to?" Kat inquired.

"Forgive me if I am going too fast too soon," Celia said and continued, "You guys have all the visible and usual signs of being in the drug business. Am I off base in even thinking this? If so, then I must ask your deepest forgiveness."

Kat stated, "No apology is necessary. Absolutely, is your answer. Randy is; my uncles and aunts are; my mother and

53

father were; and so is nearly everyone that I am blood-kin to. And it has been that way all the way back to my great-grandfather. But my sweet Celia, I never have been; I never will be; and I hate it more than I hate Satan and his burning Hell! That and that alone is what caused me to come apart at my mental-seams the first time and that is what caused me to come apart three times since. And that is why my family keeps me at a distance. And that's why I don't go home except for family funerals. I detest it!"

Kat said, "'Nita told me about it, first. We were twelve. She, Pablo, and Randy are the only ones who stuck by my side through all my problems and still accept and respect my feelings. My mother sure didn't. That's why she got rid of me by sending me to high school in Mexico and made me go to college there.

"But let me get off this and calm down. Let's get back to answering your question about why I so quickly approached you yesterday."

Celia interrupted, "Let's take a bathroom break."

Kat pointed, "His and hers are over there. You take one' I'll take the other."

NINE

Kat began, "My great-grandfather on my mother's side was a Shaman in one of the native tribes in the mountains of central Peru near Cerro De Pasco. A Shaman is not a witch-doctor like modern movies make them. They were and are among the elders in the tribe. It was quite common for one to be a female, too.

"Often-times he, or she, would be responsible for not only knowing, making, and applying the herbal medicines and storing a supply of them, but also being the teacher of the tribe's history and its spiritual beliefs, its marriage counselor, its accountant, the keeper of their food and ammunition stores, its trainer of youths into manhood, some into warriors, guiding young maidens through their puberty cross overs, the forecaster of weather, directing their hunters where to find game, and the keeper of sacred dates and rituals. Plus his or her additional duty was to be their representative to near-by tribes, requiring a knowledge of different tribal languages and sometimes including either English, French, German, or Portuguese."

Kat continued, "Since the beginning of known history in the mountains, Shamans used the leaves of the abundant coca plant to make drugs that they used in healing as anesthetics and in sacred ceremonials. It was not until invaders from the outside world showed them what profits from drug production could mean that these plants were cultivated. And my great-grandfather was one of the first to do it."

Kat added, "He received enormous amounts of gold and silver and jewels. But his tribe frowned on this. They felt it was wrong. They tolerated it until he started swapping his treasures for vast regions of thick forests and then, clearing them and planting more coca. That interfered with his tribe's hunting grounds and with their religious belief that one cannot own land, that Mother Earth cannot be sold.

"His actions became unacceptable," Kat added. "So, the tribal leaders met and threw him out, exiling their wayward Shaman towards white man's civilization and condemning his soul to forever living on earth. But he took with him proof of his ownership of millions of acres and continued his lucrative endeavors from afar.

"Greed and materialism! That's what caused it then and keeps it going now! Will we ever learn?" Kat said.

"I had my first menstruation at eleven. Back then I knew nothing about drugs. I had been tutored at home by the local teachers that came every morning six days a week at seven and left at noon. I was sheltered from the outside. I was allowed to play with one child, 'Nita. I was being reared in a strict Roman Catholic religion and believed everything that the church taught me."

Kat continued, "This is how I was when my mother's father, Grandfather Elizondo, came to pick me up to return to Peru for that summer to learn cattle on his huge ranch. Little did I know what I was in store for and how it would change my life forever. Neither did my dad or he would have killed his father-in-law.

"No more," Kat explained, "than had we gotten into his house than Grandfather told me not to unpack. Grand mother Elizondo had died the previous year at my house where she had come for the Christmas celebration. I asked why could I not go to my room? And he said, 'Because you and I are going on a trip to see some of your distant cousins. And we'll probably be there two weeks.' I loved and trusted my Grandfather and after this upcoming trip I loved him more. I was his favorite, for sure.

Kat added, "He and Mother did not get along at all. I remember the time when he found out that my mother, his daughter, was not going to let me attend the local Roman Catholic school with all the other kids and that she intended to lock me in and have me tutored. He blew up, hired a plane to rush him all the way to Bogota and gave her a big whatever. But it did no good. He tried to get my father to let him take me home with him where he'd raise his grandbaby right. He calmed down after a few days and went back. But from then on he sure kept a watchful eye on me.

"Oh, and Celia," Kat exclaimed, "as soon as he got back to Peru he put $1 million in a trust fund or whatever it was called back then and said that I could begin drawing the interest when I started college and the principal would be mine as his college graduation gift to me. I never did take any money out, though, for Mother and Father took care of all my expenses. And that account is being drawn on for our kids' educations. I don't recall him ever doing that much for any of my cousins or anyone else for that matter; just me."

Kat continued, "My uncle Julio and Aunt Freida managed the ranch then, where Grandfather stayed but lived about two miles away on the other side of the mountain. I thought that it was them coming up the dusty road to get us, but it wasn't. It was an old, beaten, ragged, school bus that looked like some nomad lived in it. I was right! He lived in it, but he wasn't a nomad."

She added, "Grandfather told me to get my stuff and Phillipe would load it and we'd be going with him for today, tonight, and tomorrow. And tomorrow night we'd be getting to where we were going to stay for ten days or more. I was scared, for Phillipe was weird looking. He looked like the wild jungle-men that I had seen in my National Geographics. And I was even more scared when he looked at me the first time.

"As we boarded," Kat continued, "I saw two double-bunks, a little gas stove, an old ice box, a portable toilet with a sheet hanging up around it, groceries, sodas and water, and several old crates with cushions on top that served as seats except for the driver's seat that Phillipe sat on. Oh, I almost forgot: and a great big hand-painted sheet over the windows on one side that read: Welcome Kat and Happy Birthday! And it had dozens of names on it, names like I had not seen before and could not pronounce, each printed by its owner with a big note at the bottom that was readable in my native Spanish: Your cousins eagerly await your arrival in the Village of The Rain Gods. Now I had a clue. But darn, I had even forgotten that my eleventh birthday was the next day!"

Kat continued, "Phillipe started the bus's smoking engine. No more than just around the first turn going downhill Phillipe hollered in Spanish, 'Uncle Juan Ts'Kolo, would you please get Kat and me a cold soda from the ice box? There are some cold beers there, too, that I got for you at the store. And would you bring one of those crates up here for Kat to sit on? I want to tell my newly found cousin what to expect for the next few days and what the village has planned for her birthday party tomorrow night.'

"WOW! Was all I could get out of me!" Kat exclaimed. "And he called me cousin, and a tribal birthday party in the mountains of Peru, and real natives who are cousins of mine that up to now I did not even know existed! I wondered why my mother never told me about this."

Kat went on, "For the next eight hours I sat next to Phillipe bouncing back and forth on the cushioned crate drinking sodas, eating cookies, listening, and using that shakey pottie. Man, did I learn a lot! And he was such a nice man. He made me laugh a lot when he was talking and trying to impress me with his Spanish and his English. He did not realize that when he got caught up in his own stories he was actually using his own language mixed with the other languages and I never told him. I let him think that he was saying something funny, and that egged him on. The more I laughed the funnier his stories got!"

Kat added, "Grandfather had gone to back of the bus and went to sleep, for he would be our night driver."

Kat said, "Hon, let's take a break. It's 12:00 now. You want some ice-water?"

"Yeah," came from Celia.

After returning, Kat informed Celia, "Celia, I phoned Randy while I was in the head and told him that you guys were getting the cabinet job. And further, that you had asked and I have told you that they are, indeed, in the drug business. Randy has already talked to Colt about it and they see no problem since you won't be involved in anything crooked whatsoever. They're up in Randy's office and will join us in this stateroom at 2:00 to discuss the job with the both of you. Snacks are at 3:00."

Kat continued from where she had left off, "When we arrived at the village about 200 people met us. Some women were completely covered, some half-naked. The men were chest-bare with leather loin covers on. Some had straps under there, some you could see everything from the side and some had huge ones, too. Kids who had not reached puberty were naked and bare-footed. Yet, everyone was very clean. Some were dark-skinned; some light tan and some nearly white. But all had coal-black hair and eyes so brown that they looked black.

"Let me go back to the night before," Kat regressed. "I skipped over something very important to the story. I woke up for about two hours during the night and went up front and sat beside my grandfather. Grandfather asked if Phillipe had talked about his people. He began, 'My grandfather, your great, great, grandfather, was born and raised a Kin Chabba. So was my father and he was nearly black. It wasn't until he left for civilization and married that our family's skin began to lighten through Spanish breeding. My mother was from Spain and my wife, your Grandmother, was a full-blooded Spaniard, too, but born in Portugal. But believe me, my precious, if I had my way and could turn back the clock, we all would be Kin Chabbas.'

"My Grandfather added, 'These kin-folks, though your mother refused to claim our ancestry, are the kindest people on God's earth. They live much like the people did in the Bible's Old Testament. But they don't know much about Jesus. They believe that their head priest, that they call Shaman, is a prophet that can talk directly to certain spirits, like your Guardian Angels, and get directions from God, whom they call Pintu Weeko, meaning: Spirit Before All Spirits. Kin Chabba means People of A Holy Place, referring to a huge temple where they go to worship Pintu Weeko. Their language is known as Chabba and their village is named Bukutu referring to their ancient rain gods. But they dropped the many gods bit a long time ago and converted to one god and put all the sub-spirits under Pintu Weeko.'

"He added, 'They have strict laws that they live by and enforce. If an outsider attacks one of their ladies, he doesn't get to leave; he disappears that night never to be seen again. And they have no crime as we know it. Their priorities are: their religion first, then their tribe and its practices, then their families and kids, and their homes, in that order. Love, generosity, and politeness are very important with them.

'Remember, Kat, that you are their blood-kin. So, if you go into one's home for the first time, they will ask you to stay and eat a meal. Not doing it, or at least having something to drink with them, is impolite and may hurt their feelings.

'If you ask directly for anything that they have, it will be given to you. So, be careful not to overly admire what you see. Possession of worldly things has very little meaning to the Kin Chabba, other than a minimum of food, clothing, and shelter. Be aware that the act of giving away their possessions is a sacred thing with them that they practice. It helps gain them a higher rank in the next level and brings their souls closer to yours while on earth. Be ever mindful of this, Honey, or we'll be hauling back a bus full when we leave Bukutu.'

'Kat, in your Roman Catholic religion, you have religious holidays like Christmas and Easter and some more honoring the Saints. They do, too, like The Day of Creation, and All Spirits Day. And everything on earth that has a name has its own guardian spirit watching out for it, similar to your Guardian Angels.'

"Grandfather continued, 'You have ceremonies like Christening or Baptism, you have First Communion and then Confirmation and some others, like Holy Matrimony and certain Holy Day Services. They do, too. But where most of yours are celebrating some form of religious meaning, their ceremonies are more in celebrating life itself. They celebrate a birth, a death, and when young boys and girls, like yourself, cross over through puberty to the adult ways. They celebrate marriage, pregnancy, crop planting, crop harvesting, the stars, the moon, the earth, wind, rain, and fire, the four cardinal directions, the night, the day, the seasons, and the plants, animals, and reptiles. In doing so, they thank their One God every day and night for all life and pray to Him through certain spirits, just like you Roman Catholics do. But they just don't have your Jesus. Eternal life for their soul is guaranteed to them from their birth, unlike some other religions.'

"He continued, 'My grandfather's sister was the grandmother of the current tribal lady Shaman. Her adult name is Embuko, meaning Living Spirit. And she's one of the finest ladies I've every known. Your grandmother was Em's best friend. We used to come down here about every other month and spend a week. We loved it. Now I don't get to come but about two or three times a year.

'When your mother became pregnant, I asked Em to do a ceremony and ask Pintu Weeko to assign a special Guardian Angel to earth to watch over you. She did, and He said that at your cross over He would send you a special gift. And that you were to use it to help yourself in your world. Em told me that your mother would be having a beautiful little girl, how much you would weigh when you were born, right to the ounce. And she said you would be pretty all your life, that you will marry a tall man whose great intelligence will match yours, and your offspring will be a boy and then a girl.'

"Grandfather continued, 'She said that you would need to have balance put into your make up when you reached the cross over ceremony, that you would encounter problems later in life. And this is why I'm bringing you to meet this wonderful lady. She is a very trusting, loving person; you'll see. You will have fun taking part in the ceremony and many gifts will be given you by your distant kins-people.

'I'll leave it up to you how you tell your mother about my taking you down here. But I'd suggest that if she asks, you tell her. If she doesn't, then it is our secret.'

'Now, give me a big kiss good-night and scoot on back to your bunk. Say your prayers and ask God to bless us and particularly your Aunt Em when she prays about you in the upcoming days during your crossing over ceremony. It will have a name but only you will receive it. She'll give it to you during your crossing.'

Kat asked Celia, "Need five minutes?" Celia nodded and went to the refrigerator.

Returning, Kat begun again, "The birthday party was nothing like I expected, but much more than I could have hoped for. I met my Aunt Em. If she just looks at you and smiles, you feel like heaven is beginning. She radiates a calmness over you. It's weird!

"All the kids in the village lined up and one by one offered me a gift and then asked me to join in with them eating tiny bites of their goodies or to sip a drop of the drink that each one brought for me to share with them. Aunt Em sat beside me on an elevated throne and interpreted Chabba for me. But some spoke pretty good Spanish and some said hello in English. I must have gotten 50 presents and was stuffed. Then the kids started playing games in front of me. And once in awhile I'd have to join in."

Kat iterated, "Then Aunt Em rose and talked in Chabba for a long time. Grandfather sat next to me, and told me what she was saying. It was a lesson for the younger ones rather than for me, except when she got to explaining what becoming a young lady meant and the responsibilities that would be placed on me. But she really wasn't talking about me in my real world, but in the Kin Chabbas' world.

"One thing did get my immediate attention when she closed with. 'And tomorrow your cousin will begin her training so that she may meet her Power Spirit, and with her Power Spirit seek and receive a Special Gift that Pintu Weeko promised for her before she was born. And she will be in full membership in Kin Chabba, for she carries some of our blood in her veins. And you will no longer call her Kat. Her adult Chabba name will be Embuko after me and you may call her Little Em for as long as I live. After I'm gone she will be called Embuko. When she returns to Bukutu you will receive and treat her as you do me. I pray that maybe someday she will return to live with us in peace and harmony in this paradise until He calls her to the next level.'

Kat kept on, "We slept in the bus that night and I finally did drop off to sleep, but it must have been 2:00."

Kat paused then said, "Celia, before I tell you about what happened next that changed my entire life from that time forward, I must prepare you, first, with some knowledge about what I was to face. I've covered already what Grandfather told me about the Kin Chabba's religion and about my Aunt Embuko being their Shaman. But I need to tell you more about their power and their mental capabilities.

"Their religion, Shamanism, has been found all over the world, for that is how widespread it used to be many centuries ago before it came very close to extinction. Twenty-five to thirty thousand year old writings on cave walls have been found in different areas of the world. A new resurgence of it is occurring primarily among the descendants of tribes, such as Native

Americans and the Aleuts in Alaska, just to name two.

"Scientists and writers have become deeply interested in what is referred to as The Old Ways. This term includes the practitioners of this unusual way of life having abilities and life styles that commonly allow them to do things unlike modern-day man. It may be that way for a number of reasons. But a much accepted basis for the differences between their lives and our modern-day ways, that we call civilization, is very simply put in saying: They live one with Nature. And they use a logic unlike ours. Plus their cultural, economic, and spiritual source is centered around their Shaman.

"History writes that it was not uncommon among those of the old ways to observe certain members of the tribes that possessed what we, today, would term Extra Sensory Perception, and not just the head priest or priestess. They had all the senses that we see today in our animals, birds and reptiles. They possessed many of these traits instinctively but some were taught and passed on over generations through the teachings of the Shaman.

"Why," Kat asked, "did these traits wane, you may ask? We really don't know. Some say that civilization's type of materialistic thinking may have replaced it, as we saved these innocent people from their paganistic beliefs. Some say white man's forced religion destroyed it. Some say it was evil, being caused by the devil. Again, no one, really, knows!

"Some doubters casually brush off this phenomenon as just not being possible. But many of us who know that this power does exist even today believe additionally that another wrong of our expanding materialistic society was perpetrated on some more unsuspecting souls.

"Because of this smothering transformation, much has been lost. As I get into telling you more you will, beyond any shadow of doubt, know why I believe in and am a student of Shamanism and still am a devout Christian and a follower of Jesus Christ's teachings."

Kat asked, "You said earlier that we should be able in our new relationship to talk about anything other than our private marital sex, didn't you?"

"Absolutely," she received.

"Then do you believe in a Creator of Everything?"

Again, "Absolutely," was Celia's response.

"May I ask you if you believe your God is omnipotent; that is, has power that is totally unlimited?"

"Absolutely!" was Celia's reinforced answer, for the third time.

Kat continued this trend of deduction, "Do the Christian religions and other religions that you are familiar with profess likewise?"

"All of them do! But what are you getting at?" was the impatient return.

"Then, my dear friend Celia, how, logically, can any intelligent human being say that Shamanism, in toto, could not possibly be another mono-deistic religion inspired by our own God?" Kat asked.

"You're right!" was the affirmation Kat got and it was sufficient to end that train of thought.

Kat returned to the beginning of the cross over ceremony. "The next morning at daylight Aunt Em came to the bus and instructed me to get up, get dressed, and then to pack my things, that I would be staying with her in her cabin for the duration so that she could have more private time teaching me The Old Ways. She woke up Grandfather and Phillipe and then made breakfast on the portable stove. Sitting around the table, my Grandfather began this Kin Chabba prayer saying to me to memorize it and think about each thought and to say it every morning before getting out of bed. Here it is: 'Pintu Weeko, my Holy Father, the Creator of me and all the things that I know and don't know, thank you for the night and for giving me rest during my sleep. Please guide me, today, through your spirits, so that my deeds will further your will for me.' Isn't that a beautiful prayer?" Kat asked.

Celia answered, "WOW! Kat."

"After breakfast as Aunt Em and I were leaving, Grandfather picked me up and gave me a big hug and a reassuring, good-bye kiss on the cheek, saying, 'Remember that you can trust this Shaman, your Aunt Embuko, with your life, as I do! Do exactly as she tells you and have no fear, for this is Pintu Weeko's way of preparing you for the future, as your ancestors have practiced it and passed on these teachings to us over millions of years.'

"Then, as if the ritual had begun, Grandfather put me down and, holding my hand, he offered it to Aunt Em saying, 'To you, Oh Holy Shaman Embuko, I offer in the name of Pintu Weeko my grandchild, this little girl called Kat, for you to help her in crossing over the bridge of life from childhood into adulthood. Please take her precious hand. Lead her. Teach her well The Old Ways and The Secrets of Shamanism, and comfort her along her ceremonial journey so that she feels the love with her of us that eagerly await the return of the adult that through these teachings and experiences she will become!' Tears of love and pride for me rolled down his face!

"Aunt Em, raising both hands palm up as if calling on the spirits, said, 'As Pintu Weeko has directed me and all Shamans before me, I prayerfully accept this great offering of your precious grandchild, my dear cousin Juan Ts'kolo. I will comfort her, care for her needs, and teach her, with the help of my Power Spirit, that which she is to learn and will faithfully return to you and to her kin in Bukutu the adult young lady, Kojo Embuko.'

"Then she said, 'It is proper that we begin your journey!'

"She," Kat continued, "took my hand and we left for her cabin, walking down a pathway lined on both sides with every single person that greeted me yesterday and last night at my party. When they first saw me they started in unison loudly chanting what sounded like 'Ku umbotcha D'lue, Pinto Weeko, kim ah Sue due tone, Kojo Embuko!' Their 200 screaming voices were deafening! I tugged on Aunt Em's hand to stop, so that I could shout to her, 'What are they saying?'

"Her answer was, 'And now our Creator, Pintu Weeko, calls unto Himself his daughter, Little Embuko! Kojo Embuko and Kojo Em are your names in Chabba.'

Kat informed, "Celia, it would take me about ten hours to tell you about all that I was taught. We don't have that much time if our guys are joining us at 2:00. So, I'll highlight just the major teachings and events that I incurred during the seven days and nights with Aunt Em and on my journey. Do you need anything before I go on?"

"No," was Celia's reply. "Please continue."

"In the privacy of her lamp-lit cabin that was as clean, as orderly, as brightly painted, and as well lit by six animal-oil lamps as a hospital's operating room, Aunt Em spoke as she placed my bag on the bunk that I was to use, 'Sweetheart, you must trust me totally when I tell you what to do. However, I will explain why and how before you begin your tasks and if you don't understand exactly what I've conveyed or if you have questions about carrying out what I've commanded, you must, I repeat, you must stop me instantly and let me know your thoughts. For this is your cross-over, not mine. And Pintu Weeko demands that I do my best, as He has taught me, to make it enjoyable for you every step of the way. Now let's begin your first lesson.'

"Aunt Embuko continued, 'It is my understanding from Juan Ts'Kolo that you have begun menstruation. Is that correct?'

'Yes,' was my answer."

'Good,' the Shaman continued. 'Has any adult explained having a period and further, have you had any instructions about reproduction and sexual activity?'

'No,' I answered."

'Do you know what the word virgin means and if so, are you still one?'

'Yes, to both those questions,' was my reply."

'Great. But I must confirm your virginity before I can proceed, as mandated by Pintu Weeko; for only virgin girls and virgin boys may participate in the Holy Cross over. So, please remove your under-panties and raise your dress above your waist and get up on that table, lie down on your back, then bend your knees upwards and outwards so that I may examine your exterior sex organs.'

"While I was getting ready, she washed her hands then whispered a prayer in Chabba, as she did before every lesson. With a lamp in hand she began examining me, saying, 'Yes, you, indeed, are a virgin. You will better understand, later, what I am about to instruct you to do when we discuss the act called intercourse during your lessons. But, now, this is very important for you to remember for your personal health and safety.

'Listen closely, Kojo Em, to my words but do not be alarmed. Before you have your first intercourse you must go to a doctor that in your language is called a gynecologist. I will spell it for you. Then you will say and spell it back to me while implanting my command, permanently, into your memory.

"She spelled it and I repeated and asked, 'Why?'

"Her answer was, 'Your female sexual attributes look very normal for a virgin your age. However, within the inner lips of the genital orifice of nearly all virgins there is a thin membrane that is usually broken once intercourse occurs. Yours looks a little thick and a little extended, though indicating no serious problem. However, it could cause you extra discomfort and external bleeding during the initial penetration by your mate. The doctor will take care of this by clipping or cutting the hymen, or maidenhead, as it is called. It is a very simple surgical procedure. Oh, it will sting a little when he does it, about like a fly's bite. I've done dozens myself with no problems. It's a common female thing. And, Kojo Em, keep this as our secret.'

"I did as she said and she proved right."

"Celia, I went into detail about this because I want to make an important point about Aunt Em," Kat explained. "Even as an eleven year old, I noticed that she seemed uncommonly educated for a tribal Shaman living hundreds of miles back in the jungles of Peru. So, I asked her how she learned all this stuff and here is what she shocked me with: during her own cross over ceremony her I.Q. was tested, as I was to be during my next lesson. And after her Shaman saw the results, he immediately called a meeting of the village elders. The elders assigned her into high priesthood training. And then after Aunt Em's cross over ceremony was concluded, they put her directly under the Shaman's tutelage for formal schooling that lasted six more years. And she never married.

"Then you know what they did next? As she finished her formal schooling, they secretly sent off an application to the Universidad Peruana in Lima, Peru where she was accepted into their nursing program! This little ole lady, my Kin Chabba Aunt Embuko, graduated in five years with a Bachelor's Degree in Nursing and taught college-level nursing courses there for a year before returning to Bukutu to take up her roll as their Shaman understudy. She speaks Spanish, English, Quechua, and Chabba!"

Again, all Celia said was, "WOW!

Kat sped up the pace, "Over the next four long days and three nights up to bedtime, she gave me several intelligence tests, then lessons in biology and physical anatomy, human reproduction, personal hygiene and grooming, courtship and basic social manners, marriage, human intercourse and love-making, menstruation and natural birth control, pregnancy and child-birth, child care, the wife's family role, the husband's family role, marriage problems and adjustments, family medical and health care, cooking and diets, homemaking and house keeping, and beginning sewing.

"Then came our history, starting with The Ten Sacred Stories that every Kin Chabba must know verbatim and must tell to at least ten others during his or her lifetime. I had to memorize them. She told me all about my unwritten ancestry and unwritten heritage.

"We began the formal training for my Shamanistic trip with her giving me the name of my cross over ceremony and instructing me how to use the words as a silent chant or mantra in aligning my conscious and sub-conscious mind with my spirit so that I might journey mentally and spiritually to my secret place and find, meet, and converse with my Guardian Angel that followers of Shamanism call Power Spirit. Further, I could never say the sounds of my sacred words within hearing distance of any human, nor spell them aloud, nor write them down or syllable them except to my God, Pintu Weeko, to my Power Spirit, or to my Shaman Teacher, Aunt Embuko. And the only exception to this was if I was ever forced to sing my death song. I was trained how to chant them until no pain is felt, my body ceases to live and my soul's journey to the next level begins. And if I become too old to be productive or fatally ill I can invoke them with Pintu Weeko's blessing.

"Detailing the training and preparations for my trip will take too much time, Celia," Kat stated. "But here's the essence: after training me on a form of self-hypnosis and practicing that again and again, until I could simply chant my mantra and quickly be in a somnambulistic state, meaning deep trance, all the while fasting for the last three days and nights, Aunt Em took me to a beautiful waterfall about five miles through the jungle where we came upon a grass-thatched, padded-floor hut. My Aunt said, 'You are to stay here, no food; just water from the falls. Use your Sacred Words the way I taught you and introduce yourself to your Power Spirit who waits for you. Build a very strong relationship with her and through her with her superior The Holy Ghost, and through both with Pintu Weeko. And may I suggest that since you profess Christianity, visit with your Savior Jesus Christ.' Notice she said her? She knew!

"Aunt Em finished, 'A Power Spirit will manifest itself in living form and usually as an animal or as a bird but it could be a living flower. Mine took the form of a female eagle. You will know it when the spirit appears to you for the third time in the same form.

'During a sacred ceremony that your Juan Ts'Kolo asked me to do for you just before your birth, my Power Spirit said that she was informed that Pintu Weeko had set aside a Special Gift for you. And further, that you will return to me from your spiritual journey with it. Also, your Power Spirit will be trained to instruct you on its use so that you may use it for your benefit and the benefit of others in Pintu Weeko's name.

'Ask your Power Spirit to show you the way back through the jungle when you two are through. Bye, my darling. I'll see you in a couple of days.' And she disappeared through the bushes."

Kat said, "Let's take ten minutes. I need to go to the head and to get a drink."

Celia wanted so badly to hear the rest that she prepared them sodas and thought that she'd never hear that darn commode flush! But it did and Kat continued, "Two days and two nights passed very rapidly. My Power Spirit and I spend a lot of time talking. It manifested itself as a beautiful spotted female jaguar. I know that you are just dying to find out what my Special Gift is. So, I think that I shall wait until tomorrow to tell you!"

Celia chided, "Yeah, you do and that jaguar Power Spirit of yours will be attending a funeral this week, Miss Smarty!"

"Just kidding!" Kat laughed and continued, "Remember us talking earlier about some of my ancestors having senses that they lost somehow along the way; senses that modern times recognize that animals, particularly, wild animals possess; senses like seeing in the dark; walking straight to water or food sources hundreds of miles away; senses like reacting early to upcoming bad weather and knowing when it has finally left. Remember that?"

Getting a "Sure," Kat went on. "Well, one of the senses that many animals have is a highly developed way of looking at another animal or human and telling if that person or animal is aggressive, afraid or calm and if any harm is meant. Tests, by today's researchers, indicate that certain gases are being emitted from body-glands and these different gases have light frequencies that are visible to special eyes; eyes that are able to receive the frequencies of these colors that are beyond a normal being's ability. For example, it can be proven very easily that we give off gases by placing one of those gauges under your arm that air-conditioning technicians use to find leaks.

"Further, scientists say that some animals and some insects, too, such as bees, see a colored halo of light completely surrounding live bodies representing their moods. Additionally, some believe that some of our higher intellect animals and in the past, certain humans, could also interpret character traits from the colors. And many Shaman were given this gift. This is one reason why they were sent as ambassadors along with their elders and chiefs to inter-tribal councils."

Pausing, she asked Celia, "Do you have any questions about this?"

"No," was her response.

"Good," Kat said, "Well, now you know my secret of secrets! In Chabba it is called, "Kulu Sin Toma", which means the gift of animal eyes. And this is how I was able to recognize you as a prospective friend. I activate the gift by relaxing and repeating my secret words until I reach a somnambulistic state. Then having called up my Power Spirit, I stare at you while she analyzes, through my eyes, the colors of your aura. By the thoughts that I received back I know my Power Spirit's summary.

"I went back to visit my Grandfather for at least two weeks during my summers home from the convent in Mexico. Then when I got into college, my father let me spend the summers with Grandfather, much to my mother's chagrin. And Randy started going with me. You know darn well we weren't at the ranch; we went straight as a bee flies to Bukutu. That's how Randy and I learned the language of the Kin Chabba. But Randy never got into the religious part of it.

"Grandfather told my father all about it once I wanted to spend the entire summer there. Father bellowed at first but then calmed down. But he wasn't ever told about my Special Gift. Mother went to the grave not knowing about any of my visits to our kin-people's village; that was her fault and her loss.

"Grandfather died some years back. Aunt Em is in her eighties and still active as their Shaman. Randy, 'Nita, and Pablo and, now you are the only ones that know about my Special Gift. You do not, I repeat you do not, have my

72

permission, at this time, to tell anyone about it, not even Colt. You can tell him all the rest, if you want to. But exclude about my gift. And be careful in sharing this. He may think that you are as weird as many think I am.

"Now let's go walk around the yacht. We've still got twenty minutes before meeting the guys."

74

As Colt followed Randy from the salon that morning, leaving Kat and Celia behind to go to the master stateroom, they had no more than gotten half way up the stairwell when Colt shocked Randy by saying, "Would I be wrong in saying that it sure looks like you guys are in the drug business?"

Randy stopped abruptly; became red-faced; took a deep breath, paused for several seconds as if trying to decide what to say, then turned directly face to face with his guest. As Colt saw Randy's reaction he thought, <u>Well, there goes the big cabinet job, you dummy!   Celia's gonna castrate my elephant-size equipment!</u>

Then Randy's face quickly faded back to normal as he shocks Colt just as much as Colt shocked him by returning with this question, "Does your wife feel the same way?"

"Yes," was Colt's truthful but very weak and very regretful answer.

Then he shocks Colt even more by adding, "Good, my friend. That relieves me and Kat from all the pressure and stress that we had loaded ourselves with trying to figure out how to break the truth to you two. Now we can get on with building the friendship, for our big wall has been hurdled. Let's skip the yacht tour for now and go to my office just ahead and break out a fresh bottle of Chivas Regal and get to know one another." And that is just what they did.

Randy was pouring their first drinks when Colt asked, "Well, Boss-man, where do we go from here and now that I've got egg all over my face?"

Randy laughed, "I don't see or smell any eggs in here; maybe a little B. S., but definitely no eggs." Pausing while looking at Colt he smiled a very wide and pearly-type smile and said, "Will you just relax Coulter J. Erhlichman? Ain't nothing big gonna blow you away. Right now, this is my party, not yours. We want to be your friends. And it's gonna freak-out your ever-loving mind to hear why we do and how much we already know about you and Celia. This ain't your mama's Oldsmobile that you're messing with! Here, have the first of many scotches that you and I are about to eliminate. Sit back and let me get out my mental shot gun and get started."

Randy started, "Yeah, we're in the drug business, big time! But I'll get to that later 'cause that isn't the most important thing that you and I need to cover. You probably don't agree with that right now. But you will later. I gair-ron-tee!

"Please, Colt, and I say please, again, don't get upset with what I am about to tell you because it could make you mad. So hear me out before coming to any conclusion. The only friends in the world that Kat and I have that we can associate with on a social basis that does not involve money or business is 'Nita and Pablo. The same is true with them. So, about a month ago the four of us were talking about how nice it would be if we could find a compatible couple who we could bring into our little tightly-knit foursome. And Kat's shrink told her that for her mental health she needed someone, a female friend, that she could trust that would take her outside of our little world of limited freedom; one that she could talk to.

"Listen to me, Colt. Again, what I'm about to tell you may make you feel like I've severely intruded into your and Celia's private life. I have. Again, I say, I have. But it has been done in order to save all of us a lot of hurt and a lot of time. We don't need to spend months and a lot of entertainment money building a deep and sincere, trusting relationship if there is anything that will ultimately interfere and end it. Not if we all can clear any potential obstacles out of the way at the start. But I have enough faith in your intelligence and understanding that allows me to know in my heart of hearts that you'll respond in a positive manner. And this is the first part of a lot that I need tell you before we meet Celia and Kat at 2:00 in our master stateroom. Further, if you will let this friendship continue, then I give you my word that in a very short time we, all six of us, will be feeling about each other: Mi casa, su casa; my house is your house! I promise!

"So, don't throw anything at me until I finish. Here goes: Colt, I run a legitimate group of about thirty corporations under one conglomerate, whose stock is worth half-a-billion dollars. The sales of those companies total about four times that: 2

billion a year. Then that import-export operation that you suspect exists, should do much, much more than our conglomerate. If this is true, then that makes me a very big heavy weight in the business world that can get a lot of things done if I want to, allowing me to have available a lot of buttons that I can push very quickly. Do you agree with what I just said?"

"Yes, absolutely," was Colt's return.

"Good" Randy commented and continued. "Colt, as I told you earlier, I studied Languages and Psychology in College and got a Master's in each. One of the courses I was required to take was <u>Understanding Human Relationships</u>. Let me highlight what I remember about it before I go further. And I doubt if you have ever been exposed to this type of thinking. It will help you understand me better and accept what I'm gonna stuff in your mouth in a little bit, ask you to chew on it, and then spit it out so that we can get on to the meat.

"Human relationships, according to my professors, can be broken down into their various parts from their beginning through their maturity. Here's some words that describe how they grow. Let's make it personal by my referring to me and to you. That'll help. In the beginning, if we are to become friends, you and I, consciously or unconsciously, must both desire a friendship with each other. The first key word is Desire.

"Then we must communicate to find knowledge about each other in order to find compatibility. The three words here are: Communicate, Knowledge and Compatibility. Then about now, as we strengthen our friendship, Trust appears, as our next word. Then it's decision time, for Commitment soon makes its presence known. Then Loyalty will slowly develop. So, here, Colt, we have what you and I need to grow through, according to my professors, if we are to become very good friends: Desire, Communication, Knowledge, Compatibility, Trust, all leading to Commitment then Loyalty, Love and Respect will follow. According to them, this takes a lot of time. And for normal relationships, that is how folks tend to find their friendships developing, that is, over a long period of time.

"How many times do you hear people say, 'Why, he's been or she's been my friend for a long time!' referring to time as if that makes the relationship strong. I say baloney! It's commitment and trust that carries a strong friendship; time does not have to be as important! We've been brainwashed!

"I say, further, that if you and I can find a way to established a deep trust today with a strong commitment to each other and know enough about one another to find compatibility, then we are on our way. We've got the building foundation finished for a big one. All we gotta do after that is stack the blocks!

"From what we told you about ourselves last night at Sam's, do you feel that you have enough knowledge of Kat and me to find compatibility?"

"Yes, you-all told us a heck of a lot. But I know very little about this other thing that I suspect you are in," were Colt's statements.

"Well, maybe all you need to know is that I am in it. But I would not want a best friend of mine to get involved. So, it should not be a factor at this time, should it?" said Randy.

"You've got a good point," replied Colt.

"Well," Randy continued, "since you know a lot about us, let me tell you that I already know a lot about you and Celia.

"You are honest and your words are your bonds. You love your children and grandchild. You are faithful and loyal to your friends.

"You are disciplinarians, except for your three-pack-a-day cigarette habit. You pay your bills on time, but you owe $33,000 in hospital bills. You need more insurance, which you are having a hart time getting and keeping. Your truck and Celia's car are paid for. You owe $28,000 on your condominium. Y'all's income last year was $87,850.

"You like to gamble $20 on your twice weekly golf game at Dove Creek and you've been known to lose $100, tops, playing poker in the locker room with the regulars after golf. Your monthly tab there runs about $150, including your meals with Celia.

"You frequent Lucky's strip joint up North 59 about once a month, alone, and leave about 50 bucks behind, half of which goes to just two girls, Anna and Jackie, for table dances. But you've not ever asked them for a date or even cursed in front of them.

"Your military record shows that you were cleared for top secret duty during you Navy tour while working in Cryptography decoding enemy messages requiring a minimum I.Q. of 125. Your police record shows only three traffic violations and two tickets for Celia. You were put overnight in the brig in California for being drunk and getting into a fight; the charges were dropped.

"Your religious background indicated that you two were members at North Bay Methodist Church until five years ago, when a new pastor arrived and you have not been back since. And you both play tennis many afternoons at your condo complex's courts.

"Now, go ahead and get mad and throw something at me if it'll make you feel better! In the meantime I'm gonna fix you a strong drink."

Colt responded, "I wish I was mad. I'd like to be mad. I'd like to be mad enough to hit you! But the funny thing is I'm shocked beyond words and that's not really adequate enough to describe how I do feel. I really feel more like laughing! How in the world did you find all that out? Every last bit of it is true and you just met us yesterday. I'm glad Celia's not in here. She'd walk out! I guess you better just pour me one on the rocks and make it a water glass full before I do decide to punch you!"

Randy handed him a weak one this time, but Colt was too upset to notice. Then he downed it and handed Randy the empty glass back for another one. Randy figured he would. He made Colt a little stronger one this time figuring that Colt would be more pensive and sip on this one. Randy was right again.

Randy sat down and looked at his friend who was letting all of this soak in while the alcohol was doing its job bringing him that needed mental-flushing feeling. About three minutes passed.

Randy did not want Colt to have a chance to talk about it for he feared that talking about it might upset him more than listening. So, Randy took control and said in a low, sincere voice while reaching over and warmly squeezing Colt's arm, "I sincerely apologize for the hurt that I may have caused you by running a background check on you two. That was not my intent; saving a lot of time and hurt feelings was. I got the report last night at midnight and it only confirmed what we had concluded earlier --we, definitely, want to be your friends. Only Kat and I read it. But Pablo and 'Nita were told that I was going to do it and this morning before you got here I told them that the report came in during the night on the fax and you and Celia got an A-Plus. And I said to my two dearest friends, "Let's go for it." And Kat feels the same way."

Randy saw Colt move from the front edge of the sofa to resting fully on the back. This was a good sign. Colt's free right arm with a tight fist was now loose and comfortably on the padded sofa arm. His eye-brows relaxed from their squenched positions. The muscles in his tight clenching jaw relaxed from his teeth-crunching bites. Colt then took a deep breath and sighed its release. Protrusion at his waistline showed stomach relaxation. Then he lit a cigarette, gently inhaled, and blew the smoke upwards and then took a slow drink. His drawn lips were now relaxed.

Randy's trained mind and eyes saw and recorded this and silently concluded, I've won! This crisis is over! Again, before Colt could speak, Randy continued, "Colt, we have a secret intelligence division of over one hundred people located in South America, in a number of U.S. cities, and in other countries that costs us over $15 million a year. And some of that, about $5 million, is spent buying information and computer access codes. I made one call as I left your place yesterday morning and put the ball in motion. Needless to say, I can find out almost anything world-wide that's not top secret. Access by computers gets us about 90% of it in about 45 minutes. Our lives are pretty much public information these days. If you have questions about my sources, I'll try to answer them."

Colt asked, "Most of that I can figure where you got it. But how did you find out about my having a hard time getting insurance?"

Randy stated, "If one makes an application for insurance and presents a history of health problems, and you, apparently, have done that, sometimes the insurance company will rate you. That is, they will apply a number that represents the increase in their premium to allow for the increased risk in covering you, let's say three times normal, for example, because of your emphysema history, your smoking three-packs-a-day and your age. If they choose they may pass the information about you having been rated by them to other participating companies and to an information source bureau. All I have to do is buy access to your file and I can get what I need. So can a lot of other people! Credit information can be bought from several sources, too. But some of the other information that I get is not quite above the table, but it can be bought also. And we use private investigators by the hundreds, too.

"Colt," Randy continued and moved to the front edge of his chair, lowering his voice while lowering his head to present sincerity and heart-felt warmth, "Right now it would be a normal feeling for you to feel prostituted; to feel like crap for my having invaded your privacy. But let me assure you that you'll know more important stuff about me before you leave today than what I've revealed about you. In fact, my reputation, and my freedom is going to be put into your hands with what I'm going to tell you.

"But let me digress to explain the most important reason why I did what I did in backgrounding you. Colt, think about this: relationships between two willing individuals can be simply evaluated at any moment of its existence by weighing the sensitive knowledge that each sacredly keeps about the other and each's strength of conscious commitment to the relationship, love included.

"Let me use a hypothetical example. Let's assure that all I now about you is all that you could and would have given me over, say, five years. Well, then I know you as well as you will let me. Then if my commitment to keep your secrets is a total commitment and if I am completely loyal to you and if we are compatible in whatever activities that allow us to share enjoyable time with each other and if the same from you applies to me, then one would say that we are true friends."

But then Randy threw in the exception. "In this example you know just as much about me as I know about you, making the amount of knowledge exchanged equal in quantity. But what if a lot of people knew all this background information on me and I knew this and could care less, because that information was not important whatsoever to me. Then my exposure of it, since you consider it so sensitive, would not allow the relationship to be equal. Does this make sense?"

Receiving a "Yes," Randy continued. "But what if I told you about my most secret secret that no one knows about me. Not Kat. Not Pablo. Not 'Nita. Not anyone, except one and I'll never name that individual. And that if you told it, I would have to kill myself and probably have you killed first for betraying me. Then if I did tell you that, can you see that I'd be more committed to you than you to me, off setting all the amount of information that I gleaned from my intelligence sources yesterday? Then couldn't you say that I proved that I wanted to be your true friend and that you could be totally and unquestionably loyal to our relationship for I had put my life in your hands?"

Colt asked after a sudden realization hit him, "This isn't just an example is it? You really intend to tell me, don't you? But why?"

Randy answered, "Because I believe every word that I've spoken to you and every principle that I've explained to you about how true, life-long friendships can be given birth immediately, and that time spent can be wasted time without a total commitment being made at the beginning. But before we talk further about more revelations, let me say some things about commitment."

Randy asked, "Do you belong to any clubs or organizations where you take a secret oath swearing to the members your sincerity in honoring them and not telling outsiders what they expose you to?"

"Yes, I am a Mason," was Colt's answer.

"Good," Randy complimented. "But let me assure you that I am not a Mason and know nothing about it other than that they do keep secrets. However, I knew that you were a Mason and I wanted to use that as an example. I saw your Masonic ring when I shook your hand the first time in your shop and knew from that, that most likely, you were a principled person since all of the Masons that I've ever met were. Would I be treading on your secret grounds by saying that I also know that from the outset Masons-to-be must make commitments like many other secret societies and fraternities that I know. I'm not saying anything new with this statement, for I've read it in articles and newspapers many times. Am I right?"

Colt's reply was, "Yes, go on."

"As a side note," Randy said, "the Mafia does similar. They call theirs Omerta, pronounced Oh-mair-tah. And death used to be the punishment for breaking their code of silence. Have I explained enough about this commitment?"

"Yes," Colt gave back.

"Then, one final point before I conclude," Randy added. "We need to cover Trust. In our Christian Society we are brainwashed by many churches to blindly accept trust as being an inherently religious thing and an integral element that everyone is expected to willingly offer other brothers and sisters, and so doing, giving it a heavenly trait. Not so! This allows them another tool of indirect control! Show me in the Bible where God or Jesus says 'Trust man-kind!' In fact, it tells us to 'Trust God and build up your treasures in heaven, not on earth.' And Jesus did say Love thy neighbor as thyself. But he did not say 'trust that sucker!'

Randy asked, "Would you trust Celia to fly you in my Bonanza?"

"Absolutely not!" Colt exclaimed.

"Would you trust me to fly you?" Randy followed with.

"Absolutely," again, Colt came back with.

"Well, my friend, you have proven that you have made decisions based on your knowledge and trust about Celia and, separately, about me. Though you trust her in many aspects, you know that she cannot pilot an airplane. And you believe you trust me enough already to admit that you'd fly with me. However, even with your commitment to get airborne with me, I'll bet you, in your heart, would feel squeamish about turning over your life control to me by leaving the ground and further that you really won't relax until you see us in the air. Additionally, your thinking and justification for the commitment will include that if I'm not telling the truth about being able to fly that Bonanza safely, then my life is in jeopardy, too. So, in this example, you combined commitment and trust with an element of caution! Am I right?"

"You bet," was Colt's feedback.

"Then Trust is not what we have been led to believe! We assign our trust in specific cases where we can depend on the outcome of the other person's actions and thoughts being acceptable to us and, further, when we can continue to expect that same action or thought in the future and can rest assured of no unacceptable changes. In other words, we trust folks only in the ways that we can predict them and their consistency. We don't just up and trust anyone! That's for sheep led by a Judas goat!

"And though as precious as some relationships may grow to be, we, still, put some sort of an invisible checks and balance system into effect in order to assure ourselves that nothing has changed. Don't we?"

"You're right again, Randy. But I've never thought about it this way. But you re correct," Colt concluded.

Randy insisted, "Let's finish this. Why don't we start our relationship with this knowledge and these principles as a basis? Plus, the first thing that I will absolutely promise you at this point, Colt, is that I will commit my solemn oath of secrecy to you and will tell nothing that you've told me to keep just between us. And that further, I swear before Almighty God that my word to you will be my bond and that all my promises to you will be kept. However, should circumstances beyond my control appear that alter, in any way, a promise that I have made to you, I will find you immediately and inform you of the same. Are you willing to swear the same oaths to me?"

Pausing to let all this soak in, Colt answered, "Yes, Randy, I am!"

"Good," Randy replied. "Then, please, stand Coulter J. Erhlichman and take the hand of Randolph Antonio Martinez.

Look me straight in the eyes, then as a sign of total commitment to your and my secrecy, our Omerta, to life-long loyalty and love to each other, to a trust that makes our word to each other our bond, you are to hug me and give me a kiss on the cheek signifying your sincere commitment before your God that seals this relationship, forever."

Then they hugged and exchanged cheek kisses. From the emotionalism of the moment, moisture showed in their eyes. With this holy exchange of vows two souls had been joined in a most unusual but forever-bonding ceremony. Randy then gave a Benediction, "Welcome into my life, my beloved brother! <u>Mi Casa, Su Casa</u>!" Randy got up to prepare another scotch for them but this time to toast their sacred, yet embryonic, gift to each other.

In conclusion to this part of their relationship, one that would never be discussed between them again, for there would be no need to, for all had been said that needed to be said, Randy began to give to Colt his deepest of secrets. "Colt, I will, indeed, have you shot if you repeat this to anyone. I am giving to you now, more than I could ever give to you when we talk about the drug industry and my involvement in it."

Looking straight into Colt's eyes, Randy relayed his innermost secret and form it Colt knew that he, indeed, could destroy Randy's world. He wished to all heaven that he had not heard what Randy had just put on his shoulders. Colt was totally caught unaware and shocked speechless! He would never have thought that Randy was capable of committing such an act. Never!

Seeing Colt's face go white, Randy suggested they take a break, and hit the heads.

TWELVE

Returning from the head, Randy answered the phone saying, "Hey darling, how is it going? Good! Does she understand your religion? Fine! Yeah, Sweetheart, I've told him a little about the business but not in detail, but I'm going to. No, it's not going to matter much between him and me. Sure, we'll see you at 2. Have fun! I love you, too, Kat. Bye!"

Colt heard all of this.

Randy, receiving a scotch, opened with, "Kat's ancestors included folks from a native tribe in Peru. They have a religion called Shamanism that is similar to the Shamanism practiced by your Native Americans for tens of thousands of years. Kat is involved in it. Some of it I believe and some of it I'm suspect. Yet, she is still a very devout Roman Catholic. You tell me how that works?

"I've visited the Kin Chabba village many times with her. We spent the summers with them during college. She and I speak their tongue, called Chabba. She's down there telling Celia all about it. Don't be surprised if Celia acts weird and does a dance for you and talks funny when you get her home," Randy laughingly added.

Randy, changing the subject said, "Before going into the stuff about my business, I need to give you some background. I'll begin while getting us some cigars from my desk. You need to sit down or lie down on the sofa for I need you to clear your mind of the shock that I gave you a few minutes ago and pay attention to what I've got to educate you on. You've been reared in an unusual atmosphere, these United States, where life and thinking is one-of-a-kind."

Having both cigars lit and observing Colt prone on the sofa watching his smoke twirl upwards towards the ceiling, Randy started, "Clear your mind and imagine this: you are now in a country unlike the U. S.! You have grown up there but know little about politics. You were a kid when the current regime overthrew the previous government by force. You cannot feel any comfort in the government's protecting you, your family, your kin, nor you business. And you know of people who have disappeared after publicly challenging their policies.

"To be in business, you must pay off everyone in authority. That is the way it operates. And though you hate it, you have to accept and participate in it. The bigger your profits are, the bigger the pay-offs become. You, literally, buy protection both for your family and yourself, for your business activities, and your business locations from the police, the government, and their henchmen through your local contributions to their various projects, through their fund raising campaigns, and through directly making individual pay-offs and bribes. Colt, is your mind seeing this?"

"Yeah!" was the reply.

"In your U.S., money comes into the government through your taxing system that is supported mainly by a very large number of working, middle-class citizens. Let's guess, for illustrative purposes, 65% of the government's income. Let's say that 15% comes from the rich and 15% of the rest collected by the IRS comes from corporations and 5% from the poor that have incomes. Oh, these percentages could be off some, for you corporations may share a little more than that but it will have no bearing in this case because the mass of citizens shoulder the bigger tax burden under your system.

"Now, what if the middle-class masses all but disappeared from your national work force and could pay no taxes because they were unable to produce enough to even qualify, and what if they all refused to file income tax returns, 95% of them being illiterate? You couldn't jail 200 million people who even if they did file would be sending no money in. Think about what changes would be brought about in your economic system. It would fall!

"Now, let's go back to the beginning of the founding of your country. Assume that the masses that make up your successful middle class never were allowed to become a middle-class because your country's future planners that influenced the government's direction by controlling its law-making would not allow a middle class to be born, period, much less develop into being the single, largest source of its revenue.

"Without this huge source of income, much would be different. Your country could not have welfare. It could not have a gigantic military or foreign aid. It could not have your space program and NASA. No farm support. No food and tobacco subsidies. It couldn't wage wars in foreign countries for its economic benefit. It could not have medicare and medicaid. It could not have your federal highway systems that allows your industrial system and your food system to work. You would not be enjoying the electricity from your huge dams and hydro-electric systems.

"Your states would not have federal government taxes returned to them for their programs such as highway paving programs and the federal school program. You would not have the federal banking system that you are so fortunate to have. And last, but probably most important to this hypothetical example, you would not have a government whose income was sufficient enough to allow it to even pay its employees a living wage much less offer them the fringe benefits plus a fine retirement program that your capitalistic system allows.

"Colt," Randy emphasized, "so, having no middle class, at all, just the very rich and the very poor, makes a total change in the results when evaluating a country and when trying to understand why a country like Colombia and Peru and even the other South American countries would turn their backs and let an industry like the drug industry not only exist, but openly assist it and to help smuggle drugs into other countries. Survival is their number one motivational reason; then comes greed and materialism. The government and its leaders and the politicians receive billions above and under-the-table for helping it operate.

"This should explain the differences between what your country offers its fortunate citizens and what Colombia, a developing country, does not and can't offer theirs? The reason is simply because the monies aren't available. So, if you understand what the conditions are as I have described them and accept them as the truth, then it should be easily understood that a basic existence, that is, food, clothing, and shelter, is the only goal for most of the people there. And it is a daily struggle for most; it consumes their waking hours. Their priorities, their motivational factors, their values of morality, legality, religion, social mores and even their value and attitude toward life, itself, are different from what your U. S. citizens so lavishly and wastefully take for granted.

"And lastly, their daily struggle for a meager existence creates a personal attitude that anything that helps them get what they need to exist is acceptable and becomes a way of life, even if it includes cheat, borrow, beg or steal. This forced poverty breeds personal danger, violence, crime, prostitution, low self-esteem, graft, corruption, and drug addiction. It, also, gives birth and life to strong but cruel and crooked, government-supported, law enforcement agencies."

As Randy walked to the head he asked, "Think about it. How would your life have been change if you had been born poor in a country like Colombia, a country very much unlike your rich America and its affluent middle class?"

Upon Randy's returning, Colt asked pointedly, "Doesn't it bother you at all to be in that business?"

"Colt," Randy replied emphatically, "you and probably another 300 million Americans would love to hear me say, "Just the idea of it makes me want to puke! I hate myself for it! I'm going to die and go to an everlasting burning Hell and I know it!" The absolute truth is it never has bothered me; not when first I found out about Kat's family's business 26 years ago. Not between then and now. And not now. Not for a second! If it had bothered me I would not have been able to become the world's third largest drug-lord. Two more bigger than us are in Colombia.

"If Forbes Magazine could find out the truth about all the currency, the gold, the silver, and the diamonds and jewels in the hands of each of the world's drug-lords, including me and the Elizondos, it would make their list of the world's wealthiest look like the wealth of a little league baseball team. And I have no idea of how much Kat and I and her in-laws are worth, but it's got to be around ten or twelve billion dollars, obtained both legally and illegally.

"But," Randy just remembered and stated, "Kat, absolutely,

positively, disagrees with my feelings on this 1,000 percent. She, to the limit, hates every bit of it. She wants nothing to do with any of it. She refuses to be in any meetings where this business is discussed. She refuses to visit Colombia and hasn't been back since we moved here. She thinks it is the worst wrong that man could perpetrate on each other.

"When 'Nita first told her about it, they were just kids. Kat went berserk and hysterical! They had to call in a doctor to render her unconscious. Her mother had to, literally, have her put into a straight jacket and fly her away to a Roman Catholic convent in Durango, Mexico in order to get her straightened out and prevent her from running away into the mountains to a commune of weirdos.

"But you know what, my friend, maybe there is a little hypocrisy in everyone, I guess. For she never asks what pays for all this luxury and she surely does not show any guilt from her enjoying it, huh?

"Anyway, I never talk about the drug business around her; the other legitimate businesses she likes me to converse with her a lot about. However, she refuses to go to any of our meetings, saying that she just doesn't understand business and that she doesn't have a business type mind. Bull! The woman has a 180 something I.Q. She's a flaming genius! She hates that her family is in it and blames them for not stopping her mother from sending her to Mexico in a straight jacket.

"But when some of her family announces that they're coming up from Colombia to visit, which is quite regularly, you'd think that it was Christmas Week in the Holy Land! Kat becomes the world's most excited and gracious hostess! And party-ing! You would not believe the amount of drinking and party-ing that goes on. And Kat is either leading it or right there in the middle of it. You'll see. I'll invite you all over to our next Colombian Rum-out, as I named them.

"No dope business can be talked in her presence. No dope, at all, is allowed at Cinco Robles, period. No way, just alcohol! And everyone respects Kat's feelings and abides by her queenly dictatorial command.

"Once, one of the gardeners lit up a joint. Kat rode by on a

91

golf cart and fired him on the spot."

THIRTEEN

Randy stated, "Because I've controlled the conversation so much, you haven't had a second to think freely and ask about my parents, the two doctors. Once that I had told them that I was going to marry into an extremely wealthy Colombian family and they met my gorgeous Spanish-genius, wife-to-be, they were like syrup all over me, completely ignoring the fact that they had found ways to keep me out of their lives during the most important years of my growing up, my childhood and my young adulthood. No sir! We were going to be one great big, happy family, again! It was like home coming at the fraternity house!

"But then, I told them that I would be moving to Colombia and planned to make a career within Kat's family's businesses and that it included illegal drug making. They told me, very adamantly, that as far as they were concerned they never had a son, good-bye, and get out! So, Kat and I packed our things and left. I've not talked to them since."

Randy's throat was beginning to clog up, Colt noticed.

"Oh, that is not completely true. I did," Randy stated, "run into them once in a mall in Miami. That was at the beginning of my setting up the Miami warehouse, before I had the bodyguards. Just seeing my father and mother for the first time in ten years flooded me with a childlike feeling of security and warmth. Once again, I felt that I was their little boy and it felt great! My emotions swept all over me with blinding control. I was so excited, momentarily, just feeling the sight of them!

"I rushed up to my father with my hand out expecting to receive one of those father-to-son manly but loving greetings. But in my little boy's heart I was hoping and praying that my father would immediately change our warm hand shake into a long, father-to-child comforting, two-armed-hug, the kind I had dreamed of a thousand times and so badly wanted from his since that day he made me leave, one that would silently mean: Welcome back home, my beloved son!

"And I prayed many times over the years for God to intervene and cause my parents to forgive me and give me a second chance; one that would allow me an opportunity to try to make up for the hurt I had brought into their lives. But I could never get up the nerve to phone them and ask for forgiveness. I was horribly afraid of the hurt I would incur if they were to slam the phone down, once my voice was recognized.

"And I just knew that my Heavenly Father would, somehow, grant my prayer for my exile to end. And here my biggest prayer was coming true! And I had visualized many times Kat and me taking our wonderful son and daughter to meet, for the first time, their grandparents. For this was so unfair to them! And it was not their fault; it was mine!

"But that day in the mall my own father and mother just stared at me with obvious disgust and contempt and hate showing in their faces. They refused to utter a single word or to even acknowledge that the grown man standing in front of them, their only son, even existed! These two old and wrinkled, gray-haired doctors just looked at each other, turned their backs on me, and hurried away in a trot as if they could not get away from me fast enough. I, as the little boy left behind who wanted their love all his life and who was now being abandoned by his parents for the third time, felt my heart being crushed to bits, breaking and falling one tiny sliver at a time.

"A grown man sat on a mall bench that day and with his face in his two hands cried his heart out, with people passing, staring, and probably wondering what could have happened bad enough to cause this man to cry like a little boy. If they only could have known the pain and rejection I was feeling and still feel!

"Some well-meaning soul told a mall guard and he told me to dry it up or leave. I bowed my ashamed head, left, and drove around the area, crying off and on for what seemed like hours. Then I had no more tears left. So, I found a bar to get drunk in, alone, again, in my abandonment with all those painful memories of my parentless, loveless childhood."

Randy concluded, "That was our last contact; twelve years ago the 3rd of next month. I sure would like to have a chance to explain my side to them and for them to see how successful I've been since college. I have one of our secretaries in Miami keep up with the local paper's obituaries for me to see if one of their names appears. Then maybe I could go down."

Colt heard Randy choke-up and saw his eyes. So he showed him some respect by not looking at him, silently getting up from the sofa and going to the head in order to give Randy some time alone, where Colt killed about ten minutes sitting clothed on the head smoking cigarettes. He flushed the toilet for sound effects before returning.

Colt didn't want Randy to be the first to speak because he knew that Randy would apologize for his emotionalism and he didn't want him doing that. As he entered the room he noticed Randy had ceased his tears, and, also, had downed his entire scotch. Colt stopped at the bar and began making fresh drinks. As he saw a silent, red-faced Randy looking at him, Colt immediately interrupted Randy's thoughts and stopped him from speaking by talking and acting as if he had been thinking about something in detail while in the head. And what he was about to say was just a continuation of this train of thought and nothing important had happened prior to his leaving the room. He began, "Randy, I've been thinking that I'd sure like to accompany you when you go back into the hills to one of those dope making operations!"

Randy recognized what his friend had just pulled off and thought, <u>What fast and brilliant thinking and what a compassionate and sensitive person Colt is to camouflage and protect my emotional feelings like he just did. That's a trait to cherish</u>! But that thinking was lightning quick and no time was lost in answering Colt with, "I'd love to, but I cannot do that because it would create a major problem with my in-laws!"

"Oh, okay! I understand. I just thought I'd ask," was Colt's apology.

Randy rapidly responded, "No, you do not understand at all, my friend!" Pausing, he shocked Colt with his strong return. Then he continued, "For if I took you there, if I'm not kidnapped for a huge ransom or maybe killed, upon returning I would be fired from being their top man and from running our conglomerate. Plus, I have never seen even one of our many marijuana fields or our coca or our poppy farms. And I am not allowed to visit our production operations. The family has kept me totally isolated and away from all of it and refuses to allow otherwise! But I'll explain it more later when we get to what I really do."

FOURTEEN

"But, now, let me get back to answering you about my attitude of not letting the ugly side of the drug business bother me whatsoever. And it is this same explanation that I would give to my parents if I had the opportunity. I think they, like you, will see a different view of the matter.

"And, by the way, thanks for allowing me a little privacy and for so tactfully getting me out of those self-pitying doldrums. Only a true, caring friend would do that!"

Randy continued, "Light yourself a cigarette or have another cigar, lie down again, and look at the ceiling. I need to paint you another picture that I firmly believe and so do many of the intelligent and enlightened people that I know; ones not born, educated, and reared in the U.S."

Colt lit a Cuban and proned himself on the expensive sofa.

Randy began his next soap box. "The U.S'. people are now depending on what has become a liberal press and many liberal television news programs to do their thinking for them; that same type of thinking that our parents, when they were young, and all the generations before them, did for themselves. But times have changed with the mass media owning the average citizen's ability to think by their resorting to using the media as their only source for new information. It has become a path of least resistance. The saddest part is that they have let themselves become brain-washed into fully accepting many things that are wrong in the eyes of a lot of people outside the U.S.; things that would have been totally rejected by the U.S. citizenry before the 1940s.

"Here are some very good examples: prior to your government's stopping General Patton's march in Germany in World II, generals ran your wars. Since then it's been politicians. Then Mr. Truman would not let General McArthur run the Chinese back to Manchuria. Look how many Kennedy left dying on the Cuban beaches at The Bay of Pigs. Then your government would not go after your spy ship, The Pueblo, captured by the North Koreans. The U.S. later left Korea not staying to win a war that killed thousands and thousands of American men who, along with their young wives back home, believed that they were there for a just cause. It left Viet Nam the same way, and did little to help your returning veterans from being castigated by your own citizens. How about Operation Desert Storm? Have your wars become operations, so that politicians can run them? Is whatever your politicians decide now the right reasons for aggression?

"Prior to Patton, the U. S. went to war to win, but not now! When did winning a war become bad? The U.S. is not the example to follow anymore. Its doing what's right has died and we outsiders see that. Your citizens don't.

"The U.S. and its states spend billions trying to stop citizens from having access to and from using marijuana, a drug that no doubt should be legalized, but tightly controlled. Why can't your citizens have a referendum on this issue? Yet, it is legal to make, sell, and socially acceptable to consume, a more dangerous drug and a true killer: alcohol. And even more hypocritical is their giving millions and millions to the tobacco industry in subsidies all the while spending millions trying to stop its use! Explain that one! Isn't Nicotine a drug?

"Here's something you need to consider. When the Russians had their first Sputnik sailing over the U.S., America became enraged and put about $60 billion behind NASA and your embryonic space industry. Quickly, did your country not only catch up, but it passed them. You people have this make it happen now, unique, national ability. You pulled the same trick in World War II when you mobilized your industry and your citizens with let's go to war and defeat the Germans and the Japs.

"Colt, don't you believe for a second that drug smuggling couldn't be eliminated if your government wanted it stopped? They didn't stop short of bombing Germany or how about Nagasaki and Hiroshima? And they could do the same in Peru and Columbia any day. And they've got all the needed intelligencia already and they'd not have to even fly down there. Rockets could take care of the job from the U.S. mainlands or from offshore ships. Or they could fly over and spray it like they did in Viet Nam. But they won't.

"How many people would be without jobs if illegal drugs were stopped or even legalized and controlled? How many Federal Drug Enforcement Agency employees would be terminated? How about the same for the U.S. Customs, the U.S. Coast Guard, the C.I.A., the F.B.I., state drug agencies, county and city drug officers, penitentiary employees, and jail employees. And how many lawyers and judges would be eliminated? Add to that all the support industries that sell them cars, planes, helicopters, boats, weapons, ammunition, uniforms, food, and companies that supply them their job benefits, e.g., insurance. How much tax money is going for these programs with the U.S. citizens' unspoken approval?

"How many billions of dollars are put into circulation and pass through your system because of illegal drugs thus benefiting tremendously your country's economy? This drug money is spent for U.S. goods and services.

"Could it be that some of the high-ranking decision-makers that actually run your country, and some of your top-ranked politicians look at your country's drug problems and at the numbers of lower-ranking citizens that eventually kill themselves with drugs and at those who die because of the drug business and think, <u>Well, drugs and our drug fight are good ways to keep folks working in order to get rid of tax money through thousands of jobs created nationally. And this lowers our unemployment figures and maybe, too, saves some welfare funds by allowing incomes to some that were previously on public assistance. And it's a good way to eliminate some bad folks without us, in government, getting the blame. And everybody knows that chemically dependent folks don't make good citizens or good voters or campaign contributors, for that matter. So, let's shuck and jive the U.S. citizens. Let's keep on doing what we're doing. It's working fine!</u> I know that the U. S. government does feel this way because of what they are doing and what they are not doing.

"So, in conclusion to why I don't feel the least bit guilty about being a drug lord, I say this to you: I employ and give jobs to thousands. Many of them would be starving in Columbia and

Peru and in other third-world countries if I wasn't so successful. I have made millionaires out of hundreds both in your country and in other countries that we traffic in. Plus we give millions to your political campaigns through a maze of P.A.C's.

"Your citizenry, because of their mental laziness, knows very little about their own government. Their apathy won't let them muster enough collective energy to resist successfully their two political parties. It is those two parties in unison that have planted a cancer seed deep into your country's originally strong, constitutional format. And your citizen's indifference coupled with the degradation of your country's initial standards by your politicians is what has allowed your government to go nuts a little at a time. And my dear friend, their goofy thinking allows me to do business under their noses. And they apparently don't want me stopped!"

Randy said, "Let's break and then I've got to speed up a little. It's 1:00 and there are a few things that we need to cover before meeting the girls."

FIFTEEN

Randy asked, "Want another drink?"

"Not thanks," Colt said, "I've had enough. Any more and I'll be drunk!"

"Me, too," Randy added, "but I need this!"

Randy continued, "There are two things we do need to discuss about the cabinet job that cannot be discussed in front of Kat. The first is: there is no way within reason, unless you hire about 50 people to work for you, that the five of you can get all our existing cabinets torn out, removed, and discarded, or sold; new ones designed; material ordered and delivered; new cabinets built, delivered, and hung in less than six months or maybe even a year. Further, I'd rather that you not hire anyone since you said that you didn't want all the headaches that it causes. Plus, if we find out when we get the girls together in a little while that they have committed to begin developing a close friendship, which Kat told me she was going to attempt, then I see no problem in your taking whatever time it takes to finish the job. For if Celia and Kat are continually doing things together Kat won't give a flip about how long you take as long as she sees progress being made. So let's go forward without even mentioning the previously discussed time factor and particularly, not if Kat is present.

"But, please, go over this in detail with Celia, and with your employees, too, since they may be around Kat some. We need to be as cautious as possible in beginning our friendship with business being a factor in it from the outset. It could make things kind of sticky if you and I don't control the situation properly.

"Now, onto the next sensitive issue concerning the cabinets. I remove from our clandestine U. S. operations tens of millions of U.S. dollars each year --excess profits that need to be put to work somewhere. We smuggle a lot of it safely back to my kin-folks in Colombia. But some of it goes directly to Swiss and other foreign banks.

"Oftentimes, I need quick availability to large, untraceable sums of money for unexpected purposes, like: if someone stateside with one of the other cartels gets in a cash flow problem, I need to loan them a million or two to bail them out. And they do the same for me. Plus, regularly, our on-board C.I.'s., Confidential Informants, are wanting money for the inside information that they sell us and they'll call my people without prior notice. And the more important the information is to us, the more it costs me. And then there are those rats with their hands out appearing on the horizon every day for personal loans that never seem to be repaid and newly-corrupted law enforcement members that need to be taken care of, financially."

Randy added, "So, I've been hiding the cash in various locations at Cinco Robles. But that is very risky, for I have no real good hiding places, none that a pro couldn't find. Could you build some false shelf bottoms in the cabinets in such a way that they would be almost impossible to detect?"

"No problem!" was Colt's answer as he continued. "I've done it before for a lawyer and his wife in California, while I was in the Navy. A couple of the guys and I moonlighted to make extra money to help support our families on an enlisted man's pay. It's really very simple, but very time consuming, therefore expensive. We assemble all of the compartment's bottoms individually. The removable bottoms are done on a random basis so that, by far, most of the cabinet bottoms are unremovable thus making it a problem to find if someone goes searching. However, we must put an extra bottom on all of them since if one looked underneath across the hanging cabinets what they viewed must show that all cabinets are the same thus concealing the storage units from the fixed bottomed ones. Then in order to identify the ones with the secret storage units, we brushed a tiny bit of varnish or paint on one of its door hinges making it look like we did the finishing after hanging the cabinet doors. The same hinge position was coded that way on corresponding cabinet doors. You'd really have to know about it or you'd never detect this tiny mistake.

"Then the owner, after removing the items from the shelf, presses a rubber suction cup against the removable shelf bottom in order to raise it for access. The rubber cups I bought at a construction supply house.

"However," Cold added, "an element of trust is prevalent between the owner and the builders of the cabinets, for the builder and his employees know the secrets involved. In my case, I can give you my word that Celia and our kids and our son-in-law only will build or help in the building and installing of your cabinets. Not a single outside person will be allowed around when we are working on the project; not during the layout, or cut-out and assembly, or during their delivery and installation."

"Great! Give me about 25% removable," said Randy, ending that issue.

"Randy, in the half hour left, tell me what your job entails," Colt directed.

"Okay, but let me tell you this, first. While I was in the head a while ago, I instructed Lou to turn around and go back to that cove that we just passed where the water should be smooth and a little privacy exists, to cast anchor so that we may enjoy our drinks and hors d'oeuvres topside on the sun deck, for him to join us, and I so informed Pablo. We should be able to make the 4:30 at Sam's. Lou reversed our course several hours back."

Colt quizzed, "Where are your bodyguards? Do you not take them with you on the yacht?"

"Good question, and you're very observant! I like that!" Randy complimented and paused while developing a thoughtful answer. "Alive, I'm worth $25 million to any kidnapper that can grab me, or even Kat for that matter. Actually, the Elizondo family would pay more than that.

"My decisions have made my in-laws, each, over $25 million a year for the last six years from all our operations. And I know our other stockholders love me, too. But I have no choice but to have security near; my Board of Directors require it. They do allow Kat, but never me, to wander unguarded once in a while, if she follows the instructions taught her during our security training classes. And sometimes they'll follow her anyway without her knowledge, just to see if she's taking proper precautions. We have to attend a refresher annually held by our Intelligence Division's best instructors. These highly-trained operatives do not work for me directly. They work for my in-law, Uncle Fernando Elizondo. I have no authority over them whatsoever. And that makes it easier for them to protect us.

"Oh, I forgot. I can leave them behind when I fly the Bonanza, as long as I don't stop and get out somewhere else. I have to return to where I departed on schedule or tell them where I intend to land and give them time, usually no more than an hour, to get some of their people there before I arrive.

"And while we are on this, I'll skip ahead a little and talk about it now. Each major division in our operations is run by a very trusted, proven, experienced and very qualified person. And that includes Kat's two Aunts. While each is responsible to me for their weekly business reports and to include me in their thinking prior to each's major decisions, they have complete authority and responsibility to do what they think is right.

"And our type of operations requires a tremendous amount of secrecy thus our code of silence, our Omerta. One of our practices, even among the family, is: <u>if he or she does not absolutely need to know do them a tremendous favor and don't tell them</u>!

"Our two top officers who run our Intelligence Division, who incidentally retired from your C.I.A., keep a top-secret list of the names of who knows what and why. If I chose to tell you a top-secret I would have to have your name added to the list of those who know that particular secret and why I decided to tell you and how this helps our business. Thus, if any kind of leak appears concerning that secret, all on the list will be called into Central and an intensive investigation done until the responsible one is brought forth, and if found negligently guilty, the person will disappear and not return alive. I've seen films of their newly-developed chemical injections. It makes that Nazi Mengele and Cambodia's Pol Pot look like Sunday School teachers. However, the final decision for an execution is made within the guilty one's own division by the person who is ranked two levels above him or her. And sometimes the decision could get as high as our Board of Directors and to me. And it has reached me, but just once.

"Now, back to what all I do. I'm responsible for the

104

marketing, sales, and distribution world-wide for all of our banana plantations and cattle ranches. But I have nothing to do with the products until they are ready for export from Central and South America, and Mexico. We have farms, plantations, ranches, plants, stores, and warehouses in Colombia, Peru, Argentina, Venezuela, Brazil, Paraguay, Guatemala, Honduras, and cattle slaughter plants in those countries and in Mexico.

"I am not directly responsible for any of our drug manufacturing operations or any of our growing fields at all, not marijuana or coca and now, not the poppy farms used for morphine production and its derivative heroin. But I do receive weekly reports from their top people and I influence their business decisions. But I am responsible for handling, profitably, the huge sums that they want laundered in the U. S. and elsewhere.

"Here's a related side story that is funny: when the family brought me in for the big pow-wow about my taking over and moving to the states, they told me I had to understand who my real boss was. That while she was allowed by me to act like it, it was definitely not Bonita Caterina Julianne! Though she controlled the biggest single chunk of stock, 20%, they had 31% among themselves, making the four of them, Kat's two Aunts and Two Uncles, my number one boss.

"Hearing this and knowing how much they adored her and loved me, this was very funny, so I laughed and replied, "Yeah, but I wonder if Her Majesty, The Exalted Ruler of Colombia And All The Outer Worlds will let you borrow her gilded throne?" Uncle Fernie, who speaks Portuguese in our Board meetings only when he wants to emphatically make a strong point, put his Cuban cigar down stood, promptly, straight up, raised his voice and shouted at me, "My beloved nephew, Randolph Antonio, whom I love as my own son, and in doing so speak for my siblings who are present and therefore observing: hear my words of wisdom advising that you go immediately, and ask your big boobed, Spanish genius Queen Wife if she remembers the old story once conveyed to her as a child by me, her mother's brother, Fernando, about the killing of the treasured goose that lays the golden eggs?

"I now, being joined by my laughing aunts, answered in Portuguese, "Uncle Fernie, are you implying that your precious blood and kin, Bonita Caterina, would do murder, even to a goose?

"Uncle Fernie began laughing, too, then looked me straight in the eye and said, "Oh, no way! But let me have you fully understand, I will, Mr. Goose; faster than a minnow can swim a dipper, if you don't do what I tell you!" The room rocked with uncontrolled laughter for minutes, and my sides were splitting! Aunt Clem wet her pants and had to change. We do have a good time together!

"The laughter calmed down and serious planning returned with Uncle Fernie asking if there were any changes that I thought we needed to make that would allow me to do my work as El Presidente more productively. I said that yes, there was one big one. I'd like to propose to the Board that they consider the fact that our banana exports and both live and processed beef exports to Europe and to the developing countries of the Far East and the U. S. were growing so fast that order backlogs were a year ahead of current shipping figures. With this in mind it would not be a good thing to ruin our reputation with these loyal customers should we get caught smuggling dope using these same products to get drugs past Customs and Import Inspectors. For our customers would then get questioned if they were the consignees of our shipments.

"My aunts jumped to my defense, but not Uncle Fernie. I relented and let him argue with his sisters. But he finally made the motion himself and it was unanimous that all exports of bananas and beef, processed or live, would be 'clean' no matter the point of origin or final destination.

"But, Colt, it did not end on that note. I've got to tell the rest of the story. What some of our white-stuff-boys, as we call the ones who smuggled the powder products out of South America, had found successful was putting one of those tiny microchips into certain cut-up pieces of meat that had drug packages inside. The receiving importer of the meat product could read this tiny transmitter with a hand-held reader about the size of a telephone, reading a nine digit number, thus identifying which hind-quarter held the drugs.

Further, they found a way to drill a green banana stalk and plant bags and a micro-chip in it before replugging the stalk's end-hole. Also, when the price per kilo shot up, they started loading plastic green bananas and attaching them onto marked stalks.

"But here's a funny one: these crazy hombres found that they could tranquilize a cow and plant 6 kilos up her vagina far enough that it took half your arm to reach it. They would then secure the implant by stitching up half of the opening about three inches from the outside, thus allowing normal usage. This <u>mula</u> was then shipped live to her waiting retriever overseas. And Customs never looked in there. These methods I stopped with their vote.

"But Uncle Fernie would not let it end there. Again, that crazy-ole–lovable coot laid down his Cuban cigar and rose to the occasion once more, saying in Portuguese very loudly to his brother and sisters, intentionally turning his back on me, 'Then, if that is the way this Board has voted, I must insist that it accept from its most astute Director, namely me, an adequately prepared expense voucher for my total expenditures for Mr. Goose's Alabama Executive Office.'

"Aunt Sophia shouted, 'Good Lord, what in the name of Heaven have you bought now?'

"From the floor beside his chair, my uncle lifted a big bag and from it he pulled a beautifully engraved, gold name plate that made the entire room rock and roar once again when we read:

R. A. Martinez
President & Director
Of Cow Butts and Banana Peels

"I'm Uncle Fernie's favorite nephew, no doubt. When I have to go to Bogota, I, absolutely, positively have to spend the first night at his home near Funza, a town just west of the big city. Usually, it turns into one of his all-nighters; slumming as he calls it. We got to the poorest part of Bogota and seek out the filthiest, grimiest bar that we can find; one that we did not go to last trip. This way, each all-nighter is somewhat different than the last. In this bar and with these people, we throw a night-long party; all the drinks and food are free, on Uncle Fernie, to everyone who wants to attend.

"In about an hour the word gets around that Senor Fernie is there and the place is sardine-can-tight with a band blasting out local music to a packed, elbow-to-elbow dance floor. Then the two most popular people in town proceed to see if they can drink this bar rum-dry, as we have tried to do in many others. We have never won, believe me.

"Then, about four or five in the morning, we stagger out and down the street or alley way as it may well be, as two knee-walking drunks! Yeah, Colt, imagine us in that scene! Then for more laughs, add six totally sober, tired and disgusted, Hulk Hogan-type bodyguards of ours in their $500 suits surrounding us as we stumble carward, praying, 'Almighty Father, please, get us a transfer!'

"I guess he's the father that I never had! And I love that old man, dearly! You've just got to go with me the next time I go. If I forget to invite you, remind me of it. You've got to meet this lovable character before he dies."

SIXTEEN

"You asked earlier about not seeing any bodyguards aboard. Colt, there are six bodyguards aboard, right now. They know when to stay out of sight. Otherwise, they have complete freedom to roam the yacht, except for Kat's master stateroom, where no one goes unless invited, except Kat's personally-approved chambermaid or 'Nita to clean. Even on charters, her stateroom is locked and stays that way.

"The security group takes charge when we embark and disembark and when Kat or I go top-side to the sundeck. Then their commander of the watch will instruct us what to do. He's number-one in control, not us. Like when we start up the stairs at 3:00 to the sundeck, you'll see him at the top where he'll say, 'Good afternoon, Mr. and Mrs. Erhlichman! Buenos Tardes, Senora and Senor Martinez! Watch your step as you climb and please, join your friends on the aft sundeck.' That means all is well!"

If the area is not clear, say there is an unidentified vessel near, he will say after the greeting, 'Sir, we are not quite ready up here, just yet. 'Nita is waiting for you with cocktails in the salon!' Then he and at least one other armed guard will escort us to the salon until all is clear.

"At the dock you will see us act like we are procrastinating in the salon until the lines are secure. The security chief will be at the rear gang-plank using his hand-held radio. Once the area is cleared between the yacht and the car, he will come for us and say, 'Your car is ready, Senor and Senora Martinez. It has been a pleasure meeting you and having you aboard, Mr. and Mrs. Erhlichman. Please watch your step as you disembark.' That's 'all clear'. Trouble is, 'I apologize for the wait. The docking will be completed in just a few minutes. I will remain here so that you may get the message as soon as I do.' A couple more guards may join us, depending on how serious the problem appears. I'll teach you more about security later."

Colt reminded Randy, "You haven't finished telling me what you do for the drug part of your organization."

"Oh," Randy exclaimed, "I forgot! I got carried away telling you about my crazy Uncle and me. You're going to go down there with me even if I have to tell Security to kidnap you! I come back every trip so relaxed after spending a few days with him, and we just goof around! Tell Celia not to be too surprised if you turn up missing for a couple of days in a week or two! Just kidding, my friend!

"Back to the authority and responsibilities given to me by my bosses: Uncle Fernie, Uncle Julio, Aunt Sophia, and Aunt Clementina. Uncle Fernie is the oldest, and the others kind of let him act like their self-appointed, senior leader. Kat's father, Alfredo, held this family spot until he got killed in that plane crash.

"Aunt Clem, with her husband and three sons, run the total banana operations. Aunt Sophia, with her one son and one daughter, runs all the cattle operations. Aunt Sophia's husband was murdered by terrorists at one of our plantations in Guatemala.

"The nick-name Uncle Fernie branded the sisters with is <u>The Two-Ruling Legit-Sisters</u>, since all their operations are legitimate and they vote the same way on every single issue that comes before the Board.

"Uncle Julio, after Kat's Grandfather Elizondo died, took over all the marijuana, poppy, and coca growing operations, which are mostly in the mountains that adjoin the Amazon Basin in Peru. All drug products are shipped to Uncle Fernie's groups in Colombia for further processing and packaging. One of Uncle Fernie's three sons, Jacinto, called Jack, heads up drug export from South America for European sales. His other son, Victorio, called Vick, handles drug exports and sales to Southeast Asia. Uncle Fernie's youngest son, Alberto, called Bert, handles drugs exports to the U.S., plus supervises the managers of the 28 power transmission and industrial supplies stores along with all the other two dozen or so fertilizer, ag-chemical, feed and supply operations.

"Vice-President Bert took my old job, the one when I was selling beef and bananas throughout all of South America. And if he keeps on doing like he is currently, in a couple of years from now, I'm going to ask the Board to let me promote him to Executive Vice-President, bring him, Phil, and their two boys to Alabama, and after that in five years or so, let Bert take over for me and I'll retire.

"Bert Elizondo has a Phd. in International Finance and Marketing, and he's only thirty years old! He went to two Ivy League Colleges and at one of them met his wife-to-be, Phyllis Ann O'Herlihy.

"Phil, Kat nick-named her, comes from Boston and has a Law Degree from Harvard. She and Bert both liked living in the states and take their vacations with us. She and Kat are like sisters. Phil and Bert are a lot of fun; you'll like them!

"And Kat adores their little boys. She calls them her grandkids and they love it. And you ought to see all the toys she buys them when they come up. Then she tells the boys they must take it all back home to Colombia. Phil screams and hollers and bellows at the top of her Yankee Boston voice! Bert and I laugh until we cry every time. Because just like clockwork Phil phones Kat two days before they leave and tells Kat she has to "Promise on your Roman Catholic Bible that you will not buy them a single solitary thing or Kat, so help me God, we are not coming!" Kat then swears and makes promises until Phil is blue in the face and gives up. then once off the phone she turns to me winks, and says, "Everybody lies sometimes! And besides, I had my fingers crossed!" Micky's six and Rick is seven, now, I think.

"And Colt, Bert's a scratch golfer! Uncle Fernie gives him a hard time about it saying, "Hey, listen here. Ain't nobody carrying a scratch handicap that works enough!"

Colt interrupted and said, "Tell me more about your activities. You mentioned your retirement. Where do you plan to go? And Randy, we've got twenty minutes!"

"I'm so sorry," Randy apologized. "I get carried away when I talk about the people that love me and I them. I guess it's because of how I was reared. But if you don't know now that I'm crazy about my family and kin-folks, you never will!

"Back to business. Our family uses the Sicilian word Omerta to designate our code of silence, also. Everyone who holds a responsible position must take the Oath Of The Code of Silence. We teach them it's sacred meaning and that death is the penalty for breaking Omerta. Further, that if they will continue their loyalty and work as instructed, they will be provided for for the rest of their lives, that their retirement will be provided them and that if they are killed or imprisoned while under Omerta, their wives and dependent children will continue to be provided with the same standards of living as they enjoyed before the unfortunate incident.

"We further promise to pay all legal charges incurred after any business-associated arrest and will provide a funeral, when necesary, according to the family's wishes. Further, I have approved continued alimony and child support payments a number of times.

"On our retirement program: we own six major retirement and vacation-type resort facilities, located one each in Colombia, the Hawaiian Islands, the Grand Caymans, Boa-Boa, Switzerland, and one in Burma. Each facility has adequate housing and the necessary whatevers for any retiring couple.

"Any employee having Omerta, after working for us for 25 years, may choose to retire. But when one reaches 60 years, retirement is mandatory. The only exception is the four Elizondos. The retiree then simply chooses where he or she wants to live and we send them and their spouses there, free. Their living quarters will be provided free but the rest they must pay for. However, they will continue to receive the same amount of pay as they received their last year of work until death. Then the surviving spouse receives his benefits if she chooses to stay until her death. After staying for a year, if they chose to move from their first choice, we'll move them once more and that's it.

"The negative side is that while their kids, kin-folks, and friends may come to visit them as often as they desire, our Omerta-retiree cannot leave for a trip elsewhere except with special permission given from the person currently occupying the second rank above the one that he retired from. The intent is to make it a hassle and therefore discourage it. And even then our Security Division people who run all our retirement facilities will send some of their folks with him for his protection and our continued security. And I plan to accept this heaven-on-earth myself just as soon as I reach 60.

"And by the way, I told Uncle Fernie one night after we had been slumming and were headed home, "My dear Uncle Fernando, since this retirement program was your idea and since I'm the one that has to keep finding ways to keep it funded, and as Chairman of The Board of Directors, I officially inform you that I expect to be treated without discrimination upon my well-earned retirement. I fully expect you to pay me a similar amount of money each year to what I made my last work year, as you voted to do for our other faithful Omertas!

"Uncle Fernie answered, "Boy, did you ever check out that minnow swimming that dipper like I told you to do?"

"No, unless you mean fast as lightning. Why?" was my response.

"Because, you keep messing with this old man and that's about as long as I'm gonna let you live after you retire, Mr. Goose!"

"He surprised me with this five karat diamond ring for my last birthday. It appraised at a quarter of a million!"

"However, may I point out that this retirement program is not a choice thing in as much as once a person takes their Omerta, they belong to us for life. But by the time one works up to their oath stage, though, they are aware of this life-long committment and either accept this as part of the life style they have chosen or simply turn us down when the first promotion that requires Omerta is made. And a refusal is respected by us without retaliation. This life is not for everyone, and we are understanding employers, in this aspect.

"Last year there was a guy, 58 years old, from one of our coke processing plants who wanted to retire and farm. He had worked faithfuly for the group a total of 42 years both there and for Aunt Clem in Guatemala. He refused Omerta many years ago and was satisfied just being a top-grade laborer. The Board bought him a $300,000 sugar cane farm and gave it to him to play with and then established a million dollar trust fund for him and his wife to live off the interest, the principle to later go towards their grandchildrens' educations.

"Now to wrap this up: the U.S. is divided into three regions - -The East Coast to the Mississippi River is Region One, from the Mississippi to the Rockies is Region Two, from the Rockies to the West Coast is Region Three. I have Vice-Presidents running each. Then each region is sub-divided into three to five areas with Area Managers overseeing. Each area is divided into five to ten districts with District Managers running them. Each district may have up to fifty geographical sub-divisions with Team Leaders running them. And then it's down to neighborhoods and local names for city areas that have Distributors who work Dealers.

"The first Omerta occurs at the district level. And an Omerta employee cannot associate with a non-Omerta employee. Further, Omertas cannot associate with any other Omerta more than two ranks above or below him. And the chain of command is strictly abided by. A serious punishment is given for breaking it.

"The Board has limited me to two levels below me also. My name and identity, my location, and any photos of me are kept from anyone lower. Each higher level has additional obligations along with taking The Code of Silence. So, as you can see, I don't get very involved with the actual distribution and sales activities. In fact, I have never seen a shipment of any kind. They keep me far from the firing line and well out of sight. So, my job is to run this huge conglomerate, Colt. Any questions?"

Colt asked, "Yes, just one. Who owns the other 49% of the stock?"

Randy said, "I'll give you a quick answer because we're five minutes late. Two brothers who are sand country oil magnates own 20%; a Turkish heroin-drug-lord that we work with owns 5%; and the other 24% is owned by a group of 17 investors hiding behind a front in the financial world in New York.

"What you and I have discussed should stay, if possible, between you and me, except what is under our Omerta and that is set in concrete! Do you agree with this, Colt?" Randy asked.

"Yes," Colt replied, "but I will expected to share some of it with Celia."

"Sure you will," Randy agreed. "And I will with Kat. That's why I'm bringing it up. But let's try to keep as much as we can between ourselves and try to stay away from specifics that give crucial names, dates, and places. Once we have informed them on a specific subject, let's take the time to tell each other what we have shared with them so that when we four are together you and I know what can comfortably be discussed and what should be avoided, if at all possible. Then, if we goof-up, we'll simply apologize to them saying that we did not mean any harm, for you and I have shared so much with each other that omissions on our part have to be accepted. Okay, my friend?"

"Right on!" Colt replied as they headed down the stairs toward the master stateroom to join the girls."

On the way Randy said, "Let me lead the conversation in the room."

Colt nodded okay.

SEVENTEEN

Entering the master stateroom for his first time, Colt gazed 360 degrees at this luxurious hideaway. All he could muster was, "Man!"

Randy asked, "How's it going, pretty ladies?"

Kat replied, "I've got a friend for life!" then looked at Celia for a positive response and got it.

Randy looked at Colt signalling that he wanted Colt to say something. Colt looked at Kat, Celia, then at Randy and confirmed, "Us, too!"

Randy offered, "Then that issue is settled? So, what do we talk about for the next hour or do you girls want to join us in getting drunk?"

Kat looked at Celia, waiting for her to speak, Celia said, "Let's talk about our relationship so that we can start off on the same foot and know what to expect."

After a pause as if all were waiting to see who would speak next, Kat took over by saying, "But before we get to that, Randy, I need to tell you about two important decisions I made and how they will affect the cabinet work. First of all, that big upright steel gun safe that you keep in your walk-in closet at C. R. is a secure one, but all it does is shows a professional thief where the good stuff is. And in it we keep a fortune in my and your jewelry. I'm not comfortable with that.

"Celia told me about a job that Colt did in California whereby they made some secret hiding places in a lawyer's cabinets. Colt, will you do that for me?"

"Sure," was Colt's response.

"Good! Randy," Kat instructed, "I want you to put the cash in those cabinets; those millions you've been sneaky with and hiding in various places around C. R. and that you think I did not know about.

"And furthermore, Celia and Colt can take all the time they need on this project. I can't understand how you figured that a month or two was enough. And besides, Celia and I have decided to make the job a fun thing for me and her by taking our time on the cabinet designs. This will give us excuses to go shopping around to see what styles are in the area's showrooms --designs that we can copy and which ones will best suit a particular room. Do you two guys have a problem with what I've said?"

With tongue in cheek Randy looked at Colt, who was red-faced from restraining an explosive laugh, answering, "Colt mentioned something about this, just as a passing comment. It's a relief to hear you girl's decisions and I admire your thoroughness in thinking of it!"

Colt exhaled and with a breath of relief being thankful that he did not blow it, immediately responded, "Great! No problem! What an excellent thought! I wish we had come up with it."

Celia then entered the conversation with, "With the guards that Colt and I saw you with at Sam's, I presume that you have more at Cinco Robles and probably a security system with cameras and all that. If I'm guessing right, then why do you need to be so protective in hiding your stuff?"

Kat answered, "With my jewelry and his business cash, together with his gun collection and my collections of antique silver serving trays and with our hobby of collecting crystal and porcelain, there's probably $20 million worth all together. Celia, if a terrorist group found out about it, they would bring in a veritable army, kill us all, and take it. But really, what we are doing is just causing ourselves to feel better by making it harder for them to find it all. Besides, most huge robberies, like this one could be, are planned with the help of an inside informant, anyway. That's why, Celia."

Celia accepted Kat's answer by acknowledging that she understood and then asked, "Randy, how can Colt and I possibly keep up our half of a relationship with you two? You spend more money in a week than we make in a year!"

Randy gave a warm, reassuring smile back at Celia with, "That's a very astute observation on your part, my lady friend; not an easy one to answer. So, bear with me as I attempt it. Celia, very wealthy folks have a hard time making and keeping friends because of their money and all that it allows them to afford, and their being able to virtually buy anything they want whenever they want it. This and the fact that they live way

118

beyond the levels that 98% of the population can afford increases the difficulty of being close friends with anyone other than like wealthy people. But, additionally, the extremely wealthy do not make good close personal friends with each other, other than their blood-kin, as a general rule. For they are too competitive when cast into the same arena, in my opinion.

"However, there is a light at the end of the tunnel; one that an old, but very wise, Mexican college professor taught me in psychology class. And this analytical, but easy to understand approach, has allowed Kat and me to become soul mate friends with Pablo and 'Nita, who faced similar feelings with us in the beginning."

Randy took drink orders and then instructed, "So, just sit back while I make us drinks and talk. And by the way, I don't remember if I told Kat over the phone or not, but we'll be having hor d'oeuvres topside on the sundeck. That's why Lou stopped and anchored."

He continued, "If you think of what is normal in your lives when it comes to spending money on fun and entertainment, that similar amount is certainly different for Kat and me. For example, pushing it to your limit, probably during Christmas season, folks like yourselves spend your greatest single amounts. Let's guess that you take your kids or friends out for an expensive holiday dinner with drinks. You'd probably plan about $50 per person. Am I off base, Colt?"

Receiving a no from Colt, Randy proceeded, "Then if Kat and I let you do that for us other than at Christmas time, we know that you are trying to match our abilities and we therefore would be allowing an injustice in our friendship to occur. And we cannot allow that to happen or eventually a bad seed will sprout.

"Pablo and 'Nita respond to us in ways that they can afford and are comfortable with. Taking you to what you two may consider expensive places is our way of enjoying with you that which God has given to us and is our way of sharing with you our normal lives. And it give us pleasure in doing so and in no way reflects upon you and your abilities. So, in the outset let's be proud of what we have to share with our love ones and not at all compare the quantity differences that exists between us. Kat and I are extremely sensitive to your feelings and are cautious about your spending on our behalf.

"And I'll end with what that old Mexican said about what the good book teaches on <u>It is more blessed to give than to receive</u>. And I'll never forget this, and I hope that you won't either. Dr. Emilio added "Yes, and the act of giving becomes more sacred and is even more blessed if one considers the value of the gift to the receiver and the value that that same gift was to the giver!"

Kat said, "Randy, you've never told me that! That was a beautiful explanation!" All agreed and Celia and Colt were comfortable with proceeding, now that they understood the money situation.

Celia asked a question to Kat, "How do we go from here with caution that we don't smother each other and eventually grow tired of being together, considering the cabinet job and all?"

Kat gave it a three or four second thinking and then said, "With Pablo and 'Nita we established a mutual understanding when they came with us up here that they needed time away from us and vice-versa. So, it works out okay with the four of us to plan a group get-together twice a month with them picking a night for hosting us and a time for us to host them. We'll do a local meal, go to a ballgame, a movie or a moonlight cruise with us up on the sundeck or something else that makes the evening just ours. They plan something within their budget keeping our eyes on the quality time enjoyed with each other. Once we just walked up and down the beach at night and had hamburgers and beers beach-side at The Pink Pony Pub."

"So," Kat added, "may I suggest that we try this arrangement by adding your choice of a night next month onto all of our calendars with us giving you ours? What do you two think of what I've said and suggested? And will three nights out a month be too much for you?"

Both indicated, "No, let's do it!"

Randy interjected, "Folks are waiting for us topside."

EIGHTEEN

They went aft to the stairs that led to the top level. Then turning into the stairs to the topside deck, they were greeted immediately by a suit-and-tie Arnold Schwarzeneger-type from the top who momentarily halted the group at the bottom with, "Good afternoon, Mr. and Mrs. Erhlichman! <u>Buenas Tardes, Senor and Senora Martinez!</u> Watch you step as you climb and please, join your friends on the aft sundeck."

Celia said, "Thank you," and she did not see Randy turn and give a secret, acknowledging wink to a grinning Colt.

As the four reached the topdeck and turned aft, what a pleasant surprise met their eyes. There was a waist-high white fence surrounding the rear third of the topside deck along portside and starboard and cross-ship and cross-stern thus identifying the aft section set aside for partying. Inside the fence was a beautifully-carved teakwood bar that highlighted a Caterina's silhouette. Outlining the rectangular perimeter were live Hawaiian plants of many varieties making it difficult to touch the side railings. Within this rainbow of South Pacific live-colors were white rattan chairs and platform rockers, the kind that one used to see on old Southern plantation porches with their fresh paint finishes, thick duck-down, multi-colored cushions and above head height backs.

In the middle about ten feet away from the dozen row-lined chairs, was a large round table piled high with a circular array of Hawaiian decorated, upwardly inclined, finger foods around a huge ice block, hand-carved, center piece with an accurate rendering of a flightless Australian bird called an emu crowning the top. Letters cut into the block's base below the three-foot-high, artists creation offered this message: <u>The Bonita Caterina's Staff Welcomes Celia and Colt, Kat And Randy.</u>

Outside the left side of the little gate entrance stood a marquee-type, tripod stand, three foot by four, hand-painted sign announcing: <u>The Bonita Caterina's Staff's First Annual Australian-Hawaiian Luau Welcomes:</u> and continuing the message across the fenced opening on its right was a second sign completing the message saying: <u>Our New Friends: Celia and Colt Erhlichman And Our Wonderful Bosses: The Senora and Senor Martinez'</u>.

Standing on the outside of the left marquee in a receiving line were the six bodyguards and on the right was 'Nita, Pablo, Lou, Chuck, and six employees. However, the suit-and-tie-gang did not have their suits on. The security team had six matching, Hawaiian short-sleeve shirts, white walking shorts, black sandals and each was wearing a head wreath of miniature orchids. 'Nita and the other ladies wore matching Hawaiian muu-muus, white sandals, a miniature orchid lei around their necks with a bird-of-paradise bloom tucked carefully above their right ear. Lou, Chuck, and the guys were attired similar to the bodyguards, but with a different set of matching shirts. Engraved, shiny-brass, first-name, name plates adorned their left breasts.

This sight halted their procession in absolute shock! Celia couldn't talk, but Colt exclaimed, "Well, I'll be a monkey's uncle! Would you just look at that?"

And astonished, but silently pleased and proud Randy turned to his gorgeous wife and in a very low voice that only the other three could hear whispered, "Now, tell the truth, you did this, didn't you, Kat?"

Kat replied in just as surprised a whisper, "I swear, Randy, I know absolutely nothing about this! But just look at all that! I've never seen anything like it! How in the name of the Virgin Mary did they get all that ordered and delivered so quickly, and get it aboard during the night without waking you and me?"

Receiving the pleasantly surprised expressions on their guests' faces, the group of smiling and clapping hosts and hostesses prepared for their entrance welcoming. Capt. Lou and Pablo followed 'Nita to the four with open-arms-hugs and warm, manly hand shakes. Leading them to a small table behind the security team's line, they helped the four slip over their street clothes: Hawaiian shirts for the man and button-down-the-back muu-muus for the ladies.

After the appropriate flower adornments were added to their costumes, the four were led to the now reformed, informal, receiving line where Celia and Colt were introduced to each that they had not previously met, and where the two very pleased and proud bosses were being welcomed by their staff.

As two of the security team quietly went below and two meandered towards the bow where two deck chairs awaited their arrival, Colt notice their departures and that they all had bulges on their hips under their over hanging shirts. He visualized himself standing next to one of the two remaining guards standing about ten feet away and guessed that his 6'1" height would top out at the guards' chin levels.

Noticing that the rest of the crowd was now walking freely about the enclosure taking in the decorations and getting drinks, the big guy that Colt was staring at caught Colt doing so and, smiling back, walked over to his guest saying, "Mr. Erhlichman, I'm Andre, the Senora's and Senor's personal security team leader. If you have a moment, may I escort you to the bar and share a drink with you?"

"Sure, Andre," Colt replied. "I was hoping for an opportunity to ask some questions when I first saw you at Sam's last night."

Two Chivas and waters were handed to them. Andre asked, "What may we talk about?"

Colt answered, "Tell me what you'd like for me to know about your unit and yourself."

Andre began, "Our Security Division is employed by the Senor's conglomerate but is headed by someone else so that autonomy is given in authority and responsibility. The Senor wishes it to be this way and allows me full authority where personal security matters concern him and the Senora. Our division receives the same company benefits and retirement program as the other divisions. We are salaried, work seven day weeks, six weeks straight, then two weeks off so that we may return to our wives and families or just R and R at one of our company's resorts. We have expense reimbursement privileges to and from our assignment locations, free room and board while working, and our suits and clothes and our weapons are furnished along with our initial intensive, six-months training. So is our recurrent training that we take annually in Louisiana or Georgia.

"Our guys must be college graduates, at least 6'2" in height, weigh over 250 after basic training; speak English, Spanish and Quechua, agree to a thorough background check, have no criminal history, take a series of I. Q. tests with results showing over 115, and pass a tough psychological profile examination showing fitness for this career. Nationality or race does not matter. For you've noticed, I'm sure, that one of my team members on the bow is a Japanese giant named like you, <u>Big Colt</u>, but after the pistol of that name."

"With all those requirements are you able to fill your quota?" Colt inquired.

Andre answered, "We hire search agencies in the major countries around the world and history shows that we take only 1 out of 50 interviewed. Our preferred choices come to us from the units of national security forces. And to answer the question that I predict you are too much of a gentleman to ask but would love to know, "How much do our beginners earn?" Beginning salary is $100,000. And their age must be no younger than 25 years and no older than 35.

"We use a military system of discipline, management and ranking. The rank bestowed upon our basic training graduate is Second Lieutenant, our Commandant wears five stars. Each assignment carries with it a specific amount of time in service, certain qualifying experience and training, and a minimum rank. For example, at Cinco Robles the security group that protects the compound has to have a type of training and experience that my current team does not require and vice-versa with us. The compound's guard team minimum rank requirements allows a Second Lieutenant to be included with a minimum ranked Team Leader of Captain.

"But since my team is assigned to The Tall Man and The Lady, as we code them, they must have other skills and since we are subject to more immediate personal risks, the minimum level of entry is Captain and the lowest ranking Team Leader is a Major. Plus, on this team the minimum field-level time is ten years; while at C. R., as we code the compound, minimum entry level is basic training."

Colt continued, "Doesn't the requirement of three languages

present a problem, particularly in cases like your Japanese friend over there?"

"Sure it does," Andre confirmed. "But in today's growing one-world-society many of these young people come to us speaking English along with their native tongue. Where a candidate fits all of the other zillion qualification points, but is deficient in one or two of the required languages, we'll hire him anyway and pay him an annual salary of $75,000 plus all expenses for up to a year. Once hired, we send him to a college in Mexico City that contracts with us for a total immersion language school. There he'll enter a one-on-one, six-days-a-week study course until his instructor graduates him.

"Once language qualified, the candidate is sent to basic training where he is taught by professionals in hand-to-hand combat techniques, weapons, a lot of physical training, diet control, basic and high-tech security systems and equipment, crowd and riot protection techniques, emergency first aid, including field surgery, jungle, cold weather and desert survival, under-water and airborne training, one defensive and one offensive martial art, and quite a bit more, including dress and hygiene, social manners, and international protocol."

Having their second scotch, Colt asks, "What rank are you and where are you from, Andre?"

"I am a Bird Colonel with 18 years in the field, Mr. Erhlichman. I'm married and have two little boys. I must apologize first before my next answer, for it may seem rude on my part. But let me explain and you will understand. Andre is not my real name. It's a pseudonym. And the rest of my identify is classified top secret also.

"Each field duty tour that we are sent on does not last for more than a year; then we are transferred. This minimizes the old adage <u>Familiarity breeds contempt</u>. And we add to that <u>which breeds death</u>. We don't want our team members to become friends with our clients, thus possibly not maximizing protection.

"Further, on my next assignment, if it is in the field, which I hope it's not, I will be given a code name other than Andre.

"This current team of mine is the 18th that has been assigned to The Tall-Man, called TTM, since he came to the states. Therefore, its number is TTM-18. So, my code name for now is TTM-18-Andre and that is how headquarters codes me on messages, work orders, and records. Thus, it makes it harder for outsiders to track me down or to get to my family. Division rules require that only two ranks below me are allowed to know my true identity. My rank being a Bird Colonel dictates that Captain Big Colt, on the bow up there, cannot know my real name since Lieutenant Colonels and Majors are between him and me. The ones who do know have sworn our Code of Silence, where death is the penalty for breaking it."

Colt asked "Two questions: you mentioned that you hope you won't have to be in the field next assignment. Why? And the next one is, why are you telling me what seems like pretty confidential stuff? You don't know me!"

"Two very good ones, sir," Andre stated. "I'll answer the second one first. Ranks of Lieutenant Colonel and above are allowed to take the responsibility themselves for qualifying an individual according to certain secret criteria without Central getting involved. And if that individual meets these stiff qualifications, this officer is permitted to assign a minimum security clearance of SC-10. An SC-10 clearance is logged in at IntelSec-Central and means that this SC-10, if I may, can be trusted with general operating policies and class 10 secrets. Sir, last night at 2400 my stateroom phone rang. The voice at the other end said this and hung up. "Colonel, Mr. Erhlichman checks out as an SC-10. Advise IntelSec-Central and your team to act accordingly!" That was a Four-Star General in our Intelligence and Security Division, his code name is The Tall Man.

"Sir, you asked about my not wanting to stay in the field," Andre added. "Our policy allows twenty years maximum as a Field Operative, unless a special assignment is then required by the Commandant. After 20-Out, as we call it, the officer must take an inside job at IntelSec-Central in order to qualify for full retirement to one of our retirement resorts. The only exception is reaching 60, the mandatory retirement age for everyone. And you're probably wondering: where's IntelSec-Central located?

That's an SC-4 so I cannot tell you that, Sir!

"Mr. Erhlichman, our Field Operatives average 15 years before burn out occurs or they are too old to keep the physical conditioning regiments that must be maintained for their own safety. In my case, I came aboard when I was 28 and next month I'll be 46! 46 is too old to last much longer with these young men kicking the crap out of me in refresher classes where, as their instructor in the martial arts, I'm supposed to rein. And 46 is too young to retire; but in my opinion just the right age to start another career within the Division. So, I've asked to be transferred after this assignment to our brand-new Satellite Tracking Intelligence Section.

"Sir, I've got a Master's Degree in physics. Plus, if I get my request, I can continue my school work and possibly get a Doctorate. Then with 18 years in the field behind me, 14 years in front of me, and beginning the new job with a Bird already, and a Ph.D. later, just maybe they'll allow me more command training and responsibility. And with that I might be able to retire at 60 with a star. Retiring with that rank and with that income will allow my wonderful wife and me a very nice life at one of our beautiful retirement resorts.

"But, really, more important to me is the fact that if I can win this transfer and get this permanent assignment, my wife and kids can join me. And The Holy Father knows that I miss them very much. You cannot be a proper father to your kids by seeing them for two weeks out of two months!"

Colt asked, "Do your other divisions use a military ranking system similar to yours?"

"Yes, Sir," Andre answered. "Similar, but not exactly. Their requirements and their jobs are very different, obviously, than ours are in IntelSec."

Colt inquired, "Does your conglomerate have enlisted man ranks?"

"Yes, again. You're very sharp, Mr. Erhlichman?" Andre complimented. "For people working for us, our Sales and Distribution Divisions assign ranks beginning at the Dealer levels with the rank of Private and Corporal. Sergeant ranking is assigned to the Distributor levels. Master Sergeant is the Team

Leaders level. Second Lieutenants, First Lieutenants, and Captains are our District Managers. Majors and Lieutenant Colonels run the Area Groups. Bird Colonels run our Regions, and one-to-two star Generals run the Divisions as our Vice-Presidents. Three to five stars are Commandants and can be Board of Directors members.

"All divisions use a similar system of ranking and the first Oath of The Code of Silence is given to a new Second Lieutenant at the District Manager's level or similar titles that the others use for their first Omertas."

Colt stated, "I saw a report on television where private army-type forces were involved in Peru with tanks and armored personnel carriers and such. Do you all have that?"

"I didn't see that report," Andre commented. "But that wasn't our group; that most likely was the Muerte a Sequestradores which means Death to Kidnappers. They're in Peru. However, we find it very necessary to protect our employees and their families from dangerous types and we spare no expense in doing it. So, yes, we are fully equipped to do so with the latest military armament that exists on the World Market including missile-equipped jets, tanks, radar, ground rockets, and the latest in field artillery and hand-held automatic weapons.

"Most of our concentration is around our coca, marijuana, and poppy fields and their related production plants. Privately funded military groups are not uncommon at all in developing countries, Sir.

"Notice," Andre pointed out, "that I said we protect our employees and their families. Until ten years ago, the Codes Of Silence of organizations around the world that dealt in our types of international business all had unwritten, but commonly agreed upon, rules of conduct that disallowed and punished perpetrators for any harm being done to another member's or an enemy's family. This was included in the Honor Statutes part of their Sacred Oaths. But now this does not apply. And I truly hate this beyond belief!"

Andre continued, "About eight years ago, one of our Field Operatives, a Major, being very drunk, let his identity be known in confidence to a prostitute in Bolivia while celebrating after an assignment that he and his team had that day successfully completed against a terrorist group of drugs hijackers. Three days later the Major's precious little four-year-old son was found in the Major's own home town, 1700 miles away, in a stinking, sloppy hog pen, decapitated. The coroner found a piece of paper stuffed inside the child's mouth with a word scribbled on it that read: Ramirez. That was the name of the dead terrorist group leader that had been the target of the Major's rifle shot.

"Since he had broken his Omerta that carries with it a death penalty, and since he had caused his own child to be heinously murdered through his irresponsible actions, their family would have to have two funerals at one time. And I, a Major at the time, was ordered by The IntelSec Commandant himself to fly from Indonesia with my entire field team and join him and some more soldiers from Headquarters Company Central to attend the family's double funeral."

Andre continued, "I was crying hard as we marched in full-dress uniform behind the 21 rifles that followed the bugler and his four drummers. Leading us up front were those two flower-draped caskets with the bodies of my identical twin brother and my precious nephew! And on that day for me, our world-wide Code of Honor had lost its meaning forever!

Colt saw his tearful eyes as a bowed-head whispered, "Please, excuse me, Sir. I've just received a coded beeper message indicating that a fax is coming in downstairs that concerns a promotion and a transfer for one of my team."

They shook hands and Colt gave heart-felt thanks to a warm and emotional human; a dedicated family man who would rather be at home; a loyal and hard-working employee; a soldier; a leader; but yet, a highly-trained and professional, ruthless killer! As the 6'8" Colonel stepped away, Colt thought, Just like our pilots dropping napalm bombs on the villages where they have been told that the enemy hides out and while doing so killing, burning, and maiming dozens and dozens of innocent men, women, and children, they were simply doing their days work; just hitting that day's target. This, too, then is the Colonel's job. Killing is Andre's way of making a living and supporting his loved ones back home. Who are we to judge this sensitive man; this husband; this father?

NINETEEN

At the same time that the Colonel had joined Colt earlier for their first drink, Celia, Kat, and Randy headed over to where Pablo, 'Nita, Lou, and three more were standing kind of in a receiving group next to the bar. Randy was the first speak. "Okay, you sneaky bunch of Sherlock Holmeses, tell us how you pulled this surprise on us? We were not gone that long last night."

Pablo spoke. "Okay, but we'll need to get Major Rick from the bow to help us. They did most of the foot work."

The security man standing beside Randy retrieved his hand-held from under his Hawaiian shirt and transmitted, "Major Enrico; Captain Carlos. Sir, the General requests your presence aft, and I'm headed to the bow to replace you, Sir."

They were receiving the last of the ordered drinks from the bar when Major Rick joined them. Pablo advised the Major, "Rick, our bosses and guests want us to tell them how we were able to get this all done without getting caught. Should we divulge our secrets or just let them keep trying to figure it out?"

The Major answered with a big smile at the ladies and at Lou, and directing an obvious wink at Randy, "Well, Senor Chef, with all due respect, I do not work for the General here. And any reprimand or transfer for me that he would request would take about six months for the punishment to reach me. But as for you, Mr. Pablo, do you have any job applications or resumes out anywhere?"

The crowd roared at this playful bantering.

"No!" Pablo laughed. "But you'd better take me with you when you go!"

The Pablo continued, "When you, Randy, and Kat left their shop yesterday morning you phoned me at C. R. saying that you two thought you had just met a couple that we should spend some time with and that it was your intention to have some drinks with them last night at Sam's. You further told me that if all went well during the evening, you were going to invite them to join us for a ride on the Caterina today and for me to expect two, maybe three, meals aboard. And lastly, that Kat and you would be staying on-board for the night.

"Several things got by you after that. Driving behind you were two of the world's best trained and cleverest night-ops officers, namely Colonel Andre and Major Enrico. If you had been looking in the rear view mirror as you drove up Hwy. 59 towards I-10 and then to Mobile you would have seen them on the phone talking to us just about the whole time. The credit for the idea must be given to Rick here. But the major planning came from Andre, 'Nita, and me over the phone."

Pablo continued, "The Hawaiian shirts and muu-muus were in our cache of party stuff at Cinco Robles. 'Nita called a Gulf Shore's catering service and they had the potted palms, the plants and flowers, including the leis, the orchids, and the hair flowers. The ice carving was started at noon yesterday and finished at 1:30 this morning over at the Hilton on 182 where one of my very good friends is the Head Chef. The emu meat I had in the freezer at C. R. The fresh fruits came from Delchamps. The signs were made at one of those all-night franchises in Mobile. The Colonel had one of his guys get a 24-foot rental van and they began picking up at 3:00 yesterday afternoon."

Randy said, "But how did you get it aboard without us seeing you?"

"Simple, Sir," the Major answered. "With our car phones and our hand-helds we were able to keep step-by-step progress reports going all the time. When you told us you were driving over to Mobile so that the Senora could make her 1:00 appointment at her eye doctor's, the Colonel and I figured we could be Party Command Central from our car. Further, we knew that you'd probably be ready to leave the doctor's office at 2:00 and head back for an hour to C. R. to rest, shower, and dress for the evening, and not go directly from Mobile to the marina. For 'Nita said that she had taken all the Senora's overnight clothes and casual attire yesterday from the Caterina to C. R. and to the dry-cleaners as the Senora had requested. So, armed with this knowledge, we simply deduced that your first arrival to the yacht would be somewhere around 11:00 after your leaving

Sam's. And we guessed right; we had about 12 hours of clear sailing, Sir."

Kat asked, "Where did you hide it all?"

"In the fresh-produce locker on board," 'Nita answered and continued. "But, believe it or not, our biggest problem was gathering everyone's sandal sizes and calling a dozen shops in Foley, Orange Beach, and Gulf Shores to find one that had all of our sizes in stock."

Then Randy got specific, "Now, hold on, you Sherlocks! How did you know that I'd tell Lou to hold the get-together topside, and to choose this cove and anchor?"

Lou replied, "We didn't know ahead. But when you made that choice, it was similar to what I had planned anyway. And besides, there are two more coves between here and the docks at Sam's, one of which I had planned to choose had you not chosen one first."

Randy followed, "You had to haul the ice-carving aboard while we were asleep. I know your group is capable of that, Rick. But how did you know that we would not see you guys moving the decorations from the locker to topside as we walked about? Seeing the food being transported would be no surprise, but how did you get the rest past us?"

Rick replied, "Sir, it is the Senora's and your personal practice that while onboard, both of you wear deck-style loafers that you keep in your stateroom. 'Nita informed us that you have two pairs in your walk-in closet and the Senora keeps three pairs in her's. Last night 'Nita brought five left-foot loafers to us before you arrived from Sam's. Our team's electronics specialist, Captain Pedro, inserted a tiny rice grain size transmitter in the seams of your shoes, thereby allowing us to track your movements throughout the day, Sir."

Celia and Kat screamed with laughter, then 'Nita, and then the rest joined in, then Randy and the Major.

Colt, now alone after the Colonel left, heard the uproar and joined them, whereby Randy laughingly told him what he had just learned. Colt joined their frivolity and the partying atmosphere. And all was right in their world!

The hot dishes were being removed from several insulated

portable chests by the galley crew when Pablo asked everyone to gather around the center table so that he might begin his little speech about what they were about to eat for the first time, for he had prepared another new recipe and wanted their opinions of it afterwards. Pablo began, "For thousands of years in the Outback of Australia, the native aboriginal tribes have used a flightless bird called the emu for a number of their needs. They harvest it at about a year old at a little more than one hundred pounds for its feathers, meat, fat, and its hide.

"The emu's feathers are used in stuffing pillows and mattresses and for adorning ceremonial costumes. Its meat is red, has a texture similar to beef, but is lower in cholesterol and fat. Its fat is used on leather, but more importantly as a salve on cuts and other skin problems to speed up healing. The natives also use the oil from the fat as a skin moisturizer. Further, with this meat as a major part of their diet, heart problems and high blood pressure are very low among the tribes. The hides are very soft and supple when tanned and make high quality, fine garments and hand bags. The birds lay large avocado green eggs in the winter months and their eggs are edible also.

"The government allows only the Aborigines to freely harvest these ostrich-like Outback inhabitants but a few ranchers have been allowed commercial licenses for breeding and commercial processing and for research. No live emus or fertile emu eggs are allowed for export but the permit holding ranchers may export their processed emu products. However, before these laws were enacted, some birds did leave for France and the U.S. From these imported emus a new, world-wide, agri-industry is developing."

Pablo continued, "This afternoon I'm offering a new recipe named The Caterina's Emu Hors d'oeuvres. And as always, I will tell you how it is prepared so that you may do it yourself when the occasion arises. And if you approve the meat dishes, then the recipes will be added as a supplement to my published cook book.

"The emu meat was ordered in pre-cut, steak form, allowing six ounces per guest. After thawing it to room temperature we simply cut it cross-grain into finger-size portions. The finger-sized pieces were marinated over night in Italian salad dressing in the refrigerator. Once time for final preparation, it was removed from the refrigerator, drained, and halved into two piles. One batch was then dipped into a milk and egg mixture and then in self-rising flour. This floured meat was then deep-fried in vegetable oil at 375 degrees until golden-brown and drained on a bed of paper towels.

"The remaining uncooked marinated emu was pan-sauteed in a small amount of olive oil and drained. Be careful not to over cook the emu meat for it has very low amounts of fat in it and will cook in about half the time of beef.

"On the table you will find small bowls of various dips for your emu meat: cocktail sauce, honey-mustard, honey-mayonnaise, hot-cajun tomato catsup, plain tomato catsup, cajon mustard, tartar sauce, and barbecue sauce. Use the toothpicks when dipping the meat into the sauces and try them all. Now if we could have the ladies lead us, we'll get a line started. Enjoy yourself and I will speak to each of you about your findings when you've finished," Pablo concluded to a resounding round of applause.

For the next hour the entire crowd enjoyed The Caterina's First Annual Australian-Hawaiian Luau. Each had an opportunity to meet the others. And special emphasis was given to Celia and Colt by the crew leaving no doubts in their minds that they were welcome aboard and would be on future visits. Major Enrico mingled with the group while keeping watch also.

From the accolades paid his two new recipes, that made another $50 grand that Pablo would soon get from his cook book publishers and he chuckled to himself, "A fellow ought to be ashamed of himself making $100 grand this way! But I ain't!"

The time had passed quickly when Lou announced, "Folks, may I ask that we begin our move to lower decks so that our crew may prepare for our trip to dockside?"

Kat and Celia were followed by Randy and Colt downstairs and into the salon where amaretto liqueur and ice awaited their arrival, making the ride to the dock very short. Randy remembered to see that their guests had the mementoes of their first time aboard: Pablo's autographed cook book for Celia, and an unopened box of Cuban Cigars for Colt. Pablo and 'Nita and then Lou joined the group in the salon for an after-dinner liqueur while the crew secured the lines to the dock. Then thanks and farewells were interrupted when Colonel Andre, holding a walkie-talkie, appeared from the stern and announced to Randy, "Your car is ready, Senor and Senora Martinez. It has been a pleasure having you aboard and meeting you, Mr. and Mrs. Erhlichman! Please watch your step as you disembark."

Colt grinned an acknowledgement to Randy and they began their walk to their vehicles, with all, in each's own way, feeling extremely pleased with today's good times and with its accompanying personal and sincere promises signifying a very interesting future for the six involved.

TWENTY

Prior to the onboard party, when Kat and Celia had left the stateroom for a walk around the yacht, they got as far as the salon door when Kat exclaimed, "Celia, there is something that I forgot to tell you that is important. Let's just go into the salon and we can talk until 2:00, then we'll go back."

Kat continued, "When Aunt Embuko informed me at the jungle grass hut that she had done a spiritual ceremony for me and learned that, among other things, I would be pretty all my born days, I was so excited for I thought that being pretty was a big blessing. Boy, was I to learn differently! It's a major burden, to say the least!

"Celia," she continued, "when I was 14 years old, I was 5'8" tall and wore a 36-D brassiere. Now can you imagine me walking into the convent's eighth-grade class room looking like that? I was taller than any girl in my class and all their boobs combined wouldn't equal mine. The Catholic Sisters made me wear under-sized bras that hurt like all get-out, because they didn't have any my size. And while they would slap the other girls on the back and say, "Hold your shoulders back and stand up straight!" they'd tell me to stop sticking out my chest. And I could not please them unless I leaned over and walked stoop-shouldered.

"Then in high school it got worse. They made us do physical education wearing those gym suits and it drove me to tears when we had to jump up and down or run. Then I started eating too much and gained a little weight and went to a 38-E. Every place, and I do mean every place, that I would go, all the men and boys would gawk at me like I was a circus freak and that is how I felt! By my junior year in high school I had gained two inches in height, making me five foot-ten and that made things worse.

"The boys over at St. Dominic's, the Catholic boy's high school, were shorter than me for the most part and my looks, height, and big boobs intimidated most of them, and the girls, too, for that matter. While the other girls were getting dates, I wasn't, and yet, they thought all the boys were crazy about me. The opposite was true. And my making straight A's and being Class President didn't help, either.

"By my senior year some of the boys caught up with me in height. I began to date some. But over 90% of the time all they wanted to do was to be seen with me at the local drive-in burger joints and movie houses then take me directly to some isolated spot and attempt to get their hands on my breasts so they could go back and brag to their buddies about it. One girl even called me a "big-titty slut" to my face and anything but that was the truth.

"The Sisters got tougher on me after one of the younger Priests visited our classroom and couldn't take his eyes off me. And by the way, I called up my Kulu Sin Toma and my Power Spirit informed me that that Catholic Priest wanted to take me to bed and to stay away from him.

"Then college was no different: big and tall, big breasted me. Straight A's, good-looking, but no dates. And I mean not a one! Then Randy came along and all that changed. I felt saved! And we went everywhere together. And I could care less what others thought. We got married our senior year. After getting my Master's Degree, I worked on campus while Randy finished his.

"In the office and in the public the lustful stares and ugly remarks returned; remarks like: "Look at those 44-magnums!" or "If my wife had those, I could sell my dairy herd!" or "Don't fall, Sugar' you won't be able to get up!" or "Where did you buy those watermelons, Sweetheart?" But when Randy was with me none were made. They knew at 6'4" and 250 pounds, he'd beat the stew out of them if they said anything. But, even with him beside me, the stares and gawking did not stop. And it has not, even up to today, and I'm in my fifties.

"This rude attention that I get in public can be a problem with other females if they are not expecting it ahead of time. And some cannot handle it. When I would go home to Bogota for the holidays my mother would refuse to go with me shopping or to the malls saying that she was not going to put up with any vulgarity caused by me. "Caused by me," my foot; I would love to be able to stop it! But I can't just hibernate.

"Once I flew to New Orleans to a doctor that specialized in breast operations to see if he could make mine smaller. After an examination he said that he'd recommend against it because while he could do the surgery that he doubted if he could remove enough to make me happy without causing me more problems than it was worth. "Further," he told me, "the size of your breasts is not your major problem. Your attitude towards them and what they cause you to have to endure from rude men is. And that is what you need to get some help with.

"So, I took the Louisiana doctor's advice and kept what God gave me, but I had to find somebody to give me some advice on handling it better.

"I don't trust psychiatrists because of the bad experiences I had with several of them when my mother put me into analysis when I was 12. I'd become depressed about my family being illegal drug lords and having to keep this an absolute secret from every kid I came in contact with, except 'Nita. And then the same at the convent was more than I could handle sometimes. Plus, I felt that I had been abandoned by both my parents and held it against my father and my mother for not letting me stay at home and go to school with my only friend, 'Nita.

"The reason I did not trust my psychiatrists was that after most sessions they called my mother in for a progress consultation and afterwards she'd chew my tail off about something that she learned I had said or done. She would blame all her bad luck and misfortunes on me when we were alone. But when we were in front of my doctors or my father or other people, she'd act like she and I were best friends.

"After I passed puberty she even hated that I developed such a good shape and big breasts, telling me that she was better looking than me before my father accidentally got her pregnant with me. But she was flat-breasted; that was her big problem.

"So, Celia, I needed someone that I could talk to and trust and Aunt Embuko was the only grown female who qualified. 'Nita had gotten married by this time and was in Europe where Pablo was attending a culinary arts college. This crisis came during the time I was working on my Master's. Randy suggested that I fly down to Lima, Peru where Aunt Embuko was to receive an Honorary Doctorate Degree from her Alma Mater and where she would be the Baccalaureate Speaker.

"The cocaine and marijuana business had boomed due to the U.S. government's lackadaisical attitude towards completely stopping their stateside drug smugglers. With this came price cutting and rivalry at the mountain growers' level in the jungles of Peru. And then little skirmishes turned into warfare among the gangs and tribes and terrorists. The major drug cartel contacted Aunt Em and asked if she would be willing to set up Red Cross-type clinics near the hot spots if she was guaranteed safety by all of the warring factions and if this was then backed by all three of the big Colombian drug cartels. Her job would be to set up a facility, then train local women and men on basic first aid and minor field surgery. Once she felt comfortable with their ability she was to move on to another area and begin another one.

"After she had met with the elders of each of the principle tribes involved and got the backing of the three drug cartels, she started on her three year journey and set up eleven such medical camps. The Peruvian government heard of her successes and wanted her recognized and honored at the Universidad De Peruana in Lima with press and television coverage. The presentation would be made by the Peruvian Minister of Education himself. And I was very excited about being there seeing my Aunt Em honored.

"This was the first time we had been outside of Bukutu together and I wanted us to enjoy a big city together. And we had a ball. She was hard to keep up with and she had to be in her late fifties or early sixties. We celebrated until the sun came up and just about everywhere we went that night everyone knew her because of the television coverage of her hour-long speech and the Minister of Education's lauding her. So, we were allowed to pay for nothing and folks were coming over to her for autographs.

"About sunrise, as we walked down the street a shady-looking character approached us. We just knew that we were about to be robbed and me possibly raped. So, we just froze and waited. He said in Spanish, "Senorita Embuko, I live away 225 miles and on a bus all day and all night I have been. On the radio I heard you were coming to Lima. When I got into town I told the police Captain what I wanted. He radioed around and told me where to look for you. And my Patron Saint has been with me for I've found you. I'm Christobal Maldonado. Three years ago, I was shot by some drug hijackers and near dying when you saved my life not only physically but spiritually. You gave me hope to live. It was near Tingo Maria. For four days and three nights when I would gain consciousness it was your smile that I saw. Then you began talking to me about my life in the Muerte a Sequestradores and about my future. But before I was released from the clinic you had gone. I swore to the Holy Mother that someday I'd find you and tell you how you changed my life. Now, my Angel of Mercy, I am a faithful husband. A father of two boys. I work at the shoe factory, and I attend mass every Sunday with my family. May I hug you in love and appreciation?

"What a wonderful sight to see! My, was I ever proud to be her Kojo Embuko! And we thought he was a robber!

"As he walked away Aunt Em said, "And that, my Kojo Em, is what keeps me young and going!"

Kat summarized, "What I learned that helped me overcome my problem concerning my breasts and accept it was that Aunt Em pointed out that Pintu Weeko keeps a balance in everything He creates. And it is so easy to see it in Nature, if we'll but look. The way she explained it to me was that for 'being pretty all my born days, for having a genius I. Q., for having a young person's body, for having good health, a great husband, a good education and for being filthy rich, Pintu Weeko's balance was my having huge breasts and the problems that go with them.

"Further," Aunt Em said, "by taking all that criticism and verbal abuse you have another blessing in that you will become a much stronger person through it all. Use the same psychology on yourself that many truly handicapped are taught to use on themselves in that you should feel better about yourself than someone without the problem because by handling it you are stronger than they are.

"And, Celia," Kat concluded, "that was all I needed. Oh,

sometimes I get pretty upset, particularly if I don't have my guard up. Like a couple of weeks ago in a mall in Pensacola, 'Nita and I were minding our own business looking in a store window when this smart aleck old goat said, "My, but those buttons on your blouse must be strong!"

"I replied before thinking, "Sir, after you die, please, ask YOUR Devil why MY God made more horses asses than He did horses?" 'Nita nearly wet her britches laughing. She'd never seen me respond so quickly. But Aunt Em prepared me to not take the abuse, anymore. And I don't!

"Let's go meet the guys, Celia."

TWENTY-ONE

After leaving the yacht, Celia and Colt were to go to their shop and Randy and Kat were to stop by the laundry, with Colonel Andre and Major Enrico in tow. Randy, thinking about their drive, began a conversation by questioning Kat, "Everything go to suit you, Hon?"

"Very much," was Kat's answer. "How about you?"

"Absolutely," Randy added. "Any reservations?"

"Yes, just one," Kat answered.

Randy instructed, "Tell me about it."

Kat began, "When Colt and you were talking last night at Sam's, he would stare at me, but not in a rude way or so much that Celia noticed. But he couldn't keep his eyes off my breasts. And it might have been the fact that I was wearing a low cut. But after I noticed it several times I called up up Kulu Sin Toma and was told that Colt was sexually motivated by me."

Randy chided, "My Heavenly Father, Kat! There's never been a man that has seen you that hasn't been sexually motivated! If a man isn't excited after looking at your attributes, something must be badly wrong with him or he is blind! Any normal male would love to get you in bed. First, they mentally undress your Dolly Parton chest. Then he'll lust over your Sophia Loren face. Then it's your Miss Universe body. Then it's your Einstein mind. And lastly, if all this doesn't drive them plumb nuts, your King Solomon's millions will. Honey, let's face it, even at 52 you've got more than enough to turn a plow mule into a stable stud. So, if Colt lusted a little and Celia didn't kick his shin under the table, more power to him! But he's not serious, Kat. I trust him implicitly."

"But," Kat asked, "would you trust him with me alone somewhere?"

Randy answered, "Well, maybe I wouldn't have last night but I would after today. But what you're implying is that you want me to speak to him about it, don't you? Did you tell Celia about your Kulu Sin Toma?"

"Yes, I did," Kat answered. "And I told her not to tell Colt.

I wanted to talk to you first. But I didn't say that to Celia."

Randy picked a business card from the visor and dialed. Colt answered their shop phone. "Colt, Randy here. Can you talk a minute? Good. Colt, I need to ask you some very personal and private questions that you can simply answer yes or no to and these questions need not be discussed with Celia. Okay? Kat is sitting beside me. And I'm calling you because she wants to be a very close friend of yours, too. However, she has a reservation about you that she wants you to know about. But before I discuss it with you, I want you to know that I love you like a brother. And if you absolutely do not feel like she accuses you of feeling, I'll wonder if you are a queer or something.

"I think I told you that Kat has a way of knowing what people are thinking and can sometimes almost read their thoughts? Well, my brother, last night she said that once you and I got into heavy conversation, you became sexually aroused by her tits. Is she right? Great! That's my pal! Now, I'm relieved to know that you're normal and not a fag. She motivates me the same way and I'm her husband! Anyway, now that we've got that straight, if you had her off somewhere by yourself would you attempt to get in her britches? That's what I thought you'd say! Can she trust you without any reservations? Will you tell her that? Okay, I'm handing the phone to her. And don't you let me hear that you apologized to her for last night because she's the one that wore that low-cut and she got what she deserved!"

Randy put his hand over the mouth piece and sternly said, "Talk to my friend, Kat. I trust him with my life. Then you talk to Celia and tell her to tell Colt the whole story about your Gift of Animal Eyes. Let's don't start this relationship holding anything back between the six of us."

Kat took the phone and in jest said, "So, you like my big boobs and want to get me in bed, huh? What do you mean not anymore? Sure, I agree. Let's play it straight with each other from now on. Yeah, I enjoyed it, too. Okay, we'll look to see you tomorrow at C. R. And I'd like to go over the cabinets to be removed first. May I speak to Celia, now?"

Kat continued, "Hi, Celia. Yeah, I enjoyed it, too. You're welcome. There'll be more fun days like today, I promise. Celia, the reason I wanted to talk to you was that I told you earlier not to say anything to Colt about my Kulu Sin Toma. I said that because I did not have the advantage of knowing how he and Randy were going to hit it off. But now that Randy and I have had a chance to talk I want you to tell my whole story to Colt from my childhood to the present, no holds barred. Will you do that tonight? I love you, too, Celia, and I'm looking forward to seeing you at C. R. tomorrow. And try to come for lunch. Bye."

Kat turned to Randy and said kiddingly, "That sure was a good one, Mr. Horse-butt; calling him like that and putting me on the spot. I think I'll just choke you for that!"

Randy replied while pulling her over to him, putting his right arm behind her neck, reaching over, unbuttoning her top button and slipping his hand inside her brassiere, "How about starting your attack when we get home and in bed."

Kat answered, "Reckon you can take it, old boy?" as she slid her hand up his thigh and into his crotch where she found what she was feeling for and thought <u>Yep, my Randy is a big man, in more ways than one</u>!

It was a long night for the two couples, for they stayed up until about 1:00 exchanging with their spouses all that each could remember about their conversations and the fun-filled day, except for Randy's secret of all secrets. Celia and Colt then fell off to sleep. But at Cinco Robles Kat turned into a hellcat in a bed and kept Randy active for another half hour.

TWENTY-TWO

The next morning Celia and Colt went to the shop and held a meeting with their three employees: their daughter, son, and son-in-law. They went over the Martinez' cabinet job telling them about the secret compartments that they were to build into the bottoms and the need for absolute secrecy concerning it and got solemn promises from all three. They talked about the current jobs in-house and decided to finish all orders but not to quote on anymore and not to take any additional orders in light of the huge job at hand. Celia told Suzie to call several suppliers and get volume price quotes and delivery on large amounts of material and cabinet hardware. Colt told Rick, their son, and David to clear out enough shop space to receive a trailer-truck load of plywood.

About 11:00 Celia phoned Kat and told her that they'd be at C. R. for lunch and that they'd like to spend the afternoon looking over the cabinets and touring the compound and that Colt wanted to spend some time with Randy alone, and she with Kat.

Following the directions Kat had given Celia they drove north up 59 turning east just south of Foley, then for 5 miles or so, then right onto a dead end dirt road that had a single-paved driveway leading south from it; through a very thick wooded area for several hundred yards that ended abruptly, and facing them as the drive continued was a closely manicured St. Augustine grass area, 50 yards wide in front of a beige 12-foot high stone wall that had razor wire crowning its top. Stadium-style flood lights on poles placed intermittently in the wall guarded the beamed entrance accompanied by security cameras covering all areas.

Colt told Celia that the wall had to be nearly a quarter of a mile wide and cost several millions to put up and that it probably enclosed 45 acres since there were 50 acres in Cinco Robles, according to Randy.

As their car broke the beam on the outer perimeter a suit and tie giant with an Uzi in his right hand and a walkie-talkie in his left moved from a guard shack inside to the middle of the double gate and waited for Colt to come to a halt and then asked, "Sir, may I be of service to you and the lady?"

Colt spoke through the window, "I'm Colt Erhlichman and this is my wife, Celia. Kat and Randy are expecting us."

The guard spoke into his hand-held, "C. R.-1; Gate-1. Sir, I have a blue late-model F-250 with Mr. and Mrs. Erhlichman. 10-4, Sir."

He turned to Colt and said, "Sir, the Senora and Senor are awaiting your arrival on the rose patio. Please enter after I open the gates and take the first left. Keep red roses on your right, make two right turns and follow the rose path from the striped parking area to your hostess and host. And Sir, I am Second Lieutenant Miguel, your day gate guard. I have been instructed to make your acquaintance. I understand that we hope to see a lot of you and your family. If I can be of service, it will be my pleasure. And enjoy your visit, Mr. and Mrs. Erhlichman."

Driving about a quarter of a mile through a tropical floral forest that reminded one of Hawaii more so than south Alabama, they came upon signs pointing to the rose patio. There were at least a dozen different varieties of blooming roses. They spied the winding rose-covered white lattice-work that surrounded the patio with Kat and Randy sitting under hanging roses watching the noon-day TV headlines. After hello hugs and small talk about the news they were served Bloody Marys and an array of fresh fruits, sandwiches, and chips.

Colt updated Kat and Randy on their shop meeting, that they needed about two more weeks to finish their current jobs, and that they would take on no more outside orders. However, they needed to make a few decisions today on just where they would start the project so that material could be ordered asap. Kat suggested that they examine the six-car garage cabinets and start there since a standard style could be quickly chosen for that area. Or another thought would be remove the existing ones, put some hidden compartments in a few, paint them some acceptable color, and re-install them, per se. Randy agreed with Kat. All that was needed now with this simple solution was for Celia and Colt to see how many were there and to arrange to get them to the shop. Plus this would give the ladies more time in planning the entire layout and visit the malls and the local showrooms for specific design ideas and for collecting other manufacturer's picture brochures.

Randy asked, "You guys got any plans for the afternoon and evening?"

Celia saw Colt's negative head-shake and said, "Not really. I'd like Kat to show me around and let you guys talk by yourselves. Too, I don't want us to over do this relationship since we've been together day and night for the last two days. Why do you ask?"

Randy replied, "'Nita told me to see if you two would stay and the six of us play some cards after she and Pablo finished work. She wants them to knock off early and join us for a draft beer and charcoal hamburger cookout over at the pool. She'll have their kitchen staff handle it. We'll play cards in the screened-in, pool-side game room until about 9:30 or ten. We won't make it late tonight. How about it, guys?"

Getting nods from the other two, Colt said, "Let's do it. Sounds like fun to me!"

Randy motioned to one of the two security men sitting in a gazebo about a couple of hundred feet away in the rose garden to come over. Arriving in a golf cart with their automatic rifles aboard, Randy introduced them, "Mr. and Mrs. Erhlichman, this is Captain Alejandro and First Lieutenant Jose. Alex is our compound security Team Leader and Jose is second-in-command. You and your family will be seeing a lot of them and their staff. These two will come to your shop and hold a meeting with you and your group concerning the compound layout and our security routines. This knowledge will make you feel more comfortable. One of them will be close by for your convenience when you start the job and will stay with each of you until you feel comfortable about getting around Cinco Robles and not getting lost. Then you'll have complete freedom to enter and leave at will. We prefer it this way rather than printing a map for obvious security reasons."

Randy instructed, "C. R.-1, please have two golf carts with hand-helds sent over. Have a cooler of ice and glasses with a chilled bottle of our Cinco Robles scuppernong wine and a chilled bottle of a blush for the ladies. Do similar for Mr. Erhlichman and me but no wine; make ours a quart of Rothschild Scotch and ice with a decanter of spring water. I want Colt to try something different. Then, please advise 'Nita and Pablo that the cookout and card game is on, that we'll be staying here until then and for them and join us when they can. And prepare them a golf cart to their choosing, also."

"Sir," the Captain asked, "may I order some cheeses and crackers for the carts and a box of Cubans for the General and the gentleman, Sir?"

"That would be splendid, Captain." Turning to Colt, Randy complimented, "Can't you see why Kat and I love these guys?"

They had another Bloody Mary before the carts arrived. Kat and Celia left saying, "We'll call you later."

Randy and Colt lit a Cuban cigar and Randy drove towards the front gate. The Captain and the other guard trailed in a separate golf cart.

Driving through the gate and turning parallel to the outside wall, Randy began telling Colt about Cinco Robles. "The wall was built about sixty years ago, even before the construction inside. A Florida railroad baron wanted a secluded place to live with bride number four. Seems he was in his late fifties and she her early thirties. The story goes that he had lost the previous three due to his lack of sexual prowess, having caught the earlier wives in amorous affairs. He figured that if he kept this one inside these walls, the possibility of another such episode would be minimized.

"So, he proceeded to building her a walled mansion. She was pregnant with her first child when he got killed in a car wreck. The mother-to-be got the place but not the railroad empire; it went to his three sons and two daughters from his earlier marriages.

"The story continues with the fact that she named the newborn boy after its father, the old man's chauffeur. And they were married afterwards. We bought the place from their estate.

"As astute as you are, "I'm sure you've already noticed the security systems. But there is one that you'll not see. Our Intelligence and Security Division that is run by my Uncle Fernie but of which I have been trained in and am a member of the Advisory Board with the rank of General, contracts with a foreign government that has a spy satellite. While very expensive a service, it is necessary that we protect, to the maximum, this compound. At any one time not only is there a lot of money here that terrorists would like to get their hands on, but frequently many of the world's top drug lords visit, also.

"So, let's both stick our arms out of the cart at the same time and give the finger to Colonel Rodrigue. Then by the time we get back into the house, he will have faxed me some form of get-even remark like, "Sir, may the bird of paradise fly up your nose, Sir." If he doesn't, then I'll be forced to phone as to why they didn't see us and the cart behind us leave the compound?"

Once having completed the forty acre rectangle, they re-entered the gates and followed the yellow-flowered drive to the right to the garage. There they looked over the existing cabinets. Colt took measurements and made notes on the numbers of hanging cabinets and sizes, and the numbers of sizes of the base cabinets.

Randy asked, "Want to see the rest of the place?"

Colt said, "I'll be down here quite a bit, later. I'd rather go somewhere where we can talk some more and get into that Rothschild. How about you?"

"Fine with me," Randy continued. "Let's go upstairs above these garages. There's a common bar up there for the guest rooms."

Looking outside the garage doors, Randy instructed, "Would you guys get the cooler and stuff for us and bring it upstairs to the bar, please?"

TWENTY-THREE

After getting set up in the bar and sipping on his first scotch, Colt commented, "This is very smooth. How come I've never heard of it?"

Randy answered, "It's a private stock for the Rothschild's and I get it out of France every once in a while. I thought you'd like it. I've got a couple of cases left, so you take home a quart with you. Remind me if I forget to get it for you before you leave. Now, what shall we discuss? We've got about three hours before I expect Pablo and 'Nita to call us. If our ladies call, we'll tell them to join us, but I doubt if they will. Kat likes to be alone with her female guests since she doesn't have that chance often."

Colt stated, "You are the first person I've ever met in the drug business. I've always thought that if the chance ever occurred, I'd like to ask a lot of questions about it. I've read about it in the papers and our kids do a little pot. And I've tried it myself, but I've never even seen the heavier stuff. Can you tell me about the industry, how it got started, and how it is smuggled into the country? I'd like to hear anything you can tell me from the beginning of its history, that kind of thing."

Randy pondered, "Where do I begin? Let's start with the coca plant's history. I've covered some of this earlier so forgive me if I repeat myself. I'll start with a little Peruvian history."

"Much of what we know about the coca plant comes from the mouth-to-mouth, hand-me-down knowledge from the more than 30 different tribes that have lived in the Peruvian jungles and forests since time began. And they have about that many languages, but the majority speak Quechua. I saw this when I first started traveling there and found some locals to tutor me for four or five years. So, I speak some Quechua, myself.

"But you cannot get by with just that and Spanish. One needs to speak the language of the people that he does business with. Therefore, Kat and I learned Chabba, her kin-folks' language. I didn't mean to imply that Kat does business with the Kin Chabbas, far from that. But I do; that is, we do. But up until about thirty years ago the Kin Chabba tribe refused to commercially grow coca and sell it to the outside world. But that all changed with the younger generations becoming more materialistic. Excuse me! I'm getting a little off my track.

"We're told that for thousands and thousands of years green cola leaves were used by the natives for the good feeling they got from it when chewed, for increasing energy, for appetite suppression, as an antidote for altitude sickness, as a local anesthetic, and they used it in religious ceremonies. Then the Spanish learned of its usage from the Andean peasants and began taking it back overseas.

"The first cocaine chemical extraction was reported in 1844 making it available for easy export. Coca-Cola used a tiny bit of it in their drinks but stopped including it after the turn of the century.

"The poorer tribes found that by getting involved with the outside world, they no longer needed to be starving and to keep struggling in trying to live off their land. All they needed to do was to clear a little land and plant coca. An acre properly planted and cared for could produce about $3,000 per crop and they could harvest it four times a year in many places, thus $12,000 per acre per year, if all worked well. It sure beat hunting and fishing for a living, or farming or cattle raising, for that matter.

"Little by little a lot of them went against their Shaman's beliefs and greed took over. Often, this split the tribe and inner-tribal fights broke out and many died. But overall, cocaine won out in the mountains and jungles of Peru and Bolivia.

"Because of the political climates over the years in Colombia, Peru, and Bolivia, some of the Spanish-speaking folks immigrated to the U. S. Once here, they became potential customers for their once available coca-leaves, cocaine, and marijuana. This began what was to become a multi-billion-dollar business in the 1970s once the supply was large enough to sell to the Americans. Now cocaine alone is about 20 billion and growing."

Colt interrupted, "Before you get too far from Colombia, go back to how they make it."

Randy regressed, "The coca plant farmer spreads the mature

154

green leaves on the bare ground or on canvas or on paper for the sun to dry them. It takes 500 pounds of dried leaves to produce one pound of cocaine. While that may seem like a lot, he may have hundreds of acres growing. Or in the case of the big boys, they'll have thousands. And remember, they can pick it four times a year.

"The dried leaves go to a nearby camp where they are crushed and hydrochloric acid is added along with water and a few more chemicals that turns the liquid in a couple of days into a paste called pasta basica which is transported to Colombia for final processing. There it is refined more, the main additives being ether and acetone. Crystallization occurs and the cocaine hydrochloride is dried and packaged in a kilo per plastic bag and tape-wrapped. A kilo is 2.2 pounds. The bags may have duct tape on them with markings showing the brand of the producer and the tape color tells who gets the shipment once stateside. We estimate, since accurate records are not available, that 80% of the world's cocaine is from Colombia, that 60% of the leaves are grown in Peru, and most of the rest grows in Bolivia."

Colt asked, "But how do you know that what you're getting from Colombia hasn't been weakened to increase the volume by the time you get it?"

"Good question," Randy added. "We call that cutting. By and large, one has to rely on the integrity of his source and most of them take pride in their product and in their work. However, when we contract for an outside buy, we send a chemist to test the shipment before we accept it. And he or she has several field tests that can give an indication as to whether the contents have been cut and to what extent. Pure coke is about 87%. Less than that we don't like to ship; we'll return it for further refinement or simply refuse to accept it at all. So far as field testing it, what some of the guys like to do is randomly select three or four kilos for inspection, taking a tiny sample from each for testing. One test includes puncturing the plastic bag with a pocket knife and retrieving just a bit on the knife's blade tip, dropping that into a test tube of a commercial laundry bleach. The coke will dissolve leaving an oily-yellow film on the top. The impurities and additives will fall to the bottom of the tube. But even then, an educated guess will have to be made about the amount.

"Another easy test is based upon the fact that cocaine will not stick to plastic. So if you see a lot of residue on the inside of the bags, it isn't coke. It's probably lactose, or quinine, or an amphetamine like speed, or powdered vitamin-B.

"Cutting is done a lot on down the distribution line where independents buy and resale the product. But since our guys are, for the most part, on salaries and incentives, ours is pretty good stuff when it gets to the user level."

"Now," Colt instructed, "go back and do the same for me with marijuana like you did with coke."

"Okay," Randy agreed. "Marijuana can be planted most anywhere where freezing isn't a major problem. And we can, in some areas, get more than one crop a year. Too, from a cost of production to street value, marijuana is a more profitable product by far. We don't have to process it twice like we do coke. My cost of making pot to street value is about 100 to 1; whereby my cost on coke to street value is 25 to 1.

"Pot has been smoked, eaten, a tea made from it, used in linen making, and canvas and rope making for as far back as 4,000 years ago in China and India. History records that pot has been in Europe for several thousand years. The Spanish introduced it into South America during the 16th century. Your Jamestown settlers brought seeds with them in 1611. And by the 19th century, American doctors were openly recommending it for insomnia, anxiety, depression, pain relief, and for helping with alcohol's D. Ts. The active ingredient in marijuana is called THC standing for delta-9-tetrahydrocannibinol.

"The most popular item to cut it with is the spice called oregano because it looks like marijuana when crushed and it smells similar to dried pot. However, if the quality of the marijuana is low-grade because of low THC levels, sometimes PCP (Angel Dust) is added. I've known some growers to let the plant go to the budding stage whereby they would harvest the buds and sell them for a higher price, then lace the inferior leaves with PCP for more profits.

Colt asked, "What about heroin?"

Randy began, "Heroin is a derivative of morphine which is

derived from the active alkaloid in opium. Opium comes from the sap of the opium poppy. The poppy just before it blooms offers about two weeks in which its bud's skin can be sliced vertically with a knife allowing the sap to ooze out and be collected.

"The opium poppy has been cultivated for tens of thousands of years primarily in the far east in such countries as Pakistan, Turkey, and more recently Cambodia. History tells us that its small black seeds were eaten also for their morphine effect. Morphine was used during your Civil War as a pain-killer. But heroin did not start showing up until the late 19th century.

"Heroin is cut many times from its pure state to street-grade. Street-grade runs about 10% having been cut, usually, with dextrose, lactose, or quinine. And the production cost versus the street value is about 100 to 1, like pot."

Colt interrupted, "How are these drugs consumed?"

"Before I answer that," Randy eluded, "let me go back to cocaine and tell you about a new product that is catching on fast. It's called <u>crack</u> and is a strong, concentrated form of cocaine. Apparently, some Caribbean islanders discovered how to concentrate coke into a rock-like form and by smoking it, a much more intense high could be attained. And for that, a much higher price could be charged, like up to ten times the price of the cocaine included, making it much more profitable than pot or heroin with a production to retail ratio of 250 to 1.

"The sad thing about crack making is, except for one prescription anesthetic which they obtain illegally, the ingredients can be bought in many retail stores. They mix it up and pop it into the oven or the microwave. After heating it they let it cool and crystallize. The <u>cookie</u> is then broken into small bits.

"An eighth inch by an eighth inch rock of good quality crack would go for about $10. And the hit would last for about ten to twenty minutes; much less time than coke but much, much more intense, and quite a bit more addictive. And it brings a lot more business volume for the suppliers because a coke addict would probably spend a couple of hundred dollars a week for his highs but a crack-head would spend a thousand or more a week for his.

"Now, if a <u>head</u> has to steal for his drug money and then sells his merchandise through a <u>fence</u> at 5 to 10 cents on the dollar, it is easy to see that crack creates quite a bit more crime where it is pushed.

"Colt, most folks that are high on marijuana or heroin are very calm and very laid-back; not violent at all when they're drugged-up. Therefore, law enforcement officers are not in as much danger when approaching them. But not so with coke or crack. Cocaine hydrochloride gives a feeling of pleasure but its side affects include increased energy levels and hyper activity, both verbally and bodily. With coke one's heart rate and blood pressure increase, their adrenaline flow increases, and pain tolerance levels are abnormally high.

"So, coke highs and especially, crack highs present quite a problem and much more danger to law officers during arrests. The police pretty much have to totally immobilize the subject and physically haul the subject off. For they usually resist and feel little or no pain at all, even if shot."

Colt chastised, "And you don't feel bad about making it tougher for the law enforcement industry, huh?"

Randy countered with, "Should we take your cigarettes and your alcohol away from you, put you in jail along with your rich billionaire U. S. manufacturers?"

Colt answered, "Two points for your team! And we, American users, make them successful, don't we?"

Randy added, "Too, it's like Americans' need for the drug caffeine. The Colombians say, "If the yanks want to be caffeine addicts, let's be their number one supplier of coffee. If they want illegal drugs, let's grow coca, pot, and poppies. It's their weakness; not ours. It's they that keep the illegal drug market sustained; without their demand we could not be the suppliers. They can destroy themselves if they want to, while they make us filthy rich! So, who's stupid, the yanks or us?

"And to repeat myself, the U. S. Government with its military capability could stop the entire world-wide drug production industry on any single day that they chose to. And you know that is true, Colt."

Colt condescended, "I wish, very much, that I could tell you that you are dead-wrong in your feelings. And that what you just said is not true. But, unfortunately and ashamedly, I cannot. We Americans are very hypocritical in our views concerning caffeine, tobacco, and alcohol. And now we are allowing this drug world to exist and grow in our country without even putting up a decent fight to stop it. We've become too liberal in our individual attitudes, I guess."

TWENTY-FOUR

"Now, Randy, would you tell me something about how you guys got started smuggling drugs into our country and how you are still able to get around our country's interdictory efforts?"

Randy regressed, "Sure, I'll get to that in a few minutes, but I did not answer your earlier question on how the drugs are consumed. Let's start with the easiest one first and I think I've already covered marijuana but I'll high-light it, again.

"By and large, marijuana is smoked either as a roll-your-own cigarette or in some form of pipe. I've never seen anyone making a tea from it but history tells us that it was once popular. Also, I've heard of people lacing cookies and cakes with pot, but I've not seen any. And I'm told that water pipes are used, too."

Randy continued, "Now on to coke. Mostly, powdered cocaine is sniffed into the nose. The first reaction that the user feels is a very strong burning sensation from the sinus cavities and some of it may penetrate the nasal passages into the upper throat. And I've been told that if a new user gets hold of some very high grade coke and ingests too much too rapidly that the smelling follicles in the nose can be permanently damaged. The next feeling caused by cocaine is a flushing warm feeling rushing through the brain followed by feeling of euphoria and well being, then a tremendous increase in energy throughout the body.

"You've seen coke consumption demonstrated on television. The user will put a small amount of coke on a flat surface, then separate the coke into several thin two or three inch-long lines and using a rolled-up dollar bill or a short portion of a drinking straw sniff up as much as a single deep breath will allow into one nostril, then do similar for the other nostril.

"The high will last two to three hours or more, depending on the quality of the cocaine and the amount consumed. I'm told that it would probably require using cocaine three or four times a week for three weeks or so for one to become physically addicted to it, but less if one has latent chemical dependency personality traits. And like most addictive drugs, the more one uses it the more their neuro cardio vascular system builds sensitivity towards the drug, thus requiring larger and larger amounts to be needed in order to get the desired high.

"Another way to get cocaine into the blood stream is to mix tobacco and coke half and half, then smoke it.

"While I'm thinking about it," Randy continued, "let me say something about over dosing. I've never heard of anyone being chemically addicted to marijuana, but mentally, yeah. And I haven't heard of anyone over dosing smoking pot. However, I have been told that if one smokes three or four strong joints very rapidly and then exercises very strenuously, that their heart may go crazy. And if one's heart was weak already, then this could possibly cause a heart attack. But any drug can be dangerous if overdone, even caffeine.

"Coke, crack, and heroin are all three, potentially, chemically and mentally addictive. Plus one doesn't have to be a chemically dependent personality to get hooked, either. And it is certainly possible to over dose and to die from consuming too much at one time, and moreso with crack and heroin due to their strength, which can be guessed wrongly.

"Crack cocaine is heated by a flame and its vapors inhaled. The bigger end of a broken automobile antenna is sometimes used as a smoking pipe by inserting a tiny crack rock into one end and using a cigarette lighter to heat the tube's filled end while sucking the vapor through the other. A socket from a wrench set held by a pair of pliers is sometimes used in a similar manner as the antenna pipe. Another street method is to crease an opened and empty soft drink can and punch pin holes in the crease. With a small crack rock on top in the crease, heat is applied to the rock with a lighter and the vapors sucked through the top's hole and inhaled.

"Heroin takes much more apparatus to use it and is not as easily concealed as coke, crack, or marijuana. While smack can be snorted, the usual method of cooking a fix is to pour the hit in a teaspoon, heat the bottom of the spoon with a lighter, a match, or a lit-candle until the powder turns into a liquid; load the liquid into a hypodermic or diabetic syringe and needle, band the upper arm with a piece of surgical tubing, clinch the fist to cause the veins to protrude at the inner elbow, insert the needle, untie the

162

tubing, and inject the drug for a nearly instantaneous reaction of a flushing euphoria. The high may last for hours depending on the quality of the heroin, the amount injected, and the user's requirements. The sharing of used and unclean needles is a constant method of disease transmission, particularly in the case of AIDS."

TWENTY-FIVE

Colt said, "While I make us a scotch, tell me about smuggling."

Randy began, "I may have high lighted it before, but okay. Our first involvement in smuggling drugs into the U.S. began many years ago when the South Americans began immigrating to the states and took with them their desire for drugs. At first, some would return and smuggle dope back. Then as a drug market began to develop, some of the locals would carry bags on their bodies and thus the industry was born.

"Believe it or not, some would swallow tiny bags of pot or coke and retrieve it from their feces, or if on a short trip they could regurgitate it after arrival. There were arrests in Miami where some females had inserted condoms filled with pot, heroin or coke into their vaginas. And even some females and some male homosexuals were caught with similar in their rectum. Too, a number of these mules died from over doses when a bag or condom broke inside while in transit or during the extraction process.

"Then hiding drugs in both checked and carry-on luggage and on babies and juveniles became popular until the law enforcement agencies and the airlines got wise to it and installed x-ray machines at check-in entrances for checking carry-on items. And if the profile fit the passenger, they would pull the suspect aside and do complete body searches. The typical profile in the beginning years before the mules became legit-looking was a Latino between 18 and 35, not well dressed as compared to yankee standards, with a round trip ticket showing no more than an overnight stay if that, traveling alone, carrying or checking something that could hide dope, frequent trips to and from the same location, no identification unless Customs was involved and then it probably would be forged. His or her eyes were always shifting around nervously looking for Narcs and if one got too close and was made he/she would quickly move out of the area. And at that time nervous sweat would appear on their upper lips and brow. And if you shook hands with him or her, their hand would be cold and clammy. Many mules were addicts themselves and because of this were very fidgety and hyper.

"Following the Feds' tightening-down, the industry shifted to the mailing of dope-filled manila envelopes, parcel post, boats and yachts, ships, planes, and cars. I'll cover each separately since each has its own interesting story.

"Concerning airline luggage smuggling, here's a very interesting technique that was carefully set up and worked successfully in shipping tons of dope before it was stopped by the Feds. Our people bribed the bell hops at one resort hotel on a Hawaiian island, bribed the baggage handlers at the island's airport and the baggage handlers at several state-side airports in order to set up the pipeline.

"Let's say that your two-suiter Samsonite baggage was chosen to be used. In order for your baggage to make your flight and since you were with a very large group whereby all of you were leaving your resort hotel for the airport at about the same time, you were instructed by the Bell Captain to have your luggage ready for pick-up and in the hall at your room door three to four hours before your flight.

"Your suit case was picked up and then taken by car off the hotel premises where it was opened with a master key, emptied, and filled with bags of dope and returned to the hotel with special tape across its locks making for easy identification and, thus, keeping it out of any local airport agricultural search. Further, upon arrival at the airport, a tag was attached that would send your suit case to a specific airport in the U.S. where it was eagerly awaited by prior-informed baggage handlers.

"From there it left the stateside airport premises to be unloaded and refilled with dope money or in some cases rags, and re-taped for further identification and back at the airport re-tagged for its return trip to the original airport and then to the off-premises spot in the islands. Once again, your clothes and articles were re-packed and it was then tagged properly and shipped to your home airport for delivery with an apology for their losing it in the system.

"The lost luggage delay, when everything worked right, was about three or four days and no one usually expected any wrong doing. If the passenger complained about their contents having been haphazardly thrown back into the case, an additional apology was given for your suitcase 'had fallen open during handling, and that probably was the reason for the delay.'

"On a normal day quite a number of suit cases would be lost and many found, drawing no suspicion, that many having successfully smuggled about half a million dollars worth of coke or heroin into the U.S. Later, our pipeline was broken when drug residue was found by the Narcs' dogs on the luggage while on the conveyers. Our Board laughed about it, when Uncle Fernie told them that "Our South Pacific business has gone to the dogs!"

Randy laughed, "I don't get involved in this type of activity and most of the time our folks even keep the knowledge of it from me. But in this case it was funny as could be how I found out about it the first time.

"Since no one knows my identity or my where abouts except in our higher echelons, and since my security team could not apprise the lower levels of our presence in the islands, there were some very embarrassed folks after I told them that the airline had lost my luggage.

"Kat just cackled like a setting hen when I told her that I found out that my own employees had stolen my suit case to smuggle dope in and additionally, what Uncle Fernie said. Uncle Fernie phoned me and shouted, "Hey, dummy, you got what you deserved! But I want to apologize for not training you better. For only a dumb gringo would let his new $25 million jet sit in that hanger in Gulf Shores and take a commercial flight all the way to Hawaii! Why you think we bought it for you, anyway! Are you broke from playing the dogs in Pensacola or just too tight to pay for the big-jet's flight time! Do you need to borrow some money or did Her Royal Majesty not give her little boy his weekly allowance? And don't try sniffing your jockey shorts, either! We don't need a doped-up, crotch-snorting Board Chairman, Mr. Goose!"

"Back to the beginning of our smuggling dope into the U. S.: airplanes offered the path of least resistance in as much as they could carry larger loads than our mules and could do it much faster. We mostly hired contract-pilots with their own planes. However, in some cases we actually put up the money for the purchase and refurbishment of the planes for the pilots that we felt had good potential. After all, what's a paltry half million dollars compared to the tens of millions we would make off its usage?

"Since payload and flying range was what we were primarily interested in, the planes were stripped of all unnecessary seats and equipment. Extra fuel tanks and rubber fuel bladders were added in order to increase the range. Since very accurate knowledge was needed in locating our somewhat hidden jungle and mountain air strips, expensive navigation equipment was added. Fifty to seventy-five thousand dollars was not unusual per plane. For weather safety we added storm scopes and weather radar. And often times we'd line the plane's cargo area with aluminum in order to make loading and unloading faster.

"Piston planes were found to be preferred because of the fact that piston engines are more fuel efficient at lower altitudes as opposed to jets requiring higher altitudes. And the planes needed to stay low to be below radar, particularly when they approached the U. S. coastlines. We used mostly the smaller twin engine and larger singles because they were better at getting in and out of shorter dirt and grass runways than larger airplanes and they require but one pilot thus giving us more pay load. Plus, to have to supply only gas and not jet fuel, too, made it easier at our loading operations, also.

"And to add to the stupidity within your Federal Government, their own FAA licensed A & P Inspectors inspected, certified, and signed off our planes after they were converted for drug hauling, thus assuring us that the planes had been re-built properly. We had many done in Pennsylvania, South Florida, and Texas.

"And here's another ridiculous laugh causer: after the law enforcement guys confiscated some of our planes and equipment, they would advertise and hold public auctions, called Seizure-Sales. We would send some legit rep, like a lawyer, to bid for us and legally buy back our planes for about ten to twenty-five percent or less of what we had put into them during conversion. For the most part, civilians don't want drug planes, thus letting many of our first bids go unchallenged.

"I remember an old DC-3 of ours that got caught in north Georgia. If I remember correctly, it cost me $100,000 and then $238,000 to get it equipped and in business. We used it dozens of times, making millions and millions of profit each trip. Anyway, we bought it back for $28,000 at the cops' auction and had it heading back to Colombia in just a week or two after the sale. We paid the Fixed Base Operator that ran the little airport a hefty fist full for his carefully taking care of it and for the oil and fuel that we bought. Besides, we were legitimate customers. That was about the fifth or sixth time that I paid for getting that same plane back, thus enjoying a great government run system that saves my initial investment for me and that helps to keep us in business.

"One would think in order to serve their citizens best, the confiscated planes, trucks, boats, and cars would be used for fishing reefs like they do with confiscated pistols, rifles, and guns. This contradiction raises some questions about the Feds' attitude concerning the drug industry, doesn't it, Colt? Or are they just discriminating against your National Rifle Association?

"In the beginning, a lot of drug trips were initiated, funded, and carried out by independents who took too many chances when it came to aircraft maintenance, fuel requirements for the trip, maximum aircraft weight limits, the trip's navigation planning, maneuvering through the Caribbean islands or Mexico, entering Colombia, finding the out-of-the-way airstrip, returning with the loaded plane, slipping into the U.S. while evading the law, finding the landing field or drop zone, and afterwards, safely flying back to home base. Because of their carelessness many airplanes can be seen in the waters surrounding the hundreds of landing sites in the islands, in the jungles and on the mountain sides. Further, many went down after being forced to do so by the U. S. Government's drug interdiction planes and helicopters.

"Additionally, in a few cases when an air drop had been completed and when the law enforcement was still in air pursuit, the pilot would set a course towards the Gulf or the ocean, let the auto-pilot fly the plane, bail out, and parachute down over land leaving the plane to keep its course until its fuel ran out. For when the pilot is making hundreds of thousands of dollars for delivering the goods, saving the plane is not desirable when it comes with jail or life in prison with no parole.

"Most of the times when a pilot jumped and left his plane on auto-pilot, the news media would tell about the plane crashing somewhere and nothing would be said about the pilot. But I remember once where a pilot parachuted into someone's yard and broke his back landing. No amount of money is worth being paralyzed."

TWENTY-SIX

Randy continued, "President Reagan sent George Bush and his folks into south Florida in the early eighties. Even then very little was effectively done to stop our planes. In fact, since Washington's concentration was centered in Florida, we shifted our inbound plane routes to the central and west coasts of the Gulf of Mexico, and the coasts of Georgia, the Carolinas, and Virginia.

"Mr. Bush did do some interesting things around the Keys, like putting up tethered radar balloons, increasing radar surveillance using their airborne radar planes, adding a few new installations along with Guantanamo, Cuba, sending out more Coast Guard boats, improving their night runs and in cloud chases by using infrared vision equipment. All that effort just made it more interesting for us.

"And they were just shucking and jiving the voters. For you never did see them get serious enough to stop us completely by entering Peru or Bolivia or Colombia and spraying our growing fields with paraquat or agent orange, thus defoliating the crops and putting us out of business. No, their effort was politically motivated and we knew it wasn't going to last very long.

"Plus, it helped in another way: I told the guys to shelf their inventory; to tell their casual buyers that supplies were limited due to the Feds' getting hot and to hit the addicts with a temporary fifty percent price increase and hold it high until Bush's heat eased off and I had notified them likewise. Further, they were to keep the extra profits for themselves and to spend it on their families as a surprise Christmas present. Some of the guys bought their wives a new home, some a new family car, and several put up trusts for college educations for their kids or their grandchildren. And we all thanked President Reagan for making things even more easy for us to do business in his country and right under his nose.

"I'll get on, in a minute, to the other forms of smuggling that we use. But while I'm thinking about it, let me tell you about an area of smuggling that you probably haven't thought about and that is just how do we get all that money out of the U.S. and to Colombia. Simple. We send it down on the planes as they come for more drugs. Of course, these <u>green</u> couriers are our very best pilots, for we cannot afford to have one of them ditch a load of ten to fifteen million dollars in the water because of their inexperience. And they all know us well enough to know that they cannot hide from us anywhere in the world if they were to steal our money. For they know that stealing a dime from us is sure death. Plus, they are paid an average of five percent for the delivery, the percentage varying one or two points depending on the amount and how hard it is to fly out from where we turn it over to them. Too, our better pilots already have five or ten million dollars hidden away somewhere and they are continuing to work for the challenge, for the excitement, for the intrigue, and for the enjoyment. Money is no longer their major motivating factor.

"With quite an excess of money on hand, our conglomerate had to find a way to put it to good use. So, what we did was make the huge sums available to large foreign companies and even to some countries, their borrowing the cash on short notice for their legitimate purposes like a large expansion and construction projects, famine damage replacement, war damage reconstruction, war machinery, and other similar needs where time is a factor. For this we get a reasonable interest rate and favorable treatment towards our drug business as well as towards our banana and beef exports.

"Concerning your government tracking our flights to our drop zones, things changed and became more complicated for us as the Feds got more experienced, better trained, and better organized. During the seventies and the early eighties, their procedures included someone spotting our inbound aircraft by radar, sight, sound, or by an informant ratting on us. Then they would order a jet to come out, identify our craft, and follow it. But with our low and slow actions, the jet had to circle above us at higher altitudes depending upon his on-board radar, or a ground-based radar or radar from the AWAC military plane above or the Navy's E-2C or a government ship's radar. But this did not stop us from continuing to our drop zone. And unless some helicopters showed up on the scene we would make the drop knowing full well that since the tracking plane knew our where abouts but not the exact spot that we were going to unload we had plenty of time to drop the goods, get them loaded, and get away before any ground arrests could be made. Plus in many cases we had the locals paid to stay away.

"But soon the Feds wised up and added helicopters to the chase once we got close to the coast. They could follow the dropped drugs down to our ground crew. So then we developed night water-drops. We had fast boats waiting nearby with homing gear to identify the transmitter-carrying, waterproof bundles. Divers were aboard to help, if needed. With four or five speed boats on a run, it made it very difficult for the law to chase the one or two that contained the drugs, even with night-vision equipped helicopters.

"But about then, the DEA added satellite tracking. This made it even more interesting. So what did we do? We'd unload in international waters from a foreign cargo ship that came from who-knows where and using a dozen or so speed boats and yachts, we'd head for some dozen or more islands or split the bunch in a lot of different directions towards the U. S. coast. Sure they caught us sometimes; about 10%. But they just did not have enough equipment at the right place and at the right time to catch us.

"If we were in the air, the only way to stop us was to shoot us down. And even though they tried to get that action approved your government's higher-ups and your citizens stopped its approval for fear that this would give the Feds the right to possibly shoot down innocent general aviation airplanes. So in the air they could follow us and that is all.

"But they had to catch us with the goods on the ground and we made that nearly impossible unless they got prior knowledge of our drop zone location. Then our water-drops made it even more difficult for them to cover since it would require so many boats on stand-by and several helicopters to chase them to ports. And even then they could be chasing a clean boat. But later, with the more sophisticated satellites that could watch the boats being loaded, they made us change some of our methods. And

I'll get to that in a minute. I need to go to the head and then get us another drink.

Upon returning and taking a fresh scotch from Colt, Randy continued, "So at that time we began to examine all of our smuggling tactics. Some of our options included shipping drugs to other friendly countries, then using air, water, and ground methods from that location into the U. S. We discovered methods that worked at the U.S. borders of both Mexico and Canada. We put money into pot fields in the rural areas of the U.S. itself. We've established some of our own crack labs stateside. And last but not least, we've gotten into the pill business by buying huge quantities of American-made amphetamines and barbiturates outside the states in several different countries and smuggling them back into the U.S. through Mexico.

"For like I said before, if the Yanks want it, we'll find a way to supply them. And where a pipeline to them doesn't exist, we'll make one. For it's their stupidity, their weakness, their greed, and their corruption that allows us to exist! And we are smart enough to profit from it all, at their expense."

About that time a voice over the hand-held that Randy had brought in with them from the golf cart and placed upon the bar, "C.R.-1 to the General."

"Go ahead, Captain," Randy answered.

Captain Alejandro continued, "Sir, C. R.-Central advises that the General has a no-code-fax from IntelSec-Central from Colonel Rodrigue. May I get it for you, Sir?"

Randy instructed, "No thank you, Alex. Tell the Lieutenant that I'll phone him from here and he can read it to me."

"Sir, I'll relay your wishes immediately, Sir."

Pressing the phone number, Randy turned to Colt, "Colonel Rodrigue and I are personal friends, also. We went through basic training in Louisiana and Georgia together. Max can out-scotch you and me combined. I want to take you down there sometime and we'll stay at his hacienda. He plays professionally in a dance band on the weekends and teaches both classical and flamenco guitar two nights a week at the local university.

"Lieutenant, please read the fax from Colonel Rodrigue,"

174

Randy said. With his hand over the phone's mouth piece he repeated, "Max says, "Sir, no disrespect to the General meant, for maybe I misinterpreted the two-finger sign language message that you guys sent to me from the golf cart while outside the compound at 2:17 p.m. your time this-date. Did that translate to how old you were when your parents got married or do I need a refresher in signing, Sir? P.S.: I understand that we have a new Johnny Red Scotch-drinker in our midst. I need a good elbow-bender. When can you two come down to my place, Sir?"

Randy, laughing along with Colt, added, "I told you that guy's a mess, and he doesn't miss a lick!"

Colt asked, "One last question and we'd better locate the girls. You said earlier that George Bush's efforts were politically motivated and did not do much good in stopping the drug smuggling but you did not identify why it was so ineffective."

Randy answered, "First, remember that I told you that we bought inside information on their activities that allowed us to know ahead of time where many of their actions were going to be directed. But probably even more of a weakness on their part was the fact that Mr. Bush tried to combine efforts from nearly every department of the government that was possible to use, including the F.B.I., his former group, the C.I.A., the DEA, the Air Force, the Coast Guard, the Army, the Navy, along with many Florida city, county, and state law enforcement agencies.

"These guys have inter-departmental jealousies and do not get along well with each other under forced circumstances like this, much less when put to all this national publicity and media pressure. Inter-group communication and cooperation was weak, to say it nicely. Plus some of them felt this was Republican Party motivated and they were not going to be exploited in this manner, period.

"Sure, Mr. Bush's anti-drug efforts spent millions and millions of tax dollars and it got many more millions worth of free air-time. But looking back what did this so-called War on Drugs amount to? It sure did not end with a governmental victory nor was there any surrender on our part, was there? But it did make us explore and open brand new drug routes, routes that we still use today. And our Distribution Division guys loved the additional profits that their increased prices allowed them personally. So, I guess one could say that Mr. Bush's shucking and jiving the voters helped us enormously, also."

Randy called Kat on the hand-held reporting, "We're headed to the pool-side game room."

TWENTY-SEVEN

Earlier, after lunch as Kat and Celia were leaving the rose garden with Randy and Colt going their own way, Captain Alejandro asked Kat, Senora, will you ladies be leaving the compound for a ride or will you be inside for the remainder of the afternoon?"

"We'll stay inside, Alex. Thanks anyway," Kat answered.

Celia asked Kat in a low voice, "What was that all about?"

Kat explained, "If I had said that we were going outside the walls, the Captain would have radioed for a cart to follow us. But since we're staying inside, we won't tie up two more guards. However, security stays with Randy no matter where he goes, even inside the compound. Colonel Andre and his team take over away from C. R. whereas Captain Alex and his crew cover us inside."

Kat changed the subject as she slowed the cart to a stop. "Celia, I did not want to bring this up in front they guys, but 'Nita and I want to talk to you about some important and private feelings of ours. So, if you will put off your tour of the place until later, I would like to call her now and have her meet us at the poolside game room where we can talk, just the three of us. What do you say?"

Celia replied, "Oh, sure. No offense meant, but that tour bit was just an excuse to get away from our guys. I'll have plenty of time to see it later."

Kat changed the hand-held to the house frequency and told a waiting 'Nita that they'd meet her in five minutes poolside. 'Nita was already there upon their arrival and had soft drinks, the two wines ordered by Captain Alex, and the cheese and crackers ready on the bar.

After the last arrivals got some wine and hors d'oeuvres, Kat began, "Celia, 'Nita and I have been going here and there, and there and here, and everywhere else with our husbands so much that we are sick and tired of it! We are so glad that you have joined us for many reasons, one of which is your adding new topics of conversation and new thought into the old ones. She and I have been the best of friends for nearly fifty years and there is probably not a single sentence that I can start that she cannot finish, and probably she'll be using my own words. And vice versa with me to her.

"But," Kat added, "don't get me wrong. We do love our husbands and enjoy very much their company, most of the time. However, everything we do is usually their idea and their decisions and not just ours or just for us. And if you'll notice, even our four-way conversations tend to have a male-influenced color about them. Additionally, Randy and Pablo play golf every Sunday together. And even sometimes on holidays they will take the Bonanza and fly somewhere to play golf for the weekend, staying over in a motel Saturday night.

"So, with all this in mind 'Nita and I have been talking about this. And then last night we decided that since you are aboard, why don't we three get together and plan something big, and I do mean <u>big</u>, for us to take up that will give us something to do that is just ours. Some kind of a project or something. Not just going shopping all the time, that's too boring. Maybe something that could take up the weekend, if we wanted it to, Saturday included. But let's think of something that doesn't take a total commitment for every weekend; one that could let us have the weekend with the guys, if we chose to. Celia, what do you think about what I've said?

Celia replied, "I love Colt and love being with him, too. But like you two, it's me going with him. Never him going with me. I feel smothered sometimes. Hey, kiddoes, let's get on with it! I'm in all the way! What kind of ideas have y'all come up with?"

Nita answered, "None. We were waiting to include you." After about ten minutes of exploring things like tennis, sailing, dog races, bowling, antiqueing, deep-sea fishing, ceramics, hunting, art courses, computer classes, golf, and civic volunteer work, nothing seemed to fit, even for two out of the three.

Then Celia hit on this: "Kat, Randy mentioned in passing that you seemed interested in learning the navigational part of flying and that you had done a good job helping him when flying in the Bonanza. Were you just smoking another Cuban cigar for

178

his benefit, or were you truly interested?"

Kat admitted, "No, indeed. Someday I'd like to learn how to fly and get a license. Why?"

Celia jovially answered as she glanced at 'Nita, "What 'da 'ya mean someday? Why not now?"

'Nita jumped in, "Count me in. I've enjoyed flying in the Bonanza."

Celia, with tongue in cheek, replied. "Why do you think I asked? In San Diego we had a neighbor that was a Navy pilot. He would take me and Colt up with him and his wife in their Cessna 182 quite often. He would let me sit up front and I probably have ten hours of time flying the plane. I'd love to get a pilot's license. Maybe we could go together and get our own plane to learn in. Then after we were licensed, we could go somewhere on the weekends when our guys are out of town playing golf and certainly on Sundays by ourselves."

Kat was so excited that she jumped up, ran around the room, and hollered and shrieked, "That's it! That's it! Celia did it! I told you she would, 'Nita! That's exactly what we're looking for! Let's do it! Let's do it! Oh, My Lord, let's do it!"

'Nita exclaimed, "My goodness, Kat, don't wet your pants." Turning to Celia, 'Nita said, "She's not been that excited in ten years!"

Kat came around to the chairs, sat down again, and said, "Okay, gals, let's get to planning and scheming. I'm so excited!"

Celia talked first by asking Kat, "Do you think you can get Randy to teach us?"

"Sure," was Kat's reply, "and for free!"

Celia continued, "'Nita, can you take off Saturdays?"

"Pablo and I don't work weekends, unless the folks from Colombia are in town," 'Nita explained.

Thinking while her friends were talking, Kat offered, "Let me suggest something. Why don't we tell the guys after they've had a few drinks and hamburgers. And we'll tell them in such a way, using our female charm and plenty of tact, so that they accept it as being our decision, not one of theirs and not one that we want them to influence, in such a way that their male egos won't be frayed. In such a way that they will know that we are strong on our decision to do this; that they had better not try to talk us out of it, and that if they are squeamish about it, then we'll not use Randy, and will hire our own dad-blamed instructor. What do you think about approaching them that way?"

Getting positive nods from both, Kat continued, "Good. Celia, would you do the talking for us? You explain things so well and they won't give you any flack like they would 'Nita or me."

"Yeah, I guess so," Celia agreed. "If that is what you two want. I'll do my best. But if Colt gives me some crap, you guys better jump in and help me."

Kat concluded, "Well, that's settled. Lordy! Lordy! We're gonna be airplane pilots! Man, that's just gee-rate! We're gonna have so much fun it's gonna be sinful and nearly illegal!

"Now let me suggest something else and I want your thoughts about this one, too. Why don't we agree to let me pay for the plane?

"If Randy accepts teaching us," Kat added," we'll have him choose what kind he wants us to learn in. Then he can find one. I'll give him the money and he can buy it. Then we'll have him lease it to his flight department for renting during the week, but not on the weekends. Therefore, they will keep up the maintenance on it, the rental income applying to the upkeep and hanger costs, thus solving another problem for us. They are to have it ready for our usage on Saturdays and Sundays unless prior approval is given by me. Further, if one of us decides to take a lesson during the week and if Randy is available, we'll check to see if it's not rented.

"And you guys," Kat continued, "could be responsible for paying for your own fuel, based on each's flight time. They can bill you monthly for it or you can just charge it to your credit card if you like after each flight. And Randy had better not want to charge us for the lessons, either, or he won't get any more moonlight swims, if you know what I mean!"

"That's more than fair," 'Nita summarized.

Celia told Kat, "If you are sure that that is what you prefer to do and since 'Nita says okay, then it's fine with me, Kat. But Colt might want to pay some on the airplane purchase."

"No, Celia," Kat responded emphatically, "because by letting our family's conglomerate's flight department have it for rental, it helps them, plus I can have it as an investment so long as we don't use it mostly ourselves and it might just end up producing a positive income in the long run, depending on how much they rent it. But either way, my part of the rental income cuts down the cost of owning the plane. And even if it just sits there during the week, surely as rich as I am, it won't hurt me to lose a little while enjoying the heck out of my time playing with my two best friends. Additionally, they will handle all the FAA bookwork and paper work on the plane's upkeep, and the required 100 hour rental inspections. This way we'll be able to concentrate on learning to fly and having fun."

Celia asked, "Kat, you seem to know a lot about it already. How come?"

Kat answered, "Several years ago, when I first expressed an interest in flying to Randy, he told me most of what I know. Some of it I just picked up listening to him and others talking about lease backs and such."

Celia continued her questions to Kat, "Do you have an idea of how long it takes to get the license and what we have to do?"

Kat answered, "We'll have Randy explain it all in detail to us. However, from what I remember, most folks do it in about six months. There're two parts to it: you have to study and pass a written test. They call this ground school. All the while you're taking lessons on that, you will also be learning how to fly the plane."

'Nita asked, "But once we have done all that and have our license what are we going to do then, just fly around this coastal area and Pensacola and Mobile sight seeing? That'll eventually get boring."

Kat added, "We can, if that's what we want to do. But there is a lot more that we can do than just that. Once we've got our private pilot license we need to keep on training. For the private only allows you to fly in good weather and not when you can't see but a certain distance and not in clouds. So, if we want to become better and safer pilots we need to keep on taking more lessons and get additional ratings as they're called. Randy says that a private ticket is just a license to begin learning. After we have it, we need to work on getting a commercial ticket along with an instrument rating. Then we'll probably move on to getting checked out in bigger and faster planes, like his Bonanza."

Celia asked, "Do you have to do all that or can you stop where you feel comfortable?"

Kat answered, "No, you can stop any time. But in this case, more is better."

'Nita asked, "Didn't I read somewhere about an all-ladies flying group?"

Kat answered, "Yes, they do have one. But I cannot remember their name; I'll ask Randy. Additionally though, there are a number of organizations we can join that have local activities as well as regional and national get-togethers. Plus, if we really get good, we can take part in precision flying events where you compete in specific airplane categories and they time you on your run and your fuel used and that kind of thing. And it doesn't matter if you are a female or not; it's how good you are in planning and flying your plane and executing your plan. And we can even go in a group to some of the Caribbean islands on trips."

Kat continued, "And there are a number of magazines you two can subscribe to that'll keep you up-to-date on what's happening and stuff like that. Randy gets them all, and I read them. And there are gatherings that they call fly-ins all around the southeast where locals have Saturday pancake breakfasts and little fund raisers almost every weekend. And that goes on year around, too. So, there's plenty to keep us as active and busy as we want to be and when we want to be."

'Nita asked, "What kind of equipment will Celia and I need to buy?"

"Randy will tell us that," Kat added. "But as far as I know, very little. Oh, he'll want us to buy some books and manuals and some things to figure navigation with. And you might want to get your own set of earphones and a flight case to keep your stuff in. But if we study together, there is no big need in triplicating everything. Let's make it a team-thing and have fun being together doing it."

"Ball-park the amount for me," 'Nita said.

Kat continued, "Oh, probably a couple of hundred dollars for the headset and about the same for a real good case and maybe a hundred for the other things you'll want personally; so about five hundred should get you first-class shape. I think Randy has the books, video tapes and course material already among his instructor stuff."

Celia asked, "If we were paying for everything that it costs to get a private license and not getting Randy for free, how much would all this cost a beginner?"

Kat came back, "Considering the ground school lessons, its instructor, and the books and material, the plane, fuel and the flight instructor, the prog-rides, your tests and the FAA examiners, all of that together would probably amount to three grand."

"What's a prog-ride, Kat?" Celia asked.

"That's where," Kat continued, "your instructor asks another instructor to talk with you and fly with you in order to help your instructor better understand your progress and how he is doing in training you. No instructor wants to have a student unhappy or to fail an FAA test. This is good for you, too, having another qualified instructor ride with you. It gives you another outlook on how different instructors teach, thus preparing you for your future rides with the FAA dudes."

Celia continued her questioning, "What does FAA stand for?"

"The Federal Aviation Administration," Kat iterated. "They are the governmental agency in Oklahoma City that among a lot of other things, controls and regulates civilian flying and all of its rules. They call us General Aviation or GA for short."

'Nita asked, "Don't I remember something about a physical being required?"

Kat replied, "Yes, before you can be licensed you must be examined by an FAA appointed doctor and pass the physical.

He's called an AME, standing for Aviation Medical Examiner. And the physicals are repeated on some form of regular basis, but I don't know much more about that than what I've said."

Celia responded, "I am amazed at how much you already know, Kat. How'd you learn so much without becoming a pilot yourself?"

Kat answered, "Well, remember that Randy has been very deeply involved in flying from the start, when we moved back to Bogota from Durango after his master degrees. He had me, in the beginning, hear him recite his own lessons. And I've helped him in keeping himself current by practicing his newly updated knowledge and such on me, and so that he can hone his teaching techniques. Too, his South American laws and rules were somewhat different than what he had to learn and pass when moving to the states. I listened to him here, too. Some of it I've retained and some of it I've let pass. However, from now on I'm gonna listen more and ask more questions and I'll share it with you guys."

Celia asked Kat, "Have you and Randy attended any of the meetings or air shows where people from these flying clubs that you mentioned were present?"

"Yes," Kat answered, "we went last October to the big annual fly-in and air show that is held about a hundred miles north of here in Evergreen, Alabama that is sponsored by the local chapter of the Experimental Aircraft Association; they call themselves the EAA. Why do you ask?"

Celia responded, "Did you see any folks wearing matching clothes or matching shirts? That kind of thing?"

"Good Lord, yes!" Kat continued. "Lots and lots of it, men and women alike, everywhere. They have groups flying in together wearing matching shoes, trousers, shirts, sweaters, and caps with their club name and their home base on them. Then there were couples with outfits that matched the color scheme of their airplane with renditions of their plane and its numbers on their caps, shirts, and jackets."

'Nita jumped, "Oh, oh! I know what she's thinking and what we're gonna do!"

Celia asked, "Kat, where do we go and get our outfits?"

Kat was excited again. "Fantastic, Celia. Just fantastic! I knew this would work out! Well, let me think. First of all, we can fly to some of the nearby FBOs. That stands for Fixed Based Operators, and they are the ones that have the planes for rent and flying schools at airports. Some of them stock stuff like we're talking about. If we cannot find exactly what we want doing that then there's a big phone in, mail order company called Sporty's Pilot Shop up in Batavia, Ohio. I've got their catalog. Additionally, there are several locally, in Gulf Shores and Orange Beach, that do embroidering and flocking. We could buy our own matching pieces, design our own logos and have them finished ourselves. What's y'all's feelings?"

'Nita getting a positive nod from Celia said, "It'd be a lot more fun to do our own. More reasons to be gone off together, too!"

Celia thoughtfully added, "But we'll need to wait 'til we get our plane before we can determine what colors to match it with and what kind of plane and the numbers.

"But," she sheepishly grinned and added, "do we have to wait until we can fly to the FBOs? We've all got cars, you know."

Kat quipped, "Just say when, loved ones, just say when!"

'Nita enthusiastically added, "The more we talk, the more fun this gets, and we haven't even had a lesson yet!"

"And it ain't stopping here, either, girls. Let's keep it going," Celia responded.

"Celia," Kat inquired, "do we need to go over with you how you're gonna handle the guys or do you feel comfortable enough?"

"No, let's talk about it," was Celia's answer.

They were as excited as five year olds at Christmas, spending the rest of the time talking about flying, approaching their husbands, and sharing more thrilling ideas about where they could later fly to and fun things to do at each destination while the arriving kitchen crew began setting up the cooking equipment and food tables poolside.

TWENTY-EIGHT

Randy and Colt drove up on their golf cart with the two bodyguards close behind in theirs.

After greetings were exchanged, Randy called Pablo on his hand-held and told him his drink was getting warm, to come on or they would start talking ugly about him. Pablo arrived in about five minutes and joined his poolside group sitting at a large round table under a giant umbrella.

After several drinks had been consumed by the guys and while the girls slowly sipped their first wine, Kat gave the nod to Celia. Celia began, "Hey, guys, listen up. We three have an important announcement to make and if you will let me explain it to you in detail first, we'll answer any questions once I'm through. So, if you will let me start, I'll tell you when I'm finished and then we'd like your thoughts."

Celia moved forward in her chair in order to be able to easily look into the eyes of each of the three men and to observe their facial expressions as she talked and to emphasize the importance of her words, saying, "In our world today, it is common for men to do things in male groups such as golf, fishing, hunting, that sort of thing. It is lovingly accepted and taken for granted by us females that you guys need time away from your spouses in order to do manly things and talk man talk; to relax and to have fun. And not only do we agree with this, we encourage it and want you to continue your segregated group activities for it gives us needed space, too.

"And like you guys, we need our separate time just like you do. And this has no reflection upon how you feel about your spouses or how we feel about you. For we all know that we six love our spouses very much; for we openly show it, regularly. And we are proud of it!

"Further," Celia continued, "by our planning three get-togethers each month, we have assured ourselves a minimum amount of group socializing time. And I'm sure that won't be all we'll be doing with each other, group-wise. I certainly hope not.

"With you two, Randy and Pablo, wanting Colt to play golf with you guys on Sundays and with Kat informing me that sometimes y'all may fly somewhere for a full weekend trip, it looks like it would behoove us ladies to plan better usage of the times that you probably will be away. And we should schedule something ourselves for Sundays; that is, at least for Sunday mornings.

"So, looking at a dozen or more things that we could do, yet still allow us to be available for your company should you guys not play, like when you are rained out or it is too cold, our list narrowed down to just one that met our qualifications; qualifications like it cannot be too time consuming; something that would keep our interest; something challenging and exciting that won't quickly get boring; something that could later include you guys; something that 'Nita and I can easily afford; and something that we ladies can feel comfortable doing from a physical standpoint.

"We have chosen a big, long-term project for the three of us as a team, and yet for each of us separately; one that definitely meets all our rigid qualifications. And on what we are announcing to you three guys we fully expect your loving understanding and heartfelt support in the same manner that we give you our loving backing on your golfing. And may I add that the three of us are extremely, I repeat extremely, excited about it and have committed ourselves fully to it. We are going to learn to fly, get our private licenses and then a commercial ticket, and then our instrument ratings, and after that who knows where it'll take the six of us literally."

Celia concluded, "Okay, I'm through. Time for questions."

About fifteen seconds passed with no word being uttered. The ladies felt the air thicken and this bolstered more strength and resolve on their part. They were now ready for a good liberated female-type stand: Bring on the fight, you male chauvinists. We're prepared! Go ahead take your best shot! Make our day!

Colt was first to react and it shocked the girls. Looking at Randy and then Pablo, he shouted, "Let's give the girls a big hand, guys! That was one heck-of-a-speech, Mrs. Erhlichman!" Then Colt jumped up and rushed over to his wife, pulled her out of the chair, grabbed her under the arms, lifted her off the concrete pool apron, and swung her around 360 degrees. Then, still laughing loudly, he let her down and kissed her hard on the mouth saying for all to hear, "I love you, gal. And I'm proud of you, girls! You can count on me 150 percent!"

Seeing this burst of emotion, the other two guys got up and kissed their wives. Then the three hugged each others' wives as if saying to each lady: We're proud to be your husbands and friends! and showing their unanimous approval.

Sitting back down, Kat took over. "Randy, we want you to be our instructor; at no charge, of course. Will you do it for us?"

Randy answered, "My Lord, girls! I'd be heartbroken if you didn't let me! Of course, I will!"

"Great!" Kat continued. "Then here's the beginning that we talked about. Randy, we want you to decide what type of airplane that you want us to learn in, all the way up through our instruments rating. You find a good one that you like and buy it with my money. Then I want you to lease it to your Flight Department for their renting to others, but during weekdays only. Have them credit my part of the rental income to my account and to bill me monthly when there is a debit balance, with them doing all the upkeep and inspections. And I want you to see that they give it first class attention and care. Equip it with those state-of-the-art radios and instruments, including a stormscope or a weather radar, or both, like our King-Air's got. For, later, we want to join some flying organizations and plan to enter some competitions and timed events."

Kat continued, "We girls will pay, individually, for our own fuel charges and costs other than the plane, such as prog-ride instructors and the FAA guys and such. Additionally, you tell us what study equipment and materials to buy, not triplicating the purchases unless necessary. We'd like Saturday mornings to be your instructional class time and sometimes, when convenient with you three, Saturday afternoons also. We'll do our studying, as a group, on Sundays while y'all are off golfing. We'll be ready to get our physicals next week. You tell us what doctor you want us to use. Does this sound like we're serious, guys?"

"Does to me!" was Pablo's reply as Colt and Randy nodded their agreement.

Randy said, half-serious/half kidding, looking at Pablo, then Colt, "Hey, partners, you guys want to play golf in Scotland and Ireland this time next year? We'll have three pilots then that can fly us there in the King-Air! And best of all, we won't have to pay them a dime; they'll get to sleep with us at night!"

After the laughing stopped, Randy said, "Sounds like you ladies have done a thorough enough job of planning it to me. Kat, I don't know of an AME in Orange Beach or Gulf Shores. Most of the guys at Jack Edwards Airport and I use a doctor in Daphne named Dr. Geraldo Javier Gondolo. You met him. He's that guy from Bogota that was our speaker at last month's "Business Night Out" that the Chamber of Commerce sponsors. He talked about problems with medical insurance; remember! Plus he and I worked together as a team on that county-wide Sheriff's Boys Ranch fund-raiser last year. Phone him Monday and tell Jerry that I want him to give you girls a third-class medical. He'll tell his office staff to work y'all in on stand-by if you ask him; that's what he does for us. And then y'all go over and wait.

"And by the way, girls," Randy concluded, "most insurance companies won't cover a flight physical unless you are required to get it as part of your profession. So you ladies will have to pay the doc yourselves. We've been paying $75.00, but some other places are higher. And after filling out your medical history and such, once you're in, it'll take about 30 minutes at the most."

The hamburgers were ready now. And for the rest of the daylight hours their rejuvenated enthusiasm fired up their conversations covering many, many exciting future group outings; outings that were founded around the girls' new flying adventure. Later, their penny-nickel-dime poker games were laced with delightful verbal interruptions.

190

TWENTY-NINE

The girls were so pumped with adrenaline about their learning to fly that they individually kept their husbands in bed and awake until about 1:00 talking about it before turning out the lamps.

But at Cinco Robles about midnight, Kat slipped out of their bed and walked around and stood beside Randy in the soft lamp light. Facing him, she slowly lifted up her short nightie, the only thing she ever wore to bed, just a bit to reveal before Randy's staring eyes her thick, wide patch of soft, coal-black pubic hair. Once she felt that he had stared enough at her love-triangle, she eased the nightie with her finger tips slowly over her big voluptuous breasts, holding the nightie over her face for about twenty seconds so that Randy could lust in his private look and become consumed in pure voyeuristic pleasure. And he did.

Randy reached over and slid one hand between her thighs smoothly storking her hairy outer lips. He eased his hand gently through her thighs and upwards, then pulled against her smooth round buttocks, moving her pubic hair towards his face while the other hand reached around her firm, wide hips and pressed her close to him so that he could kiss her where it was now very moist. And for a minute or so he did what she wanted him to do with his wet, warm tongue. And she loved his doing it.

Kat slipped her nightie over her beautiful Latin face and let it fall on the soft carpet, gently leaned over and gave her lover a long, warm and tender kiss, slipping her hot tongue far into his mouth. She slithered her warm body in beside him allowing him to, for a moment, suck the breast she was cradling in her two hands while he gently palmed her other hardened nipple.

She slid atop Randy tightening her thighs over his, with her left hand finding and stroking back and forth his stiffened proof of readiness across her now completely wet outer lips. Easing slowly under the covers, she softly dragged her sensitive nipples across his hairy chest and down over his stomach, both enjoying this physical pleasure. Then kissing and licking and tongue-teasing his firm, tanned body at least a hundred times, she inched downward. Once getting to where she wanted to be, she found what she was looking for and wanted. And it was in the extremely hard form that she wanted it to be and she loved its bigness. Then she became aware of a deep feeling of inner joy from pleasing her lover.

Her head rotated from side to side and up and down as she let slip out deep cat-like purrs, sighs or pure pleasure, moans that only female lovers can emit. And Randy was glad that she was doing what she was doing and tenderly thought, <u>What a lady and what a lover! And she's all mine! And at 52, man; if the world only knew!</u>

Then Randy whispered, "Honey, I can't take much more of that!"

When she heard this proof that now she had Randy aroused to the point where she wanted him to be, Kat slithered upwards and with her hot wet lips and tongue she found his. Then with her right hand she reached between her thighs, got a firm grip on his full erection, found her wettest spot, and did what Randy so badly wanted her to do.

Both Randy and Kat let out a low, intense moan.

When he felt their first deepest penetration, he got a hot tingling sensation that seemed to have started somewhere inside her as if it was emanating from her body and she was intentionally passing it into him through his thrusting erection. And he basked in this flushing feeling as it slowly spread through his body with fleeing warmth.

Randy gently but firmly began squeezing and twirling both of her hard nipples between his index fingers and thumbs causing a rushing sexual rapture to envelope and capture her mind. Her thrusts were getting stronger, her thighs were tightening around his thighs, her pelvic pressure was increasing. The faster her rhythmic motions became, the harder he excited her breasts, rapidly building her desires to a sexual crescendo and into a totally euphoric, mind-spinning explosion.

With Randy holding back and timing his physical release with hers, their simultaneous burst of uncontrolled emotions began with both lovers making many loud, involuntary, animal-like sounds. Through their climaxes the two were completely fulfilled beyond words; even beyond thoughts. They then spiralled downward into a spent-lover's, private oblivion.

After being absorbed for nearly ten minutes in this wordless, colorful dreamed of warm, blissful, sweet-nothingness, they slowly returned and then consciously wrapped each other in tight, loving arms, soft body pressed against soft body; legs intertwined; and cheek gently against cheek. Then with each becoming aware of just how tired they were after enjoying a great day and after their super but exhausting love making, they slipped from their tender, hugging togetherness.

Kat slipped out of the bed. After returning from the bathroom, along with a hot wash cloth for Randy, she gave him a passionate goodnight kiss, and said, "I am so lucky to have you."

He whispered, "I love you, too, Kat, very much."

Then neutralizing their thoughts, the in-love lovers drifted off into a deep and well earned sleep.

THIRTY

In 1983, after deciding to take up flying as their female thing, Kat, Celia, and 'Nita met with Randy to discuss their plans and desires. Randy gave them a detailed explanation of what was to be expected; things for them to buy and how he'd handle their lessons. Together, they'd meet on Saturday mornings in his office at the airport for ground school lessons and when flying lessons were started Saturday afternoons would be used. Then when he and the other guys played golf, the girls could get together and study.

He explained they must pass a formal written test administered by the FAA, the government institution that controlled general aviation. They would take the test over in Pensacola when he signed them off as being ready. The previous Monday, the three already had successfully received their Third Class physicals.

He explained he would get to work finding a plane that week and try to get it ready just as soon as possible. He added that if he could get what he wanted, and he thought he could, that all four of them would be able to fly together, thus allowing the two in the back seat to share some of each flying lesson's knowledge as it was being relayed up front, thereby cutting down a lot of flying time. Then once they had passed their written tests and were ready, he'd sign them off and they could take their check ride for their Private License with an FAA Designee.

Normally, he explained, most students were ready for their first solo in 10 to 15 hours. Then add another 40 hours to that and most had earned their privates. But the required minimum for it was 40 hours with several cross-country flights included of 100 or more miles from home base, one of which would be done solo.

After getting their Private Licenses they could continue to accumulate flying time to 150 hours when Randy would begin their lessons towards their Instrument Rating, which had a minimum requirement of 200 hours. However, prior to that they could work towards a Commercial ticket. This, they wanted to do.

In Trade-A-Plane magazine Randy located a three year-old Piper Aircraft PA-28-161, Cherokee Warrior II at Peachtree-Dekalb Airport in Chamblee, Georgia in north Atlanta, with no damage history, for $93,000. 2,157 hours was the total time on the airframe. And it had a zero-time factory remanufactured, Lycoming 0-320, 160 horse-power engine in it with a full IFR-King panel, a newly reupholstered interior, and air conditioning. He paid a competent A & P Mechanic from Mobile to fly up and check it out. And it got an A-Plus Condition Report. So, Randy flew to PDK in his Bonanza and bought it.

And before having it ferried to Gulf Shores, he had Epps Aviation do a fresh annual on it, put new rubber on the ground, and install a Ryan Stormscope and a Fly-Buddy Loran-C. With all this equipment, the four seater could just barely legally fly four grown men with full fuel. But with Randy and the three ladies aboard, who did not weigh as much, it would be safe. And he felt they'd love their little low-winger since it was freshly painted a light beige with a beautiful, medium-brown interior; Kat's and Celia's favorite colors.

Waiting for the Warrior II to land at Jack Edwards Airport that afternoon, the girls were like kids in toy land. After giving it a thorough fine-tooth combing, along with their three proud spouses in tow, they opened two bottles of chilled Dom Perignon and properly welcomed their new love and soul mate: Cherokee 7999 Zulu and the beginning of a whole new world full of hours and hours of fun experiences.

From the outset of their training, the three student pilots talked frequently over 99 Zulu's radio with the FAA's aviation services in Pensacola, named Pensacola Clearance Delivery, Pensacola Departure, Pensacola Approach, the Pensacola Regional Airport's Ground Control and Tower. Over the years, as an instructor, it was Randy's practice to take his students several times over to visit the FAA facilities and their personnel, called ATC's. Before their first visit, off the microphones and among themselves kiddingly the ATC's had nicknamed the ladies The Troublesome Threesome.

Then Randy had the ladies fly him over three or four times, allowing them to meet most of the guys and gals who worked on all three shifts. The female student pilots began bringing fresh home-baked pies and cakes and sandwiches with them and joining in the ATC's coffee breaks and bag lunches. From then on, The Troublesome Threesome became The Terrific Trio. And if a favor could be granted, or if extra help or patience was needed by these student pilots, they did not have to even ask for it. It was automatically given!

One evening 'Nita was in the pilot's seat, Kat was co-piloting and navigating with Celia in the back seat observing. Kat called, "Pensacola Clearance Delivery. Piper Cherokee Warrior 7999 Zulu."

PCD: "Piper Cherokee Warrior 7999 Zulu. Pensacola Clearance Delivery."

99 Zulu: "Pensacola, 99 Zulu's at Jack Edwards with Pensacola information Mike; departing runway 35; IFR to PDK. Please read the clearance in detail for our practice. Ready to copy."

PCD: "Piper Cherokee Warrior 7999 Zulu cleared IFR as filed to PDK; Al-15 direct MVC; Victor-20 direct MGM; Victor-20 direct LGC: direct. Expect Vectors LGC to PDK. Fly runway heading after take-off; cleared to 3,000'; expect 7,000' ten minutes after departure. Once off contact Pensacola Departure on 119.0. Transponder Squawk 3273. Departure Time 3:15 local. If not off by 3:30, contact Pensacola on 120.05 by Clearance Void-Time 3:45 or Anniston on 123.6 or telephone Flight Service. Pensacola altimeter 29.97. Read-back when ready."

99 Zulu: "Roger. Understand 99 Zulu cleared IFR as filed to PDK. Jack Edwards direct to Monroeville VOR. Victor 20 to Montgomery VOR. Victor 20 to LaGrange VOR direct. Expect Vectors from LaGrange to PDK. Fly runway 35 heading; cleared to 3,000', expect 7000' 10 minutes after departure. Contact Pensacola Departure on 119.0. Squawking 3273. ETD 3:15 local; off by 3:30. Clearance Void-Time 3:45; Pensacola on 120.05 or Anniston on 123.6 or phone FSS. Pensacola altimeter 29.97. Thanks."

PCD: "99 Zulu. Read-back correct. Kat, Atlanta Approach, normally, will send you from LaGrange up the west side of

Atlanta, north over Fulton County-Charlie Brown Airport then east towards Peachtree-Dekalb to intercept the ILS for 2-right or around for the ILS to 20-left. Tell Atlanta Approach initially that you just got your new instrument ticket at Pensacola, that it's your first time flying into the Atlanta area, and if he or she has time, you'd appreciate any extra help. ATC's, everywhere love to help our female aviators! Where's The Terrific Trio headed today?"

99 Zulu: "We're going for dinner at a neat little burned-out World War II French villa called The 57th Fighter Group located on the airport there in Chamblee. Celia's been there before; 'Nita and I haven't."

PCD: "Have a good trip, ladies! Switch when ready."

99 Zulu: "Thanks, Charlie. We'll talk to you guys later tonight. 99 Zulu switching to CTAF-Jack Edwards."

The trip up was a beautiful ride; snow-white puffs of scattered clouds below them at 2500', nothing above but a contrail-striped, azure-clear sky, unlimited visibility with wind at 7000' at 20 knots from the south adding about 10 miles per hour to their ground speed, according to Kat's calculations using the Loran-C, making it 135 miles per hour. She figured that Atlanta Approach's vectoring them would add about twenty minutes to their time. But still they should be on the ground by 7:30 p.m. Atlanta time, having added an hour for their crossing over from Central Standard Time to Eastern. So, with the forecast in mind, they knew that they did not have a lot of time to waste.

A slow moving cold front was over Louisiana and moving eastward. The forecast for their return trip to PDK included a ceiling forecasted for 5000' overcast, visibility 15 miles, 5 knot winds from the southeast with possible fog after 11:00 local time. The Pensacola area forecast for their estimated landing time, about 11:30 Central Time, for Jack Edwards was winds south 10 to 15 knots, visibility of 5 miles and a ceiling of '2,000' scattered to broken with fog and light rain inland.

They planned to get a weather update at PDK before filing their return as IFR and maybe fly VFR on top. Too, they wanted to take off before any fog could get started at PDK and that cold front brought low ceilings, bad visibility, and rain to Gulf Shores.

On their way up Kat calculated they were burning about 8.5 gallons an hour from their two 25 gallon tanks and that they'd probably use less than 30 gallons total getting to PDK at their current rate. Further, she suggested that they switch from the left wing tank to the right one over Montgomery, thus leaving about half in the left, making wing leveling a little easier on the pilot. And they ought to have their tanks topped off at the PDK ramp, thus not having to pay a possible tie-down fee, plus making it easier to ask the FBO to let them have a free courtesy car to use in getting around the airport to the restaurant and back.

'Nita jokingly told Kat that the auto-pilot was flying the plane and it never complained to her of being tired! And she asked Kat if she needed some lessons on how to operate it. While they were in a jovial mood, 'Nita reminded them that since she was flying them up she got to ride in the back going home. And that meant she could have some drinks with dinner but they couldn't since the FAA rule was <u>Eight hours from bottle to throttle</u>! Celia laughing, told her, "Bull! What one does, we all do! Remember, that was our deal, Miss Smarty?"

They had great prime rib steak-dinners! First-timers 'Nita and Kat were thrilled viewing all the restaurant's World War II memorabilia and the restored vintage fighters on the pads outside the windows that overlooked the active runways and taxiways at PDK. But they did not have enough time to see it all. Maybe next trip they'd come up for the day, have lunch here, and go over to nearby huge Perimeter Mall. But it was nearing 9:00 and time to go.

Kat had gotten a weather update, filed their IFR flight plan, and was airborne at 9:30 p.m. Eastern Time, a half hour later than they had anticipated. The forecast for the Pensacola area for their 12:00 Central Time landing at Jack Edwards Airport in Gulf Shores was 1,000 feet overcast, 2 miles visibility in light fog or light rain, southwest winds at 10 knots gusting to 15. This meant that the cold front was picking up speed. But Kat, an excellent bad weather pilot, was in the left seat flying the plane now with Celia co-piloting and navigating in the right; 'Nita was in the back.

But they were not worried, for if the weather at Jack Edwards was below the minimums for its non-precision VOR approach, they could still get into either Brookley Field in Mobile or Pensacola Regional and have one of their spouses come get them. Both of those airports had precision ILS approaches that allowed lower ceilings and visibility.

They had used less fuel going up than expected, only 25 gallons, due to the winds helping with their groundspeed. But on the return trip the winds had switched to the southwest and increased to 20 knots as the cold front got closer, therefore causing more fuel to be used and a slower ground speed of 110 according to Celia. They were flying in a slightly bumpy cloud layer at 6000 feet as they approached the Montgomery VOR where they had planned to switch tanks, which all three forgot.

About sixty miles southwest of Montgomery on the inbound bearing to Monroeville VOR, 'Nita reminded them that they had forgotten to change tanks. The fuel lever was on the wall panel left of Kat's leg and was operated by a pull button knob on a handle showing Left-Off-Right.

Kat reached down to make the switch and screamed in terror, "OH, MY GOD! IT'S STUCK IN THE OFF POSITION! TAKE THE PLANE, CELIA!" as she switched off the auto-pilot.

Kat tried again and again, but it wouldn't move.

'Nita screamed, "KAT, PUT YOU FOOT ON IT AND PUSH!"

Kat followed her instructions, only for the three to hear something snap and saw the lever rotate freely.

The engine went silent; the prop was slowly wind-milling. Kat shouted, "I got the plane. I'm setting up on best glide speed of 73. Celia, do exactly as I say. Handle the radios! Tell Atlanta Center we're declaring an engine out Emergency, switching to 121.5, squawking Mayday 7700, and need immediate vectors to the nearest airport. Then you hit the Loran for the nearest airport for back-up!"

Kat continued, "'Nita take the calculator from Celia and figure my glide distance mileage using 9 to 1, 6,000', giving 54,000 and divide by 5280. Take this sectional chart and show me where we are when Atlanta gives it to you."

Celia radioed, "Atlanta Center, Warrior 7999 Zulu declaring engine out emergency, about 30 minutes southwest of Montgomery, IFR to AL-15 in cloud at 6000', three souls aboard, our fuel lever's stuck in the off position with its handle broken.   Request   immediate   vectors   to   nearest   airport, squawking 7700, and switching now to 121.5. Please help us!"

Atlanta Center answered on 121.5, the emergency frequency: "Warrior 7999 Zulu, Atlanta Center, Roger all that. I show 99 Zulu seven miles west of city of Georgiana, 23 miles northeast of Monroeville, and 18 miles north of Evergreen. Last weather showed zero-zero for both Monroeville and Evergreen airports, fogged in with light rain. Say your intentions."

'Nita, realizing their problem first, was crying now, but said, "Kat, we can only glide 10.2 miles maximum. We won't make it to either airport! We're gonna crash before we get there!"

Kat shouted, "'NITA SHUT UP! Don't speak unless I ask you something! Put our purses and everything else on the floor! Here, take these charts and this Jep-book. Get three pillows from behind you and hold them until I say so. Then tighten your seat belt and shoulder strap! Celia, watcha got on the Loran?"

Celia answered, "Closest airport is Evergreen, heading 190, and 17 miles."

Kat keyed the mike, "Atlanta, 99 Zulu request distance and vectors to interstate I-65. We'll land there. Please notify Alabama Highway Patrol. Phone the name and number on my flight plan (Randy at home) and get three EMTs rolling from Georgiana."

Atlanta Center: "Roger, 99 Zulu. You're six miles from the southbound side of I-65; no other traffic in area. Fly 090; I'll call your turn to the south, and we're phoning them now."

Kat said, "Be calm ladies; we're gonna walk away from this. I've called up my Power Spirit and my Kulu Sin Toma. There's nothing to fear! We'll use the emergency highway approach technique that Randy taught us. Celia, just before we land, I'll shut off the master switch, then you hand me a pillow. Exactly when I say so, release the overhead latch, pull the door handle, and push it open. Then we'll all get in the crash position, if necessary. Check your seat belts. 'Nita, hand two pillows to Celia and keep one for yourself. Nobody talk, just pray."

Atlanta Center: "99 Zulu. All phoned as requested. Mr. Martinez and your spouses are on the way. You are two miles west of I-65. Monroeville altimeter: 29.15. Say your altitude and expect to begin a standard right turn to heading 195 on my call."

99 Zulu: "Atlanta, we're descending through 2500 feet at 500 feet per minute in cloud."

Atlanta Center: "Roger, 99 Zulu, begin turn to 195 --now. You are a half mile south of the Georgina Exit and one quarter mile west of the south-bound lane."

99 Zulu: "Atlanta, I don't see it! Am I over it! I'm still in the soup! NO! NO! WE BROKE OUT! Thank God! There're tail lights! It's right below us! Good visibility! I'm landing south-bound!"

Kat set up the landing just like Randy had taught them: pick out an eighteen-wheeler and get close to the rear of his trailer and a little above it. He'll be going 70 miles an hour but confirm that. Then you slow down 5 miles per hour less than the tractor-trailer's speed, giving the traffic behind your plane plenty of time to slow down. They will see you and your lowering down in front of them, thus clearing out a landing space ahead for you and giving a visual warning to those behind. Then it's just a matter of you setting up for the emergency highway landing and bleeding off your airspeed.

Kat calmly said, "Girls, watch the best dead stick landing that I've ever made!" And she did just that!

Stopping the plane in the middle of I-65, she keyed the mike and said, "Atlanta, 99 Zulu is on the ground and we're unhurt. Please phone the alternate number on my flight plan and tell our spouses we made it down just fine and are at the 111 mile marker in the median. It's our car phone. And thanks a million for the help!"

Then she said to her friends, "Open the door, Celia, and let's push this bird into that grassy median. Then, I'm gonna find me a bush. I'm about to pee in my pants!"

THIRTY-ONE

In the fall of 1984, about the same time that the cabinet job was coming to a close, Colt's son, Rick, approached his dad one afternoon and said, "Pop, there's something that I need to discuss with just you in private. When can we talk?"

Colt asked, "Just how important is it, son?"

"Very!" was Rick's answer.

"Well, how about after work?" Colt continued. "Your mother's over at C. R. with Kat. I'll phone her and tell her that you and I are going out for a drink after work and I'll be home later. How much time do you need? You wanna have dinner somewhere, too? What's this all about, anyway? Can't we talk here and now?"

Rick said rather emphatically, "No, we cannot talk now with the others around. And further, it's too personal for talking here. Let's plan to drive over to the Mobile Bay Causeway and get some raw oysters and some seafood."

Colt was getting miffed and countered, "Nothing's been so dad-blamed personal before that we couldn't talk here. Is this about you-personal or me-personal?"

Rick adamantly replied, "All I'm going to tell you right now is that it concerns me, you, and yours; not me and mine! That's it! I'm not saying anything else right now. I've got some doors to glue and hardware out for tomorrow's hanging. Call Mom and I'll talk to you about 5:00. Mickie knows I'm gonna be late."

Colt was visually upset. He called Celia and told her what he had said he would and she suspected nothing. But Colt tried and tried to concentrate on paying the bills and getting last week's purchasing tickets organized, but could not do either correctly. Rick had him very shaken up and he lit one cigarette after the other, racking his brain.

Rick had never been this serious with his dad. And when he even came close to it, he talked about some problem that he had that usually ended up with Colt loaning him some money, all of which he promptly paid back on time and most of it early. And the last time that had happened was over three years ago.

Colt thought on, But he said on 'me, you and yours'! What could he be talking about? Is Celia cheating on me and he's gonna tell me about it? Is Celia sick and I don't know about it? Is he going to tell me that he is quitting? No, that would be about 'him' not about 'me and mine', or would it? Does he have some real bad stuff about Randy? Ain't no way he could have found out about Randy's 'secret of all secrets'. He doesn't know that part of Randy's history. Plus that wouldn't be about me, anyway.

Looking at the clock, Colt saw that it was just 2:30. He got up from his desk and over the shop intercom said, "Rick, I'm going to the bank and then over to the lumber yard to get some stuff. I'll be back at 5:00."

Rick waved <u>okay</u> to his dad as he walked out the door but thought, Darn, I should have waited until about four. Now he'll go straight to The Blue Dolphin and be half drunk when he gets back and I need him sober this time. Will I ever learn to be more patient with the ole man and not do him that way?

And he was right. By 4:45 Colt had downed four or five Johnny Walker Reds and water. Colt had been solving more and more of his problems with alcohol lately, and lately he had more and more problems to solve.

It was 5:30 now and the two were on their way. Rick was driving his company S10 Chevy pick-up, while beside him, Colt sipped on his sixth Johnny Red from a to-go cup he had brought back with him. Rick glanced over, pointed to the cup and said, "What I want to talk to you about, among other things, is just that. Dad, you're drinking all the time now, even in the mornings, from those bottles that you keep hid in the men's room in the cabinet under the sink behind the toilet paper and towels. And Mom's told me you're back to smoking over three packs a day. And your emphysema is not getting any better. Also, she told me that you guys lost your medical insurance back about the time that we dropped all our other customers and took on y'all's doper friends."

Looking at his dad straight in the eyes for emphasis Rick said, "Get mad if you want to, but don't say a single word until I finish, okay? I've never talked much to you and certainly not this way or certainly not to you about you and your business. I've always been <u>Little Rick</u>, your little boy in our relationship. But I'm a grown 32 year-old man now, and you need to listen to me."

Rick reached over and squeezed Colt's arm and said, "I love you, Dad, very much. And that's something you've never said to me; not man to man, anyway. And we've never hugged each other, not as men do that love one another. And it's high time that we changed our relationship to include some of that. And furthermore, I'm not gonna just sit by and watch you slowly destroy yourself, physically and financially."

Rick continued, "I have not talked to my two sisters about any of this. And I don't intend to, and don't want to, for that matter. I don't have that kind of a relationship with them or with their spouses and don't want one, either. I live in a totally different world than those four. They are so wrapped up in their own little worlds that they aren't even aware of any problems that you and Mom might have."

Rick continued, "We don't even see Suzie and David socially outside of the shop. And even when Mickie and I run into them at a shopping center or somewhere, that bible-pounding son-in-law of yours is on my tail in a second about my beer drinking and grass smoking. And I don't need him preaching to me; not with as much devil as he used to raise himself before he <u>got saved</u>. And I don't call California. And Jackie nor Bill never phone me."

Rick said, "And you, Dad, you don't know me or much about the world that I live in, either. You think you do. And you act like you do. You make Mom think you do. And you tell people that you do. But believe me, Dad, you don't know me! And that needs to change. At least, I want it to. And believe me, we both, need it to. That's what tonight's all about, Dad; getting to know each other as what we really are; not this father and his little boy bit. Not anymore, not ever again. Not after tonight. But beginning now, Pop!"

Rick added, "Besides loving you as my dad and placing you up on a pedestal as one of my life-long heroes, I happen to like you as a person, too. And I'd like to see if we can be friends.

207

You and I think alike. Folks tell me I'm getting more and more like you every day and that makes me feel proud! But the only change that needs to be made is for you to start thinking of me and treating me as a man and not your little boy. Won't you give me a chance, Pop? We both need it."

Colt's eyes teared up. He wiped them with his sleeve and said while reaching over his hand, "You better believe I will, Rick. Starting right now. You're right; it's high time. And I love you, too, son, more than you know! Boy, did you hit the nail on the head this time."

And they shook on it, long and hard, but this time man to man.

Rick acted as if he didn't see his dad roll down the window and toss his half-filled cup of Johnny Red out onto the roadside, something that Colt just did not do, ever. Then Colt said in a very serious tone, "You're dead on center, son. Talk. I'm listening."

Rick continued, "Dad, week before last, I think it was Tuesday, some big rough-looking dude came by the shop while you guys were installing cabinets at C. R. and just walked in the side door as if he owned the place. I thought at first he was a cop. He walked straight over to me and asked if my name was Erhlichman. I told him it was. He proceeded to tell me that he was from some collection agency in Mobile and wanted to know when I was going to pay the $18,360 owed for over six months to some laboratory in Mobile for the Cat-scans, MRIs, x-rays, and a whole bunch of lab tests."

Rick continued, "I asked him did he have some identification and some copies of the bills to show me proof. He did. So, I told him to wait at the Coke machine and I went into your office and looked up the lab's name in the yellow pages in order to confirm that he wasn't some con-man and I phoned them. I told the lady I was you and asked her to verify the bills and who my doctor was that ordered the tests and to name the collection agency that they had hired. She was correct in both cases. I then phoned your doctor's office and had his nurse confirm that your doctor had ordered the tests and that you had gotten them, and they had the results in your life. Even though some of the machinery they used is located in the doctor's office, it belongs to a separate company, the lab that billed you."

Rick went on to say, "I locked up the shop and had the dude follow me to my bank in Gulf Shores where I got a cashier's check for $18,630 and I gave it to him. Now, Pop, will you please open up and be honest with me and tell your grown son just what the blazes is going on with you and Mom?"

"Pull over to that package store up there. I need a drink bad now," Colt ordered.

Rick instructed, "No, Pop, I'm not pulling over. You're not going to get drunk on me; not tonight. I want you stone-cold sober this time. We're just beginning to talk and that 18 grand is not very important compared to what else we're gonna get into! You can wait another fifteen minutes and we'll be at Petro's. Then you can have a drink, but no more than two an hour. We've got a lot to talk about and your head needs to be clear. You may have left the shop with your little boy, but you're gonna return tonight with the man that is going to help you get your act back together. And I'm going to get my father back as well as making me a new best friend. And the way we're gonna do it is to put all the cards on the table and play straight with one another; nothing held back or hid. And I mean that, Dad!"

Tension was released by idle chatter about the Auburn Tigers, the Alabama Crimson Tide, and the New Orleans Saints football teams and the Atlanta Braves until they were at Petro's where draft beers plus two dozen Apalachicola Bay oysters were ordered. Colt thought that since he couldn't get drunk, he might as well drink beer, plus it goes better with seafood anyway.

THIRTY-TWO

Colt turned to Rick, "How'd you come by that kind of money; that 18 thousand?"

Rick began, "Dad, what I'm about to tell you may shock you at first. But don't form any lasting opinions until you've heard the whole story and have had a while to mull over it. I'm asking you to think about all this that we're going to talk about tonight for a couple of days before coming to any conclusions about it or about me. And wait until a week or two before discussing any of this with Mom. Will you promise me you'll do that?"

Receiving a yes from his dad, they shook hands to seal this promise, too. They silently agreed that this longer than usual hand gripping of theirs was going to become their new and secret way of swearing an oath to each other, man-to-man; and not father-to-son and vice versa anymore.

"Dad, I keep thirty grand in the bank, but I've got over 800 thousand hidden in the walls of my house," Rick shocked him with.

"GOOD LORD!" Colt, unconsciously, blurted out. "What in the world have you gotten yourself into, son?"

Rick iterated emphatically, "SEE! That is just what I'm talking about. So, don't jump to any more quick conclusions until you hear the whole story. You just don't know much about me, Dad. Let me start from the beginning and then you'll feel easier about it. And relax! Enjoy your oysters and beer. This is MY NIGHT with MY DAD. Man-to-man. Just you and me. One-on-one. LISTEN, POP. JUST LISTEN! I ain't your little kid anymore! You can't tell me what to do!"

Colt thought about what Rick had just said while staring at Rick eye-to-eye without saying a word for about ten seconds, took a deep breath, exhaled, and let his mind join Rick's thought pattern. Now he was open to accept whatever was coming and this intentional change of attitude began to relax him. Rick saw this subtle change reflected in his dad's face as Colt took a big mouthful of beer and concentrated on the oysters and crackers. Rick had won their little mental tussle. Now Colt was ready to hear the rest of the story.

Rick began, "Remember four Christmas Eves ago, in 1980, when I brought some marijuana to your family get-together and you got loaded on scotch and you tried some?" Getting a nod from Colt, Rick continued, "You asked where I got it and I told you that a friend of mine sold it to me. Then you said that I'd better leave that guy and his kind alone? Well, not only did I not leave him alone, he offered me a deal and took it. Now, don't jump to any conclusions! I'm not dealing dope, honest! Just listen."

Rick continued, "When Mr. Bush squeezed the south Florida drug smugglers with his so-called War On Drugs, this whole Gulf Coast area opened up to become one heck of a big pipeline for marijuana both through air-to-ground drops, air-to-water drops, and by shrimp boats, yachts, and even cargo ships. What my friend Tony was doing was running a crew that would go out at night to a certain farm and once a plane had dropped the bales of marijuana, his men would load the stuff onto the waiting trucks. Sometimes the burlap or plastic-covered bales would bust open upon hitting the ground and they would literally rake the stuff up and put it in plastic trash bags. Because of this they were called Rakers."

Rick continued, "Tony would receive a beeper call about 6:30 p.m. and returned the call to some local pay-phone getting instructions as to what shopping center to drive to where an empty car or van was waiting with the keys in it. He would use this vehicle to meet his three guys at some other place. He'd pick them up and later return them to their cars or trucks. For this Tony was paid, before he left the drop site, $25,000; he'd keep 10 grand and pay the rest to his rakers, giving $5,000 to each of them for three-to-four hours work."

Colt interrupted, "Can I ask questions as you go along so that I might understand things better? I may forget them later."

"Sure. Go ahead," was Rick's approval.

Colt asked, "Were four guys all it took?"

Rick answered, "Depends on how much was to be dropped. I've seen as many as four raker crews working at one time on a King-Air drop."

Colt interjected, "So, I gather that you're running a crew."

"There you go," Rick chastised, "jumping to conclusions again! You're right, though. I am now. But I started off several years ago as a raker under Tony until they got to trusting me and let me get my own guys."

"How often are you doing it now?" Colt asked.

Rick answered, "With the house and everything paid for and with all that I've got stashed, I asked them last year for permission to cut back to a subs-level. Now I get a call only about once or twice a month, unless they have a problem. But I cannot get into anything else, like smuggling or dealing, unless they give me permission to. And I have to stay in close contact with my superior, their local made-man, a District Manager as we call him, about once a month by meeting with him and some others in some bar after they phone me. My rank is called a Team Leader. They just ask me a bunch of questions about myself and my life and Mickie and what I'm doing. That's about all. Otherwise, I don't come in contact with them unless I want some grass. And they give me all I want for my own use, free; coke, too, if I'd ask for it. But I've never even tried the hard stuff. Alcohol and grass are good enough for me."

Colt asked, "Have you ever met any of their higher-ups?"

"Yes,' Rick added, "I met my boss' boss when they promoted me. But they only called him by his first name; which is fine with me. The less I know, the better I like it."

Colt asked, "So, Mickie knows about all this?"

Rick answered, "Sure. I would not have gone into it if she had refused. Oh, she was scared to death of it at first; I was, too. But after we met several dozen guys and gals that have been in it for over ten years and with not a single one in this area having been arrested, we felt it was worth a try. Plus, if you do get caught, the upstairs guys pay for everything plus gives you a hundred grand when you get out for each year you serve on their behalf. And they try like all get-out to see that you don't go to jail; not the first time, anyway."

"Is she doing it, too?" Colt asked.

Rick stated, "No. She and I decided to keep her out of it. But she does know some of my crew. Plus that year-old Oldsmobile that she has was bought as a surprise for her birthday last year by my boss and his wife from the car auction over in Pensacola. His company owns a bunch of car lots from Panama City, Florida to Gulf Port, Mississippi. Mickie baby-sits their three kids and house-keeps for them a lot when they have to go on trips to Colombia or Mexico; sometimes for one or two weeks at a time. And she and I do parties for them when folks come in from out of the country."

Colt asked, "Are you involved with cocaine?"

Rick lowered his tone and leaned closer, put down his beer, stopped eating, and talked slower while looking directly into his dad's eyes in order to emphasize his words and said, "Dad, I've learned a lot about this dangerous and shady side of the world in three years. And one of the most important things they've taught me is this: <u>Once you've told someone all he absolutely needs to know, do him a big favor and don't tell him more. For his knowledge can get him killed, if it is mishandled.</u> So, Pop, unless you can convince me why you need to know more at this time, I've gone as far as I need on this subject tonight. Won't you agree?"

"I'm shocked, Rick. I had no clue!" Colt confessed.

"Yeah. I'd be surprised if you weren't. But are you disappointed or mad at me?" Rick asked.

"No, not now that I know quite a bit about the drug industry from Randy," was Colt's reply.

Rick bounced back, "What about Randy? How's he involved?"

Colt answered, "Well, like you just said, it's best that you don't know about Randy in that respect. Plus I'm sworn to secrecy. I agreed with that when we first met him and Kat. Randy and I are very, very close, personally. But while your mother and I are aware of it, we are not in any way involved with Randy's business activities, period, other than our building the secret compartments in those cabinets. Plus, I might mention to you now that you've told me what you have, it probably is best that Randy never finds out about your involvement and you never, ever, mention his name among your cohorts."

Rick agreed, "Great advice! But I thought about that a long time ago and have been practicing that. So has Mickie. Let's keep it that way. And you need to make Mom aware of this, too, once you've talked to her.

"Dad, what other financial problems do you and Mom have?" Rick queried.

Colt lowered his head, as if ashamed, and started, only glancing up once in a while, "We never were able to get completely out from under the medical debts from Virginia and add to them the cost of the move down here. I've accumulated another hundred grand of bills between five doctors and those three of four trips to the hospitals both in Foley, Pensacola, and Mobile. We had to take out a second mortgage on the condo. And when that wasn't enough, I tried to get a consolidation loan from the bank but they turned me down because I had missed notes to them several times."

Colt added, "With no place to turn to, I, last year, found some guys in Mobile that take cases like mine but who charge up to 12% interest. But right now I'm only just barely able to make the interest payments to them. And they don't seem to care; not with the rates they charge. Plus, they have everything I own as collateral, except for our cabinet business. All we, actually, own is the wood-working machinery and they did not want it. They even made me pay off the bank's 11% condo mortgage and put that in the lump sum at 12%, too, or they wouldn't bail me out of any of it."

Colt continued, "I was so shook up about all of this mess that when I approached those Mobile dudes I forgot about the 18 grand owed that lab company. Afterwards, I knew I was behind on it, but they never wrote me threatening letters or called or nothing like that. Thanks for handling it like you did, son. Please don't say anything to your mother; she's already worried to death about everything."

Colt continued, "She's got forty to forty-five grand in the bank left from her mother's estate and she has tried and tried to get me to take that. But I won't hear of it because if something happens to me she'll need it to get by on until social security kicks in. I tell her that that is her play money. And she'll draw some out every once in a while to spend on herself and her flying lessons and such. And that helps me even though I feel awful about that, too."

"Dad," Rick sincerely offered, "let me pay off your debts. I don't need all that money."

"No, son! Absolutely not!" Colt uttered strongly. "I got myself into this situation by smoking and drinking too much and it's up to me to find a way to get myself out. So, don't mention that again, ever. If I let you do that, my opinion of myself would be destroyed and I'd fall down so low that I'd commit suicide. No way! But thanks a million for the offer, anyway."

They both went silent and pensive while finishing off the oysters. Having ordered fried seafood platters, Colt broke the silence by stating, "Son, we've covered enough serious talk for tonight. Give me a week to think about all this and I'll get back to you with some ways to get me out of the mess I'm in. I don't have a clue what they'll be, but I've got to come up with something quick. You do the same. But let's begin our new relationship on a man-to-man, equal level starting right now. And I love you, <u>MY BEST FRIEND, MR. RICK ERHLICHMAN</u>!"

Rick laughed at his Dad's now calling him Mr. and responded as they, once again, shook on it, "That's a deal. Let's talk about something else." And they did.

THIRTY-THREE

A week went by after their meeting at Petro's before Colt and Rick got back together. This time they went to GHEP'S, a Gulf Shores restaurant and bar known for their great barbecue. After their plates were delivered, Colt asked Rick, "Don't I remember you saying that your boss was named Carlo and that he was a made-man?"

Rick replied, "Yes. Why?"

Colt answered, "Son, I'm just months away from Chapter 7 Bankruptcy. Even with the money from Randy on the cabinets, it is not enough to get me ahead on my notes. I'm desperate! I'd rather die than continue to do this to Celia. If I could get a big life insurance policy, I'd kill myself!"

Rick asked, "Why are you asking about Carlo? Dad, you're too old to be tossing heavy bales."

"Son, I have no choice!" Colt exclaimed. "Put yourself in my shoes. I've got to do something or die! I want you to call Carlo and vouch for me. Then you tell him about the mess I'm in and ask him if there is some place he can use me other than dealing. Then if he thinks there may be a chance, set up a meeting for me and I'll handle the rest. I never in my life thought I'd do something like this. But suicide, in a case like mine, is a coward's way out."

About bedtime that night Rick called Colt and said, "Carlo wants you to meet him at Hazel's Restaurant in Gulf Shores at 6:30 in the morning for breakfast. I told him what you look like and he said he'll be waiting for you in his black Lincoln. He's American-born but Spanish-looking with a mustache and goatee. His last name is Arguello. He knows about my sharing the bit about the rakers with you and he knows Tony. He knows nothing about Randy. I've never mentioned Randy to Carlo or to anyone else for that matter, other than Mickie and she knows to keep her mouth shut. Good luck and let me know how it comes out. Oh, I almost forgot, Pop, he said to tell you that you will be going with him all day tomorrow, to visit a number of his car lots starting in Fairhope and ending in Gulfport. You'll be getting back late tomorrow night."

Colt and Carlo met as planned, had breakfast, began chatting about their childhoods to adulthood, families, education, work experience, and related background information, nothing serious, just the usual get acquainted type of stuff. They were on the way to the first of eleven retail car businesses that they'd visit before heading back to Orange Beach from Gulfport at 9:15 that night when Carlo asked, "What do you know about my other businesses, Colt?"

Colt cautiously answered, "First, with no disrespect to you meant, Carlo, I really don't know much and don't want to know anymore than I absolutely need to know. I know that my son and Tony work for you as Team Leaders on raking crews. Rick has told me what that means and how his part of the operation works and also that you know that he told me. He told me that you and your wife own a number of car lots between Panama City and Gulfport. I know that, apparently, you and your wife think a lot of my daughter-in-law, Mickie, in that you entrust your kids with her quite often and I know about the Oldsmobile that you guys gave her. Other than that, Rick refuses to tell me anything, warning me that knowledge can get me killed, if I mishandle it."

"You're right about that and about our feelings, too. My wife, Martina, we call her Marty, and I love and trust Mickie and Rick like they were our own blood. You and Celia have done a great job in rearing you son. And he's got a great gal for a wife. Y'all're lucky. And if you are anywhere like him in honesty, integrity, and hard work, you and I can definitely make some money together, legally and otherwise. But we need to spend the day talking about how and getting to know each other."

So, between calls on his lot managers and driving to the next lot, they talked in progressive stages. Carlo began feeling Colt out by asking, "Are you willing to step over the legal limits and take calculated risks?"

Colt answered, "Yes, if I know that the odds are in my favor and if the end rewards more than justify the chances taken."

"Are you willing to take risks that could possibly end in jail time?" Carlo asked.

Colt replied, "Rick told me that at the raking crew level one could expect 100 to 1 odds in being caught. Further, that the first time you usually get them off. But if they do have to serve any time on your behalf you pay for everything and then you reimburse them for time spent in jail on the basis of one hundred grand per year. Is that true?"

Carlo answered, "Yes, but that's at that level. The higher up one goes, the bigger responsibility and risks he carries and the more he makes for us. So, with that in mind it can be said that what you've been told applies to the beginning level. For the higher one goes, the bigger that chances he takes, but the bigger the rewards he enjoys. And once accepted, the movement upward is placed by the individual on himself, not by us. How high do you want to go, Colt? Rick told me about your financial problems and your health situation. A couple hundred grand could set you straight. That's easily attainable, if you are willing to take a risk or two."

Colt responded, "I'm willing to discuss anything that will get me out of my predicament, legal or illegal. But Rick doesn't seem to think I belong tossing bales or raking. So, I guess that I should say that I am at your disposal, but don't know what services I can perform for you, not at this point, anyway. So, as my dear son and my beloved daughter-in-law have done, I put my life, the welfare of my wife and our marriage, my faith for the future and my blind trust in your hands. Mi nuevo compadre! And via con Dios!

Carlo complimented, "Muy elecuente! I'm impressed! You and I will do fine together! No molestar! Nothing to worry about!"

Colt felt relieved and that he had been accepted, up to this point anyway; not so much by what he had said to Carlo but more than anything by his son and Mickie having been what they had been to this man and to his wife. But not belittling himself, he felt confident that he had achieved and was going to get his chances. And after all, that was all he wanted.

So, he relaxed the conversation by getting back to the mundane. Rick had told him that Carlo was about as crazy about golf as he was so he used that to change the subject and give Carlo time to think and for the tension of the day to be eased.

Colt would just wait for Carlo's next move. And he expected Carlo would wait until the next day to let him know something.

No more on this area of business was talked about for the rest of the drive from the last Mobile lot to first one in Pascagoula. Then Carlo began explaining the problems in detail concerning the upcoming car lot as they left the last one and he asked Colt to give him some thoughts on how to solve each. Surprisingly enough to both, Colt quickly became valuable to Carlo in this area of expertise. And soon Carlo was introducing him as <u>My new business consultant, Mr. Erhlichman</u>.

Over lunch and drinks at The Tiki in Gautier, Mississippi, Carlo remarked, half-laughing/half-seriously "Colt, <u>mi nuevo amigo</u>, how does this sound to you: a new Lincoln to drive, a full expense account, 1500 bucks a week, and you run these car lots for me? In a month you'd be doing a better job than me. Besides, I think my Johnny-Reb managers would rather deal with a gringo that talks like they do than a Latino like me. And I could teach you how to buy cars at the auctions in Pensacola, Mobile, Gulf Port, and Slidell, Louisiana. Then I would not be tied up for four days a week. And I've got a lot more areas that need my attention. I don't know if you know it or not but we've also got thirteen more car lots in the panhandle of Florida."

The rest of the day and early night were spent visiting with car lot managers and driving. Once back, about midnight at Hazel's Restaurant in Gulf Shores where Colt had left his pick-up truck Carlo turned to Colt and asked, "Do you know where Frisco's Marina and Yacht Repair is located over on Cotton Bayou in Orange Beach?" Getting a yes-nod from Colt he continued, "We own it. Can you meet me there at 8:00 in the morning?" Again getting a nod from Colt he concluded with a handshake. Great! I'm going to offer you a contract on something that we've not talked about, yet. Something pretty big! You and I are going into business together. You're the business minded man I've been looking for and praying for. And forget about your debts; you'll be able to take care of them all in a couple of months. And we're gonna get you some good doctors, too. Thanks for going with me today, and tell Celia I'm looking forward to meeting her. And pray to Saint Jude to bless

our meeting tomorrow and our future together, my friend."
Carlo drove off. Colt was shocked!

Celia was waiting up for him and as he walked in she said,
"Rick and Mickie's up, too. Call them first so they can go to
bed. We'll sleep late in the morning."

Colt responded, "No we can't, either. I've got to meet Carlo
at 8:00."

Then Colt phoned Rick. Mickie was listening on their other
phone so they both could hear and Celia was standing by as he
told them in detail what had transpired that day. Then they all,
happily but anxiously, went to bed.

THIRTY-FOUR

To Colt, Frisco's Marina and Yacht Repair looked typical of others in the area with its large metal building with yachts inside being worked on, yachts on dollies and racks all over the yard waiting their turn, tall sheds with boats of all sizes and descriptions moored out of the weather, dozens and dozens of similar yachts tied in covered slips along wooden piers, two long wharves lined with sport-fishing charter boats, at the end of two of the piers two bottom fishing boats were tied, a combined charter office and fisherman's supply store was dockside. Colt noticed not one Latino in sight; all looked American.

Colt asked a black man driving a huge fork-lift carrying a large inboard-outboard boat where he could find Mr. Arguello and was pointed to some stairs leading to the offices above a hanger-type, boat dry-storage building. Upstairs at least two dozen desks occupied this floor where mostly females were busy before computer screens and numerous small and large walled-in but windowed offices surrounded the open area. A small gated-fence with a pretty Spanish-looking receptionist at a desk behind it asked if she could help. Colt appraised her of his name and she said, "Buenos Dias and welcome to Frisco Industries, Mr. Erhlichman. My name is Rosita, but everyone here calls me Rosie. We've been eagerly expecting you, Sir. Please follow me to our kitchen and breakroom where Senior Arguello awaits you for breakfast."

Following Rosie, Colt could not help but notice how immaculately she was dressed, high-heeled shoes and all the rest and looking around, so were all the other ladies. And all the men wore ties. This was very unlike most of the businesses on the coast where informal attire was the acceptable dress code. And the office equipment and the decor was up-to-date, and expensively, very first-class.

A suited Carlo sat along a benched table with some other shirt and tied executives. And after a warm welcome and introductions, he asked Colt if he'd like some smoked country ham and eggs. Spying boxes of Krispy Kreme donuts on the serving counter, Colt answered that coffee and donuts would be fine. The others ordered full breakfasts from the uniformed chef behind the kitchen's window. Colt, sipping on a cup of freshly-ground and brewed gourmet Colombian coffee, said, "Carlo, I'm amazed. I had no idea that Frisco's was anything but a marina and a boat yard."

"Good. Then our efforts to keep a low profile are working. Actually, I run four businesses out of here, including the car lots, with 73 employees on site alone." Then he leaned over and whispered in Colt's ear, "And they are all legit fronts."

After breakfast they went to the back of the open desked area to Carlo's office. Upon sitting around a coffee table Carlo began, "After our talking all day and into the night last night I decided to call my boss, the Area Manager, and ask for permission to create a special place for you. Based upon my strong desire and my opinion of you, and upon the boss' knowing of Rick's work for the last three years and having met him when we promoted Rick to Team Leader, he approved my request. I'm sticking my neck out some, so don't let me down, Colt."

Carlo advised, "I'll explain what I have in mind. Then you and I will take a walk around the marina and talk some more." On the word talk he winked at Colt indicating that something special would be discussed as they walked and talked elsewhere that could not be discussed in the office. He continued, "Here's the deal: I, indeed, do want you to take over supervision of all the car lots. I'll train you and stay with you until you are comfortable. I suggested $1500 a week yesterday, but my boss said to make it an even two grand since taxes and social security will be taken out. You'll get a company car, a new Lincoln, plus expenses. And I'm told to get you some company supplied medical insurance, if our plan will take you or elsewhere if I have to.

"Further," Carlo continued, "my boss and I figure you should be tied up five hours per day five days a week on a two week turn around. With a couple dozen lots, that means you'll need to visit about three a day. And we will fly you. I keep a full-time pilot here and have two planes that we keep in those little T-hangers that you see at Jack Edwards Airport in Gulf

Shores. One's a foul-weather-equipped Cessna 182 RG and the other is a twin engine Cessna 414. My pilot will be re-assigned to you. You can leave at 7:00 and be back to your shop by mid-day or fly out at noon; I don't care. We'll put a used car at every airport and he can drive you locally back and forth. If the weather is too bad to fly, he'll pick you up and drive you. Now, while you digest all this, let's get a cup of coffee to-go from the kitchen and take you on a tour."

With cup in hand and leaving the upstairs offices Carlo continued. "Only legit business is ever talked upstairs. We never know when or where a bug is going to be placed and we've found some. We have a world-wide security division that we call IntelSec that trains us and furnishes the security for most of our operations. They keep our cars, offices and homes swept but it does not pay to take chances. That's why we're walking. Any questions about that?"

Receiving a no from Colt, Carlo continued, "Listen closely, here's more of the deal: my district owns over three dozen boats and yachts of varying sizes and purposes, all under various names and docked at about as many different marinas and places. Plus dozens of charter fishing boats are under contract to me for special trips. We've begun a program to refurbish their interiors to include places to hide merchandise and money in their walls and in their cabinets and under their tables and bunks. Very seldom are we ever caught unless we are told on by someone inside. And about the only time we get accidentally exposed is when the local Marine Police, Game Wardens, or Coast Guard make routine stops and become suspicious of what they see. If nothing is in view they usually just write up some life-jacket charge or something like that and we're off the hook, except for minor fines."

Carlo continued by asking, "Is it feasible for you to get together with your wife, and Rick and you guys arrange your schedule for you to take over the car lots? Additionally, maybe let Rick hire some help at your shop and you guys take on my entire boat and yacht refurbishing needs? You could build the cabinets and whatever at your place and install them here using my facilities and even our dry docks when needed. This part will be legitimate business and you'll invoice us and be paid by and be under a contract with Frisco Industries. I'd want it on a cost-plus basis, with advances to you, of course.

"Now, here's the third and final part. As a Team Leader, you are in lower management. One of the jobs that Rick knows very little about and is not involved in is what we call off-loading. We send night crews out regularly into the Gulf's international waters to unload merchandise from shrimp boats and even cargo ships. We've never had the first person jailed.

"Your job," Carlo explained, "would be to go out about two nights a week supervising the off-loading. You'll be supplied with a coded expected inventory list and your responsibility is to see that we get all that we're supposed to from the mother ship and in turn which inbound boat of ours took what. We'll have eight or ten boats or yachts standing by. You'll write down on a form the boat registration number and what each received as they are one-at-a-time loaded. The Team Leader on each vessel will then sign off for you for his loaded cargo. You give him a receipt; you keep the signed original.

"When finished," he continued, "you'll sign off for the mother ship using your assigned coded identification, hopefully agreeing on any overages or shortages. You'll have two armed IntelSec Field Operatives beside you at all times. If it is a cargo ship, you'll need to board before unloading begins, meet their supervisor and his interpreter and our on-board IntelSec representative. To him, identify yourself and your bodyguards. You'll instruct them on how you want unloading to be done."

Carlo continued, "Your code name will be The Silver Eagle, for obvious reasons and you'll be given a different trip identification number for each job. Our onboard IntelSec officer will verify you and your number to the boat supervisor. The boat that you'll go out on, you'll return on, and it will not carry any merchandise; just hi-tech radio and navigational equipment and two qualified boat captains. But sometimes you'll sign for and take money outbound. This is one way we get it back to Colombia and that's why you'll have at least two armed guards with you onboard. And for about eight hours per round trip, I'll pay you $25,000. You can use this to pay off your bills to those

226

dudes in Mobile. That's it! What do you think now, compadre?"

"GOOD LORD, CARLO!" was all Colt could muster.

Carlo instructed, "I thought you'd say something like that. Now go to the shop and talk it over with your wife and son. I want their solemn approval, too. Get back with me in a couple of days and let me know when you guys can be ready to start. I've got three 48' Bertrams and one 55' Hatteras waiting in dry dock now."

Needless to say, Celia and Rick were apprehensive about Colt getting involved in drug trafficking. But this could solve a number of needs. First, and obviously, it would give Colt a way to get out from under his Mobile financial problems and possibly get some medical insurance for Celia and himself. Secondly, it would give him a way to not only rid himself of all their debt, but a source of income to prepare for eventual retirement. And thirdly, this opportunity allowed their shop to continue with a single source of work, not to have to go back to seeking individual orders with the ups and downs that that brings, and even to expand their operation some. Another advantage was that it gave a new lease on life to Colt, for he was getting stagnant and bored around the cabinet shop. And now he was excited as he was when he made his first golfing hole-in-one. So, they all agreed to back Colt and Colt phoned Carlo and accepted the responsibilities.

Carlo said, "Great! Now, tomorrow morning, go over to Mobile to Metzgers and charge to me a dozen expensive suits, shirts, and ties and a half dozen pairs of Johnston and Murphy's. I'll phone ahead. Then go to Louie's on Royal Street and get yourself a hair cut and a shave and have your fingernails manicured; he'll be expecting you. I want you to look the part, running our car businesses. Then at 6:00 take Celia to Hemingway's Restaurant in Orange Beach. A bottle of Dom Perignon will be waiting for you two in the bar. Enjoy yourselves! Marty and I will join you later, at eight, for dinner and a super celebration. Congratulations; you've made a great decision! See you guys tomorrow night."

THIRTY-FIVE

During the fall of 1984, the converting over from making cabinets for Cinco Robles and beginning to do similar installations aboard yachts did not take much adjusting. Rick hired four more people --guys that he could trust from his raking crews. Rick was managing the shop now with brother-in-law David Cannon being promoted to shop foreman. Celia and Suzie ran the office. Colt was left to come and go as he saw fit because of his new work schedule. He joined in when he could, particularly with the initial designing and layout of each new job, and watching their paperwork for costs and profits.

When Randy inquired about their shop business, he was told they had taken on another huge job furnishing yacht interiors, and that satisfied his curiosity. And whenever he phoned the shop for Colt, they'd immediately page Colt no matter where he was. And as Randy had promised, he gave them a $25,000 bonus for their year's work on the cabinets at C. R. and for the good quality done. Colt shared it equally with the other four.

Colt's car lot supervisor and auto auction buying training period under Carlo lasted about six months before he was put on his own in the spring of '85. His off-loading training was done by another Team Leader and within a month he was supervising all their shrimp boat transfers. But it took about another year, the spring of 1986, before he was assigned to a cargo ship, for this would be in the tens of millions of dollars category.

Another six months passed of those twice weekly trips offshore, they being about two-thirds shrimp boats, another third cargo vessels. After two years, in the fall of 1986, everything had become routine to Colt; no problems whatsoever with the car lots now that he had them reorganized with three group supervisors handling eight lots apiece under him and all the business computerized. Plus he had hired and trained three full-time car buyers and contracted with four independent car brokers to bring him cars from the Atlanta and Orlando auctions. All was going smoothly.

Then during on off-loading one night in August, the IntelSec officer aboard the Panamanian ship called over his bull-horn for

Colt to return aboard the vessel just as it was about time to clear the last boat to approach. Earlier, the officer had requested that this yacht be the last to load yet, it had been scheduled by Colt to be in the middle of the pact. This was unusual, but not uncommon, for it normally meant they were going to put some duffel bags of money on it that would be smuggled into the states for laundering.

When Colt got back up on deck, the Colonel said, "Silver Eagle, we have a major problem facing us. One of the off-loaders on that Hatteras, the Latino with the bald head and full beard, has been identified by one of my loaders as a Narc from Panama that was exposed then transferred last year to the U.S. If he is correct, the Narc will have the tattoo <u>Vindicta</u>, which means revenge on his left wrist under that wide leather watch band that he wears. Take your two Operatives and go aboard quietly, saying that you want to check their storage facilities before you load some money. Have your men overcome him, then handcuff him and see if he has that tattoo. I've radioed and got disposition orders from IntelSec Central. They have confirmed that he also has a joint missing from his right thumb. If you, yourself, confirm both these signs, tell the Hatteras' Team Leader that you want him and his crew to board your boat for their return trip home. But if we are mistaken, apologize to the man and order the Team Leader to pay him an extra grand for the insult."

The Colonel continued, "If he is the suspected Narc, once the crew is aboard your boat, order your Operatives to render him unconscious and have them slit his throat. Then you get off and have your men shoot holes throughout the lower forward berths below the water line and have them abandon it before it sinks. Most likely the Narc has bugged it and it is to be apprehended near the shore. We will then off-load the money to your boat, sign off our manifests, and you may leave. You will be paid an extra 50 grand for carrying out these orders. Your and my superiors will hear of your loyalty and this piece of work. Good luck, Silver Eagle, and I'll see you back here in a little while."

Colt thought initially that he, himself, would be fear struck.

But actually he had no problem with it at all. In fact he further surprised himself by noticing a inner feeling of hatred toward the Narc. The collaring of the Panamanian went smoothly, for the man did not resist, was not armed, and acted as if he expected it when he saw Colt and the two Field Operatives come aboard. The tattoo was there and the missing thumb joint sealed his fate. Transferring the Hatteras' crew went very orderly and the only violence witnessed by the others were the reports of the automatic weapons as holes were shot in the hull. All of this only took about twenty minutes before the money was off-loaded, the manifests verified and signed, and they were on their way home after another good night's work. Almost!

Later, about ten miles out from Perdido Pass, the Team Leader from the Hatteras asked Colt to stop the boat and explain to him and his crew what had happened aboard the Hatteras. Colt told them the details and was about to order the captain to proceed home when out of the corner of his eye he saw the Hatteras' Team Leader step up on the stern's gunnel, put an automatic 45 caliber pistol in his own mouth, pull the trigger, and fall overboard backwards. The Team Leader knew a violent death would soon have been his fate also since, though innocently done, he alone had mistakenly hired the Narc and thus by doing so had vouched for his trustworthiness. Plus, this was the best way to handle it; for now Carlo would not have to order the man's demise and could tell his family that he got swept accidentally overboard in a storm or something.

This night and its happenings changed Colt's relationship with Carlo and the Colombian Cartel forever. With this action the Silver Eagle now became committed and labelled throughout the cartel's lower ranks as a <u>connected</u> <u>man</u>!

THIRTY-SIX

By 1986, a lot had happened that drastically changed the lives of Celia and Colt. Not only had they gotten completely out of debt but they were enjoying life again. Colt had been flying to New Orleans, Houston, and Atlanta in Carlo's airplanes seeing the country's best emphysema specialists and he was much, much better. His weekends were filled with his playing golf with Randy and Pablo, or separately and unbeknownst to them, with Carlo. Celia was happy as a pig-in-a-poke, too, having a ball playing and socializing with Kat and 'Nita.

During April of last year, 1985, Celia and Colt drove up to Blairsville, a town in the mountains of northeast Georgia. Nearby, they found and bought a secluded five acre lot on Lake Hiawassee, whereby they contracted and had built one of those large shell homes. Then Colt, Rick, and David drove up for three weeks in June and finished the insides with their own brand of special walls and cabinets. Here they began to hide most of the large amounts of cash that Colt and Rick had accumulated, over two million dollars combined. This would be the family's vacation retreat and, hopefully, one day become Celia and Colt's retirement home.

David and Suzie Cannon, the son-in-law and daughter of Colt and Celia, wanted nothing, absolutely nothing, to do with the drug business or even any money acquired directly from it. But they hypocritically did not turn down the frequent ten or fifteen thousand dollar bonuses that Rick, Celia, and Colt would give them, supposedly from the cabinet business. Both had become Born-again Christians and had joined a huge charismatic, Pentecostal, evangelical, revival-type church near Pensacola. Also, they chose not to see their sinful in-laws other than at work. And they attended church services and religious work shops every free night and most weekends and associated socially only with fellow church members. Respectfully, they did not push their religion and their new way of life on the others at the shop. And after they had paid everything off, they began pouring most of their money into the church's coffers.

Celia and Colt were beginning to feel that maybe, just

maybe, all of this drug involvement was a big mistake. They both agreed that they and Rick and Mickie weren't really free; not anymore. They could not come and go like they used to. Further, they could not openly spend large quantities of their money for fear of it attracting attention from their neighbors and maybe the local cops and maybe even the IRS. Too, they feared that their house was bugged. They became aware that they just did not want more materialism. After all, how many new cars can a couple drive at once? How many clothes should one have in the closet? How much jewelry does one need? How many homes can one use? All this owning things meant more to care for and more to worry over. Hiding $100,000 a month and worrying if somebody will find out about it and steal it or maybe kill them for it was becoming reoccurring thoughts to all four of them! They saw how tied down Kat and Randy were, too. But these feelings were becoming rather insignificant in light of their fear of what could be happening to them next as they exposed themselves to more and more danger in their ever deepening involvement in drug smuggling!

About 2:00 one afternoon in September, 1986, Celia got a phone call at their shop from Carlo saying, "Celia; Carlo. Colt will be arriving at Jack Edwards Airport about 6:00 from Panama City. Something very wonderful and very important for Colt and for you has transpired in our company. Is it possible that you could take the rest of the afternoon off, go home, get a shower, get dressed, and let my wife, Marty, and me and another gentleman pick you up at 5:30? We'll surprise Colt when he lands and go to Pensacola for a great meal. We'll tell you and Colt what this is all about once he joins us."

Shocked, but agreeable, Celia responded, "Sure. I'd love to."

"Good," Carlo continued. "Then we'll see you at 5:30. We'll be waiting downstairs in your condo's parking lot. And be prepared to have some fun!"

Right at 6:00 the Cessna 182 RG with two aboard taxied up to the front of the small terminal building at Jack Edwards Airport and shut down its engine just long enough to let the executive with the brief case climb out of the co-pilot's side. Just as the silver-haired and mustached passenger raised up from

234

his stoop and cleared the wing, a white super-long limousine came through the side gate from the parking lot and drove quickly across the ramp to the startled and staring man. Out stepped Celia, Marty, Carlo, and the other gentlemen. Shocked speechless, Colt shouted, "What the blazes is going on?"

After a hug and brushing kiss, Celia said, "We're taking you to dinner in Pensacola."

After a warm hug from Marty and a handshake from Carlo, Carlo said, "Salvatore Aristaqieta meet The Silver Eagle: Coulter Erhlichman. Colt meet my boss, Sal, our Area Manager."

Colt asked again, "What's this all about, Carlo?"

"Like Celia said, we're taking you to dinner," was Carlo's response.

"Bull; in a big limousine?" Colt commented.

"Get in, Mr. Coulter Erhlichman, Silver Eagle. It's your big night!" responded Sal.

Opening a bottle of Dom Perignon from one of the two ice buckets, Carlo poured the ladies a glass each and then the guys, saying, "Here's to our very successful and brilliant Team Leader, Colt, and to his bright future!"

Sal took over as if it was his time to begin a little presentation, speaking first to Colt then including the ladies. "Not long ago Colt, you were working with a Colonel on a Panamanian cargo ship. Do you remember that night and the Colonel? He never told you his code name."

Getting a yes nod from Colt, he continued, "Good. Well, it seems that about one month later he was promoted to a one star general. Subsequently, he wrote a meritorious letter of recommendation on your piece of work to the Commandant of IntelSec and suggested that you be offered a promotion to a District Managership. Yet, oddly enough, the new General did not and still does not, and for that matter neither does the Commandant, know your real name; just The Silver Eagle from the Gulf Coast. To get this done one needs two more similar recommendations from managers within our organization that know about the character of the applicant. Having received a copy of his recommendation, since it happened in my area, I asked Carlo about you. He agreed to write a second letter and guess what? A certain Team Leader who has worked so faithfully for us for over six years did the same; his name is Rick Erhlichman."

Sal said, "So with that, Mr. Silver Eagle, would you like to become a made-man? You will be required to take the oath of secrecy called Omerta. You have been given special permission to work past your sixtieth birthday and not be automatically forced to retire. Plus, your retirement qualifications have been waived. So, you and Celia will be guaranteed a lucrative retirement, if and when you wish to take it. We want you to understudy Carlo and be his replacement when he thinks you are ready. He will take my job and I will move up to a newly created Vice-Presidency. You will not work night jobs anymore. And you will be on an annual salary of $250,000 plus bonuses that should bring your income to over $300,000, plus your benefits package."

"May I ask questions now?" Colt asked.

"Shoot, <u>mi compadre</u>!" Carlo answered.

"Who will take my place?" Colt asked.

Carlo answered, "Rick will be offered the opportunity, if you accept. And if he accepts it, he won't take over until you are ready. And then not until y'all can successfully hire someone and train them to run the cabinet shop and continue your boat contract with us. Your cabinet shop is very important to us. We've got boats all over the coastal U.S. and South America that need your work done on them."

Colt asked Celia, "Did Rick tell you anything about this, Hon?"

Celia replied, "You heard it for the first time just like I did. He said nothing to me."

Colt turned to Sal and Carlo, "How soon do you guys need an answer?"

Sal answered, "Take as much time as you like; a month if you want? How much time do you feel comfortable with?"

Colt looked at Celia, then said to Carlo, "Pick up that phone and tell the driver to pull over at that Circle K up there. Celia and I need to walk around for a few minutes."

Out of the car and by themselves, Colt asked, "Tell me the

honest truth. What are you feeling and what do you think we should do? Stall, decline it or take it on faith and go on?"

Celia told him, "Sweetheart, we've got all the money that we'll ever need. So has Rick. This is dangerous work and these are dangerous people. But on the other hand we could begin living openly in luxury and have a very good time on all that honest money that you'll be getting above-board. Whereas we cannot do that on our hidden money. Plus it will be great fun for you. And you seem happiest when you are working under extreme pressure and under a monstrous challenge. But I'm behind you 100% whatever you decide."

Colt continued, "Well, I'm not under their secret oath yet. So, I'm going to tell you something that cannot be told to anyone, not even Rick. That piece of work with that Panamanian Colonel that Sal was referring to was bad news. A Narc was discovered on one of the boats that was under my off-loading supervision and I had to verify him as such, both personally and physically. Then I had to order him killed on the spot and the bugged yacht sunk. That's what's getting me promoted; my having ordered a hit and carrying it out myself, making it a double credit to me. Anyway, I really don't have a clear-cut choice and it'll be a good break for Rick, too. Plus I'll have him working with me, also. I'd like that very much. He and I are each other's best friends now. So I'm gonna take it. Let's go back and have some Dom Perignon."

Following Celia back into the limo, Colt laughingly said, "Marty, reach over here and give a big hug to your husband's newest District Manager!"

All clapped and laughed and the champagne flowed all the way to Pensacola.

Upon arriving at Gotti's Restaurante Italiana, Sal asked the ladies if they would mind going ahead into the restaurant and telling the Maitre D' to seat them at his reserved table while he and Carlo had a few more words with Colt. Upon parking, Sal told the driver to get some fresh air for about ten minutes.

Then Sal told Colt, "Raise your right hand to God Almighty and answer with I do."

Then Colt answered the following questions: "Do you, Coulter Erhlichman , swear to keep all secrets when told to you as such by any known made-man within this organization, allowing them to only those who properly should receive them, they having revealed themselves to you as being worthy of such knowledge?

"Do you solemnly swear that you will not lie to a known made-man in this organization and further that your word will be your bond? And do you further promise and swear that should you find that circumstances beyond your control alter your ability to keep completely your promises to this organization's made-men that you will make every effort to notify those affected as soon as you possibly can?

"Do you solemnly promise and swear that you will not have sex with another male human or any animal? And do you further promise and swear not to have sex with a known made-man's wife, daughter, mother, or blood-sister?

"Do you solemnly promise and swear to protect as best as you can the good reputation, the welfare, and the safety of any known made-man in this organization should you be aware of his need as such?

"Do you solemnly promise and swear to keep the operational rules and policies of this organization as they are revealed and taught to you?

"Do you solemnly promise and swear to obey any and all direct orders from your superiors provided these orders do not interfere with the welfare and security of yourself, your wife, or your immediate family?"

With Sal pausing Colt answered, "I do."

Sal continued, "Good. Then Coulter Erhlichman, take the hand of Salvatore M. Aristaqieta, a made-man in this organization and your Area Manager. Look me straight in the eyes; then as a sign of total commitment to your sacred oaths just made and to the secrecy that they denote, to this your and our oath of secrecy, our Omerta, to your life-long loyalty, and to a trust that makes our word to each other our bond, to love for your fellow members, you are to hug me and give me a kiss on my right cheek signifying your soulful commitment before your

God that seals this relationship between you and our organization, forever."

Sal said, "Now, reconfirm this by hugging and kissing your brother, Carlo!"

Colt recalled, very accurately, where and when he had heard these words, almost exactly, before. But he could never tell these guys about that; for his greater loyalty was to Randy, and somewhat less to these men. But, yet, he could not tell Randy about this, either. Ever.

When approaching the ladies, Sal said, "We now have a newly made-man, ladies. Let's celebrate this precious occasion."

And they did, until 4:00 the next morning; all over Pensacola. However, as the night went into morning the guys were getting knee-walking drunk. At Trader Jon's Marty motioned for Celia to follow her to the ladies room and said, "Celia, Sal has been leaving several hundred dollar tips at the last three bars that we've made. That's ridiculous! Let's tell him to give us his money and we'll handle the bills from now own since you and I are staying sober."

They did and he did. From this wad of hundreds, Marty and Celia had eight hundred each at the end of the night that Sal wasn't aware of. The all night binge ended with Celia winking at Marty as she kissed Sal on the cheek good-bye saying, "Yeah, Sal, you're right. It's been a fun and profitable night for all of us!"

THIRTY-SEVEN

For the past two years, now 1988, the Erhlichmans had been enjoying life. Plenty of money coming in, a new half-million dollar, 2,000 square feet condo in the exclusive Horizon Towers At Alabama Point, overlooking the sparkling, fluorescent, rolling, multi-green water of the Gulf of Mexico at Perdido Pass, --the place to live in Orange Beach. Celia had a new Mercedes convertible and Colt had bought himself a year old Corvette over at the car auction in Pensacola to go along with his new Lincoln Town Car that the company furnished him. Then there were the trips to their mountain home in Hiawassee, Georgia. And they got to take their two grandsons, Suzie's kids, with them often.

Celia was playing a lot of tennis with the local area-wide condo-league team. She also flew with Kat and 'Nita on Saturdays when the guys were off somewhere, which was quite often here lately.

Colt was playing golf every Sunday morning with Randy, Pablo, and one of Randy's security team; they rotated their fourth player from his bodyguard group. Sometimes he and Carlo would slip off to a course, too. Colt just loved his job running the four companies for Carlo.

When Colt was being trained, he learned about the other three companies that he would eventually supervise. They owned and operated a retail seafood store over in Bon Secour, a little fishing village on Mobile Bay. Out of this location ran eleven shrimp boats manned by Vietnamese and Thailanders. They used these nationalities because they were stopped less by the local cops and therefore they could haul dope with less intervention. Eight more boats were under contract when they needed them for off-loading.

The third business taught Colt was a company that contracted to haul cars from the car auctions located in all the five southeastern states and also between their own 24 retail used car lots. When Colt asked more about the operation, Carlo answered, "Have you ever seen a dope-sniffing dog try to climb one of those portable parking lots? Man, we ship tons of drugs in the trunks of those cars and have never been stopped. That explains our need for the car lots, too, doesn't it?"

The fourth company they managed from their Orange Beach headquarters was one that had small offices all over the South that transported used mobile homes across state lines. "Why?" Colt inquired.

Carlo responded, "Can you just imagine how many bales of grass can be hauled in the two halves of a double-wide without suspicion?"

Colt also was told his division, the Transportation Division, was not involved in buying and selling drugs; just getting them stateside and then to prescribed locations, that's all. Other divisions handled the rest. And Colt liked it much better that way.

THIRTY-EIGHT

During one of the last all night off-loading runs Colt made before he was promoted to District Manager, just as he was about to leave the mother ship, the IntelSec officer asked if he had noticed the big, tall gentleman who had appeared on deck earlier just before they began loading the first boat. Colt told him no. Then the officer said that he asked who you were and he was told, "That's the famous Silver Eagle of the Gulf Coast!" He added, "He wants to see you in his cabin and I'm to take you there."

After opening the cabin door, the deck officer left the two. The giant said, "Hello, Colt Erhlichman. So you're The Silver Eagle I've heard so much about. Remember me?"

Colt said shockingly, "Well, I'll be darn. How are you, Colonel Andre? What a pleasant surprise!"

As they shook hands, the big man laughed and said, "That's right I was Andre then, wasn't I? Call me Fred, my friend. My real name is used now: Frederico Espinosa. And guess what, Colt? I did get that transfer to Satellite Tracking and a promotion to Brigadier General!"

Colt responded, "What a pleasant surprise to see you! I've often wondered where you went after leaving us. Did you get back to college and earn your Phd?"

"Yes, Sir," the General responded. "In fact, the Doctorate was conferred on me just last month."

"Great!" Colt continued. "I'm very happy for you. But what in the world are you doing on this cargo ship?"

"Good question," Fred continued. "The Commandant, at my graduation, told me he felt I had been putting in too many working hours between our SatTrac lab and the college campus. So, he was assigning me to a special inter-divisional project that involved SatTrac and our Sales Distribution Division. This project would have me aboard this cargo vessel for three weeks, then to Russia for five weeks of which one week would be at a training school on a new spy satellite. I am to have my wife and two sons join me in Moscow after the training class and we are to tour Russia for a month, all at company expense. Then, when we return he will announce my promotion to SatTrac Division Commander."

"Super!" Colt complimented. "I knew from that brief talk we had aboard the Caterina that afternoon that you were destined for great things."

Fred asked, "Does the Tall Man know of The Silver Eagle?"

"No," Colt answered. "In fact, I've told him nothing about what I do outside of our personal relationship. He apparently just assumes it is our cabinet business that keeps me so busy. And additionally, my division superiors do not know anything at all about Randy, or that The Tall Man, actually, lives and runs this organization right under their local noses. So, I guess you can say that I've sworn to an Omerta with this organization without being made, huh?

"General, you have my curiosity aroused," Colt added. "Is it okay if I ask, why on this ship and not one going directly to Europe?"

"Oh sure!" the General answered. "We're testing a new inventory control and off-loading system involving our onboard merchandise handling and accounting. You may have noticed how fast we loaded your boats this time; it took 90 minutes less than it normally would. And as we perfect it, it will decrease our down time; that is, our time anchored, and thus minimize our exposure time to possible DEA or military intervention."

He continued, "What we'll eventually do is change the way we're identifying each package, bundle, or bale during final packaging from written markings showing content, weight, and customer destination information to bar code/laser read outs and add an automatic, high-tech, computerized conveyor system replacing most of the onboard manual handling. Tonight's test load, though, had to be marked both ways. We're also developing a ship-to-boat portable and flexible conveyor transfer system to eliminate the current manual to crane to manual methods. Additionally, a containerized freight system is under development for use in countries where marijuana importation problems don't exist.

"Later," Fred concluded, "you Supervisors and your boat

Team Leaders will be trained on and will use a hand-held reader about the size of a walkie-talkie instead of doing your verification and validations visually and manually. Once you and the ship's Off-loading Supervisor and the IntelSec officer sign off on the off-loaded merchandise, the shipment information will be up-linked to a satellite, and immediately our Control Office Central will receive the figures.

"This will be a much more accurate and time saving system. And further, it will cut down tremendously on what is called our float. Float, in our case, means costs and profits tied up in released inventory not yet invoiced and paid for, and we're talking about hundreds of millions. Plus it will save us additional monies by eliminating over half of our mother ship's off-loading crew by cutting the required numbers of men and substituting the conveyors. Further, with fewer men we have less exposure, thus cutting our chances of having a Narc slip into their ranks like you did that night when you did that great piece of work for us. I'm here working out the kinks on the satellite up-link portion of the project. And, Sir, please keep this to yourself until we announce the new project."

It momentarily irritated Colt that Fred knew about his having that Narc killed. He wondered just how many more within the organization knew about it. And further, he felt very uneasy about the general bringing up that point about Randy not knowing of his being The Silver Eagle.

They chatted for about thirty minutes about the golf games they had played together, about their wives and families, Kat and Randy, Pablo and 'Nita, and Cinco Robles before good-byes and good lucks were exchanged. Yes, they had become friends and maybe their paths would cross again. They hoped so.

THIRTY-NINE

In October, 1988 two loaded, large military-type helicopters flew below radar from somewhere in Baldwin County. As they reached north Wolf Bay and the secluded walled-in 50-acre compound named Cinco Robles, they hovered above it just long enough for all four opened sides of the two choppers to dispel about four dozen canisters of a deadly nerve gas, covering the entire compound with an opaque cloud of death-dealing fog. Once landed in the compound's open area, and as the two empty helicopters made their escape, it was obvious to the 12 jump-suited and gas-masked, armed terrorists that no one appeared alive, but they shot them anyway just to make sure. As planned, they had caught all the occupants, including the compound's Ground Security Team, off guard. Next, they shot out all of the security cameras and the security control room. All telephone and transmission lines and equipment were the last to go.

Then, individually, they began loading in duffel bags the hidden millions in cash, silver and gold bars, diamonds, rubies, and jewelry. They knew exactly where to look, for each uniformed assailant had a map showing his assigned area and a detailed drawing depicting where all the money and valuables were hidden. Just as the automatic weapons started to fire, a large, blue passenger van, the kind that can hold up to 18 people, drove up, shot the front gate's lock and then proceeded through, its driver suited and masked for chemicals also. While in the main kitchen, a late-night dishwasher heard the choppers' approach, and panicked as he saw out the window compound security guards falling unconscious. But he managed to dial 911 and reported the situation just seconds before the nerve gas killed him.

The 911 dispatcher phoned Foley Police. Two Alabama State Highway Patrol helicopter pilots, who were monitoring the local police band and just happened to be on stand-by at the Foley Airport while the Governor was nearby at his farm, decided to get airborne and head for Hwy. 59 south of town.

In less than ten minutes the van was loaded with all the still-masked men, weapons, and loot. It left the compound with all the van's windows open in order to air out any possible trace of the nerve gas. They headed the five miles to Highway 59 towards Foley. About half a mile from Hwy. 59, the van stopped abruptly. Everyone got out, removed their protective clothing and gas masks and tossed them into the roadside ditch.

The State chopper pilots knew where the compound was located, having flown over it numerous times, and were approaching the feeder road. They saw the stopped van's lights and the commotion beside it. The terrorists heard and saw the chopper. Its group leader ordered, "No shooting, unless I say so! Don't' attract any attention! Load, NOW! Drive north to Mobile! Maintain the speed limit."

The chopper's co-pilot switched to the Foley Police's frequency, identified themselves as <u>The Governor's Chopper</u> and advised the lady dispatcher that they had a blue van in sight full of military-dressed occupants who had apparently, discarded their clothing in the ditch on County Road 12 just east of 59, that the subjects' vehicle's rear window was stuffed with what looked like duffel bags.

The Foley Police's Shift Commander felt that he couldn't get a proper road block set up fast enough. Plus that would be stupid anyway, since the 911 report he got said that "everybody at the place was being gassed and machine-gunned down by a hundred soldiers." So, the Lieutenant got on the police radio and ordered that no patrol car was to directly pursue the subjects until he could phone his Chief for further orders. All officers listening, on duty and off, were to take the closest route to Hwy. 59 and stand-by there. Then he ordered the Shift Sergeant and a patrol car to head to the compound; not to go inside, but keep everyone far away until he could get the Fire Department's Haz-Mat Crew there to clear it for entry.

He ordered the dispatcher to phone the Foley Fire Department, to call the Gulf Shores Police, the Orange Beach Police, Summerdale, Robertsdale, Loxley, and the Bay Minette Police Departments and ask them all to stand-by. She was told to notify the Baldwin County Sheriff's Department, the local office of the Alabama Highway Patrol, the County Coroner, and tell all local Paramedics and EMT services to head to the scene and report to the Police Sergeant and the patrolman.

He also asked the chopper to stay with the van but out of firing range and keep him appraised of the vehicle's movements. But under this tremendous amount of pressure and pandemonium, he forgot to tell his dispatcher to call the Mobile Police, the Mobile County Sheriff's Department and the FBI. And, unfortunately, she forgot to phone the Bay Minette Police and the Alabama Highway Patrol.

By now, fully understanding what they might be faced with should they accidentally confront this armed team of highly trained, professional assassins, Foley's Finest found reasons to be slow in getting activated and arriving at Hwy. 59, intentionally giving the killers plenty of time to get past their spot and out of harm's way. So did most of the rest of the notified towns and cities.

The helicopter's pilots talked about it and decided to stay with the vehicle and at a safe distance behind regardless of where it went, for they had full fuel tanks. They kept reporting back on Foley's frequency, and asked Foley to advise the Governor, giving them his unlisted number. But the other agencies did not have the advantage of listening to their on-going reports, for they did not know what frequency to use; at least, so they claimed later. Further, the chopper pilots willingly decided that they did not have the authority to shoot at the van. For they had not been ordered to even be in this dangerous situation, much less shoot without direct orders from their Montgomery headquarters. For they were assigned to the Governor, not to the State's SWAT team. Plus all they had aboard was their side arms and those would be totally ineffective against these guys' automatic weapons. Too, they might hit some innocent people down there if they fired while flying at these heights.

The van made the 22 miles up Hwy. 59 to I-10 driving the speed limit with no visible interference. As they approached the left turn lane onto the interstate's west-bound entrance ramp, a black van of similar size with only a driver in it and a red Buick came from the nearby BP Station's parking lot and fell in behind. Together, the three vehicles proceeded over the ten miles on I-10 to the Mobile Bay-Way and uneventfully drove the next seven miles across the causeway and entered the double-laned west-bound tube of the George Wallace Tunnel that crosses beneath the Mobile River connecting I-10 through the city's downtown area.

Earlier, the chopper co-pilot radioed Mobile Approach and identified himself and his aircraft. He advised them that they were at I-10 and Baldwin Hwy. 59 at 1000 feet on hot pursuit west-bound and asked them to clear away all air traffic over west-bound I-10 up to 2000 feet all the way to the Alabama-Mississippi state line. Mobile Approach gave him a transponder squawk code number so that they could track him on their radar screen if he stayed high enough. They said they would notify the Houston Air Route Traffic Control Center and the Mobile Regional Airport's Tower but that the Downtown Mobile Airport's tower located nearby at Brookley Field had closed earlier at 10:00. Therefore, the helicopter would have to VFR it through the next eight miles, meaning that he would have to watch out for any local airplanes not listening to this frequency until he was out of the Downtown Mobile Airport's traffic pattern.

Being occupied with this, the pilots did not notice the black van with the red Buick behind it pull up along the left side of the terrorists' vehicle just before the tunnel entrance. Nor did they see them intentionally slow down to about 30 miles and hour as the three entered, thus backing up the two lanes of traffic behind them. Just inside the tunnel and creeping along together, the black van went ahead just a little, leaving a gap between it and the following red Buick. Immediately the blue loaded van in the right lane slammed on its brakes, skidded left across both lanes and in front of the creeping on coming Buick, and quickly backed up to touch the right wall. The Buick then veered left to the wall and stopped, thus blocking the open space in front of the van causing both lanes of traffic to be blocked.

The driver jumped out of the Buick as did all occupants in the blue van. They immediately unloaded all the duffel bags and gear and within less than a minute were loaded into the waiting adjacent black van. Then it sped off, leaving behind their two abandoned vehicles and a blocked tunnel.

250

The tunnel's Policeman guard, who is supposed to be continually monitoring the four television screens in his control room, was watching the Dave Letterman Show on another television and did not see any of this. Once his peripheral vision became aware of no movement on one of the screens, he phoned the Mobile Police and advised them that a red Buick had collided with a large blue passenger van inside the west-bound tube with people hurt.

Just a few minutes before this, seeing the blue van enter the tunnel, and realizing they had about three minutes before it could exit the west-side, the chopper pilot asked the co-pilot, "See any sign of a road block or any blue lights?" The co-pilot nodded no. The pilot continued, "I'll bet they're going to nail them at the Virginia Street exit; plenty of room and not congested like downtown is. We'll be able to tell when we get up there. The east-bound side will be blocked off at Michigan Avenue. Man, it's gonna be a lot of fire power going on. Glad we're up here and not down there. Dial up Mobile Police's frequency; but they'll probably be on a discrete channel. If so, get it."

Just as the co-pilot switched to Mobile, they both heard, "Car 320."

"320. Watcha got, Dottie?"

"320, 10-32 on Tach 3."

"10-4. 320 switching."

The chopper's co-pilot changed channels on his transceiver also.

"Sergeant, T-67 phoned and said he's got what looks like a Signal 8 inside the George Wallace Tunnel's west-bound tube near its east entrance involving a large blue passenger van and a red Buick. Mike couldn't say how many's injured. Traffic's blocked and backing up. I've got Morgan's on the way with two EMT-units; Fire Central is sending one Rescue Unit and two hose trucks. Who do you want me to assign it to, who'll back-up, and how do you want me to work it? 10-4?"

"10-4. Assign it to 317. 319 can back-up Smokey. 19's 10-7 at headquarters on paperwork. Tell Vicky she can be the first to go 10-8 afterwards. Put Motorcycle Unit M-33 at Church and Water Streets and M-35 at Church and Auditorium Drive. Tell

317, 319, Fire Central, and Morgan's to 10-40 prior with me in the auditorium's parking lot. Advise the Shift Commander we'll stage there and use Church Street to enter the Water Street west-side exit ramp after clearing traffic. Move two department wreckers to my 10-20. Then phone T-67 and tell Mike to walk down there and get me an injury report. And ask the Commander to see if two downtown Vice Units are available if I have to re-route the west-bound Bay-way. Tell the two bike units to 10-32 with me now on Tach 2. And advise the rest to go on Tach 2 until going 10-8. 10-4?"

The helicopter co-pilot screamed, "Gene, they ain't got no road block! They don't even know! They'll be slaughtered!"

The pilot shouted back, "Call 'em and tell 'em not to go into that tunnel! We're landing at the auditorium, right now! And advise approach!"

In the meantime, the loaded black van had already cleared the tunnel and left I-10, was downtown taking Water Street northwards towards the I-165 by-pass and would continue unscathed on north I-65 to exit 22 in Creola. There at the Mark Reynolds-North Mobile County Airport's grass runway the bags of money, silver, gold, and jewelry would be loaded aboard two Cessna 421s and flown to Ft. Lauderdale where a Cessna Citation would jet the loot to Bolivia to the terrorist's headquarters. Also, both of the army-type helicopters that had been to Cinco Robles would be waiting in Creola to return the killers to their starting point, for their night's work was now successfully completed.

Once warned and brought up-to-date by the chopper pilots, the Mobile Police Department and the Mobile County Sheriff's Department were called out in full force --SWAT Team, dogs, and everything. News cameras and reporters scurried to the scene. It was too late to stop T-67; his hand-held would not work in the tunnel.

Then to everyone's shocked amazement, 13 minutes later, T-67 had walked back out and radioed on his transceiver that the vehicles in question were empty; that something was wrong! No drivers were present and it wasn't even a Signal 7; no bent metal! But the Sergeant knew! So, a dragnet was ordered, this time including the FBI and the Alabama Highway Patrol, throughout a fifty mile radius around Mobile with television's on-the-spot coverage with their well-meaning words that ended with nothing but embarrassment to all those hard-working badge wearers. And the bad guys got away again!

But Foley had their hands full. Two hours and ten minutes after the 911 call, the Fire Department's Haz-Mat Team gave the other departments clearance to enter. Thirty-seven mutilated bodies were found; no survivors. Pablo and 'Nita were found on their bedroom floor in their bloody pajamas. Unfortunately, a cameraman and reporter were following the officer when he entered their door. And this scene was picked up and beamed out live over the national networks. They had been shocked awake by the noise of the exploding gas canisters. Then the gas immediately got to them through the air-conditioning ducts while the panic and confusion of the moment rendered their screaming minds useless during those last few minutes. Pablo had eleven bullet holes in him and 'Nita had six in her, according to the coroner's report.

Newspaper and the liberal news media, local and national, would castigate those Southern law enforcement agencies for not doing their jobs. Politicians would form their usual investigation committees. The public would have something to talk about for months. And worldwide terrorism could continue; this time at the dope cartel's expense. But what a price had already been paid, and by so many! Yet, more would be killed because of this; for murder begets murder. That's the way this game is played!

FORTY

Kat and Randy were in Bogota, Colombia that terrible night in October, 1988 when C. R. was raided. Aunt Clementina had died at 80 years old from an unexpected heart attack.

Colt and Celia were awakened from a deep sleep by the phone with their son, Rick shouting, "Turn on the television, quick. Something horrible has happened at C. R.!"

The news anchor on WKRG-Channel Five from Mobile was saying, "And now we go live to the scene on north Wolf Bay in Baldwin County, Alabama."

The on-the-scene reporter began, "There has been a bloody massacre here tonight at this exclusive, walled-in compound located on north Wolf Bay that has the name <u>Cinco Robles</u> in wrought-iron over its entrance gates. The Foley Police Chief, who is handling the investigation, told us earlier that 31 bodies have been found so far. And evidence indicates that the entire place has been thoroughly ransacked. Nearby witnesses reported that they watched two army-type helicopters with troops aboard fly over the area, just above the tree-tops, about 10:00 p.m. After hearing first what sounded like dozens of shot gun blasts, they saw the helicopters leave about five minutes later. Then, for about ten more minutes, hundreds of shots apparently fired from automatic weapons filled the air. Another witness told us he was driving east on County Road 12 when he saw a west-bound, blue van pull over and stop and a group of gas-masked and jump-suited men got out. The Foley Fire Chief told us that a deadly nerve gas was the cause of the deaths, but the victims were also shot, most likely afterwards."

Colt turned off the television; they had seen enough! They were shocked speechless!

Celia was crying and screaming again and again, hysterically, "'Nita and Pablo! Oh, My God! 'Nita and Pablo!"

Colt, sobbing and shaking, also mumbled as he went for his bottle of Johnny Walker Red, "Thank God, Randy and Kat are in Colombia!"

For three more days Colt, Celia, Rick, and Micky tried to find out what had happened. But they could not let on to Carlo or to any of his people anything about their involvement with Cinco Robles. But there was no doubt in anyone's mind, anyone even remotely close to being in the know, that this was anything other than an inside job. Even the news media, once allowed inside, showed that the cabinets had been selectively ripped open.

Colt continually phoned Randy's Jack Edwards Airport office trying to get a return call from Randy or Kat, all to no avail. It was obvious to him that a blanket of silence had been ordered. Finally, Colt talked Randy's Executive Secretary into giving him Uncle Fernie's unlisted home phone number in Funza, Colombia. After three attempts, Uncle Fernie accepted the call.

Colt started by saying, "This is Colt Erhlichman calling from Orange Beach, Alabama, Sir. I think you may know of me. All of us here are so sorry for the catastrophe at the compound, Senor Elizondo, and also for the death of your sister. I've tried for several days to reach Kat and Randy. Are they okay and is there anything that we can do to help? Can you tell me anything, Sir?"

The old gentleman answered, "Oh, yes. I indeed know of you, Mr. Erhlichman. Kat and Randy spoke many times very highly of you and your wife, Celia. Yes, I will answer any questions you may have. But before you ask, let me say what I need to tell you, then I shall answer your inquiries. I've arranged for the bodies of Pablo and 'Nita to be cremated in Foley, then their ashes shipped here for burial. Their requests were in their living wills. Kat has asked me, should I hear from you, to tell you that she and Randy will not be returning to the U.S. In time, she will write. The rest of the needed help in your area will be handled by our IntelSec Division. But it is kind of you to offer."

The IntelSec Commandant and Five-Star General continued, 'May I point out, as I'm sure you already are aware of, that that massacre and robbery was done with inside help; someone who could supply detailed knowledge of where each money cache, the diamonds and rubies, their jewelry, and the gold and silver bars were hidden or stored. Randy estimated the value to me at $100 million. May I also say that you and your people installed the cabinets, thereby automatically including you and your family among the prime suspects."

He continued, "However, using our expert Field Operatives, we located the guilty parties. Now, listen very closely, Mr. Silver Eagle, for your life and the lives of your entire family depends on your understanding and carrying out, exactly, my direct orders to you. Our Off-loading Division knows nothing about you and your family's involvement with Kat and Randy, for they know not of them at all. They must not be told, ever!"

The General added, "You along with your son, Rick, must resign your positions with Carlo and his group immediately. Tell Carlo that you want to retire to your mountain home in north Georgia. Since Rick has made enough money to never have to work again, tell Carlo that he and his wife are going with you and Celia. You and your family are to have nothing to do with anyone associated with this cartel, the drug business, or any of my family for the rest of your lives. For your and Rick's faithful service to us and for the millions made by us from you two's efforts, our appreciation is being shown in this manner. No company retirement benefits will be forthcoming; you've made enough. You and your family must keep silence and you must maintain your individual Omerta."

Continuing, the Commandant said, "Should any of these orders not be carried out in full, all of you as well as your daughter in California and her entire family will be eliminated! Now, you may ask other questions if you completely understand my orders."

Colt, with a lump in his throat, uttered, "I understand, fully. But you did not mention David and Suzie!"

The Senor finished, "It is obvious by your calling me that you have not been watching your local news station today! Good-bye, Mr. Erhlichman, and never phone me, ever again or I'll have you shot!" The phone went dead!

Colt, with the phone still in his hand, screamed in fear to Celia, "Celia, turn on the television! Something's happened to David and Suzie!"

Again, live from the scene, this time in front of David and Suzie's home, the reporter said, "For those of you who just

257

joined us, I'll repeat our earlier report. Two more major tragedies have occurred today in south Baldwin County. This time here in Orange Beach at the home of David and Suzanne Cannon, and separately in Lillian, a little town east of Foley, Alabama located on the Alabama-Florida state line. At about seven this morning, Mr. Charles H. Stunstall, who resides on a farm on MacReady Road near Lillian, was feeding his livestock when he discovered the decapitated body of a white male half-submerged inside his hog pen. A Baldwin County Deputy Sheriff, who attended the same church in Pensacola as the victim, identified at the scene the severed head as that of David Wayne Cannon of Orange Beach, Alabama."

The female reporter continued, "Baldwin County's Sheriff's Office phone David Cannon's wife and informed her of the tragedy and asked that she drive to the Magnolia Funeral Home in Foley to officially identify the victim's body as that of her husband. Apparently, Mrs. Cannon loaded her two young sons in their family station wagon and turned the ignition key, igniting a car bomb that took all three of their lives."

She added, "When contacted by our news department's producer, the Baldwin County Sheriff himself informed us that the only clue found so far was a wadded piece of paper found by the coroner stuffed inside Mr. Cannon's mouth along with his penis. The note had six words scribbled on it: <u>For Pablo, 'Nita, and Five Oaks</u>.

FORTY-ONE

Almost a year later, in the summer of 1989, Celia left their beautiful mountain side home, walked down the gravel drive to their mail box and retrieved from among the usual six or seven pieces of junk mail a strange looking, thick letter. It was from South America! Running as fast as she could back up the drive, she was hollering to Colt, "It's from Kat! Colt, it's from Kat! We've got a letter from Kat!"

Colt handed her a glass of ice water as Celia opened the letter and began reading aloud, "My dearest darling Celia: I've waited until now to write because I wanted to have some time to get my life on an even keel again, but mostly to give you some time for the immense amount of pain that I feel I brought into your lives to ease somewhat, if that is at all possible.

"I am so very, very sorry for what happened that ruined our happiness. And I pray every day to Pintu Weeko for forgiveness. More than anything, I pray that one day you will forgive me for the terrible afflictions that Randy, I, and my family brought upon you guys. I love you so much, Celia!

"Since you probably have no way of knowing what transpired down here during all that horrendous time, I want to detail it for you. Some of it you know from Uncle Fernie's conversation with Colt; most of it you don't. Some of it was told to me much later by my uncle.

"At Aunt Clementina's funeral, some IntelSec officers asked Uncle Fernie and Randy to please come with them, that something terrible had happened in the U.S. Randy left with the group.

"Without Randy, Uncle Fernie arrived back late at his home where we were staying and took me into a private room. There he began to unravel for me this horrible story."

The letter continued: "He told me all the details about the terrorists' successful raid on my wonderful home, Cinco Robles, and the death of Pablo and 'Nita, the only true friend that I ever had other than you, my sweet, Celia. He told me that they had already found the inside informants and justice would be coming in two to three days for your Suzie and David. Both had been in on it and were to be paid $2,000,000, all of which they had planned to give to their church, none of which they lived to get, except for $25,000 up-front money."

She wrote, "Uncle Fernie informed Randy that afternoon that the organization had a super-productive <u>made-man</u> that for several years had been helping to produce hundreds of millions for the cartel, that The Silver Eagle lived in Orange Beach. Further, he told Randy that this Omerta District Manager was Colt. It was a major mistake on Randy's part for not knowing and a violation of his Omerta for having a personal relationship with a made-man far below his level.   And the Board of Directors also felt Randy was indirectly responsible for the security of their 62 million in cash taken from Cinco Robles. Randy was fired on the spot."

Continuing, Celia read, "Then the real shocker that crumbled my life began when Uncle Fernie said, "Kat, I know this is going to hurt you very, very much. I am terribly sorry that I have to be the one to tell you. For over ten years now, your husband has kept a condominium in downtown Bogota that you did not know about and he thought that we didn't. But he was wrong about our knowing. Each trip down here, and there were many, he would spend at least a night or more there. He had met a young black homosexual in Miami and moved him to Bogota for his own sexual pleasures. Today, after meeting with me and the IntelSec officers and after being informed by me about our stand on his responsibilities concerning Mr. Erhlichman and our lost money at the compound, Randy left by himself. I had him followed. But after I was informed that he had gone to his secret condo and before I could get to him, he shot his lover and then turned the pistol on himself. Kat, your husband and his homosexual lover are dead! I'm so sorry for you, my precious niece, for I have loved you all of your life as my own daughter!"

The letter continued, "Celia, my world fell apart. I had never been happier in my life than I was with you and 'Nita nearby. I tried and tried to face life by living back in my home town of Funza, outside of Bogota. But nothing helped; I was planning to kill myself. Then one night while praying, my

Power Spirit appeared unexpectedly out of nowhere and said, "You cannot go back to the Gulf Coast of Alabama for 'Nita is with us now and Celia has moved. Go, my child, to where you have always felt wanted and were happy. Go home to the Kin Chabba, for your Aunt Embuko is failing now. She needs and longs for you, as does all of your relatives."

Kat continued, "So, Bukutu is where I plan to live out my life. The tribe has me under studying Aunt Embuko. I will soon replace her as their tribal Shaman.

"My darling friend, happiness is slowly returning to me. But true happiness cannot until I see you again, and hear you say that I am forgiven. When the time is right for you, I want you to phone Uncle Fernie and ask him to get the word to me that you will come visit me and the Kin Chabbas. I will have sent to you a round-trip airline ticket. I'd love to have Colt accompany you; that is, if he would indeed ever want to see me again."

Then the letter ended with, "Thinking back over the entire details from when I first met you in your shop that morning until our last time together, all I can offer is: remembering that night at Sam's on the Intracoastal Waterwary when I asked you and Colt to join us the next day for a boat ride on the Bonita Caterina, I guess that I, alone, am to blame for all of this, having asked you to go what has proven to have been ONE STEP TOO FAR. But had I not done that, I would not have had you in my life at all, nor all the love that you, without reservation or limitation, gave to me.

"With tears running down my cheeks now, I say to you in Chabba: K'lyjo Pintu Weeko simtoka k'yo a p'sodo a Key simtokas lim kli mito z'mino pitol somo, eto Celia: May God bless you as much as He has blessed me by my having known you, my Celia!

"I miss you so very much, My Best Friend."

Through eyes blinded with tears, Celia read the signature: Kojo Embuko.

EPILOGUE

As instructed by Uncle Fernie, Colt and Celia, as well as Rick and Micky, moved to the beautiful mountains of northeast Georgia.

Uncle Fernie moved their U.S. headquarters operation to Ft. Lauderdale and sent Bert and his wife, Phil, up to run it. And their business continues to increase as more and more Americans stupidly kill themselves with drugs!

January 1990: Carlo and his wife, Marty, were killed in a one-car accident on Canal Road in Gulf Shores at 4:30 one Sunday morning after leaving the Flora-Bama Bar on Highway 182 at the state line.

1997: Sal, Carlo's boss, is still at it as a Regional Vice-President under Bert, lives in Atlanta's elegant Dunwoody, and coaches his son in Little League Football at nearby Murphy-Candler Park.

1998: Colt died in October due to liver failure. So, cigarettes didn't kill him after all; alcohol did. Celia sold their place and is living with Rick and Micky. Micky had twins eleven years ago, a girl and a boy. Rick's building mountain homes now, and is a scratch golfer.

Celia has not gone to visit Kat in Bukutu. For if she does, Uncle Fernie will have Celia and her entire family killed for violating the orders he gave to Colt under which they could never contact any member of his Elizondo family again. But Kat doesn't know that. And maybe it's best that she never finds it out and all else that goes on in the real world outside her Peruvian jungle home, for that matter.

THE END

ABOUT THE AUTHOR

Following a thirty-five year career of marketing and manufacturing, Vern spends much of his time writing stories about the many interesting people that he met while traveling the U.S. In between chapters, he is an avid Harley-Davidson rider. He resides next to the Mobile River Delta in Creola, Alabama.

Printed in the United States
38992LVS00001B/19-39